THE COOK'S ENCYCLOPEDIA OF
VEGETABLES

THE COOK'S ENCYCLOPEDIA OF
VEGETABLES

A visual guide to vegetables and how to use them, with
100 delicious recipes for soups, salads and main courses

CHRISTINE INGRAM

southwater

This edition is published by Southwater,
an imprint of Anness Publishing Ltd,
108 Great Russell Street,
London WCIB 3NA;
info@anness.com

www.southwaterbooks.com; www.annesspublishing.com

If you like the images in this book and would like to investigate using
them for publishing, promotions or advertising, please visit our
website www.practicalpictures.com for more information.

Publisher: Joanna Lorenz
Editor: Rosemary Wilkinson
Food for photography: Jane Stevenson
Photography and styling: With the exception of sources noted, all photographic material
    supplied and styled by Patrick McLeavey and Tom Odulate. Anthony Blake Photo Library:
    68tr; Gene Coleman: 76b; Holt Studios International: 21m; Robert Estall: 42t; Michelle
    Garret: 95t, 95m; David Jordan: 85t, 85b; MC Picture Library: 51, 80b; S E Marshall
    & Co Ltd: 40b; Debbie Patterson: 24tl; Tessa Traeger: 29b; 90r; The Garden Picture
    Library, Mayer/Le Scanff: 69b; Sunniva Harte: 72b; Mayer/Le Scanff: 100b, 124b;
    Unwins Seeds Ltd: 61b, 69t, 104b
Designer: Patrick McLeavey
Production Controller: Ben Worley

NOTES
Bracketed terms are intended for American readers.
    For all recipes, quantities are given in both metric and imperial measures and, where
appropriate, in standard cups and spoons. Follow one set of measures, but not a mixture,
because they are not interchangeable.
    Standard spoon and cup measures are level. 1 tsp = 5ml, 1 tbsp = 15ml,
1 cup = 250ml/8fl oz.
    Australian standard tablespoons are 20ml. Australian readers should use 3 tsp in place
of 1 tbsp for measuring small quantities.
    American pints are 16fl oz/2 cups. American readers should use 20fl oz/2.5 cups
in place of 1 pint when measuring liquids.
    Electric oven temperatures in this book are for conventional ovens. When using a fan oven,
the temperature will probably need to be reduced by about 10–20°C/20–40°F. Since ovens
vary, you should check with your manufacturer's instruction book for guidance.
    The nutritional analysis given for each recipe is calculated per portion (i.e. serving or item),
unless otherwise stated. If the recipe gives a range, such as Serves 4–6, then the nutritional
analysis will be for the smaller portion size, i.e. 6 servings. The analysis does not include
optional ingredients, such as salt added to taste.
    Medium (US large) eggs are used unless otherwise stated.

PUBLISHER'S NOTE
Although the advice and information in this book are believed to be accurate and true at the
time of going to press, neither the authors nor the publisher can accept any legal responsibility
or liability for any errors or omissions that may have been made nor for any inaccuracies nor
for any loss, harm or injury that comes about from following instructions or advice in this book.

CONTENTS

INTRODUCTION

As a child, there were two basic types of vegetables for me: the ones my mother cooked and the ones given to us at school. My mother only ever bought fresh vegetables and she knew how to cook them, so they were simple but good. Vegetables at school were overcooked and invariably tasteless. Travel then broadened my outlook.

From my teenage sojourns around Europe, I recall, even now, the stalls in a Barcelona produce market, piled high with tomatoes, (bell) peppers and aubergines (eggplants). The exotic-looking produce of The Orient, Asia and Caribbean countries cannot fail to spark off an inquisitive, creative enthusiasm in those who are unfamiliar with them and even basic ingredients – potatoes, onions and carrots – do not look like everyday necessities when they are displayed with pride.

HISTORY

Plants have formed an essential part of our diet since the early existence of mankind. Hunter-gatherers progressed towards a more settled life as they learned how to cultivate crops and rear domestic animals. Archaeological evidence indicates that forms of wheat and barley, believed to be the first crops, were farmed in the Middle East as early as 8000BC. Many edible plants are native to this area, so we can assume that vegetables were also eaten, not least to relieve a monotonous diet.

As plants became a regular part of the diet for satisfying appetites, and those that caused stomach upsets were discovered and avoided, people realized the necessity of growing edible crops. Beans and

Left: Italian Roast Peppers.
Above: Roast Asparagus Crêpes.

Left: Shallots.

By the Middle Ages, a wealth of vegetables was available and many recipes for them were recorded in the first cookbooks.

Early explorers displayed exotic ingredients, the spoils of their travels, in their native countries and created a huge appetite for new tastes among the wealthy classes of Europe. Marco Polo travelled to China and carried aromatic spices on his return to Europe. Christopher Colombus and subsequent explorers found potatoes, tomatoes, peppers, squashes and maize. Such produce was greeted with a rather lukewarm reception and potatoes and tomatoes were received with suspicion and grave misgivings!

It is only in recent generations that people all over the world have expressed interest in vegetables cultivated in different climates.

Nowadays, of course, we have the option of buying exactly what we want, when we want it. This is a luxury we have come to expect and we are ready to pay the price for international variety. Gluts of vegetables, once common seasonal occurrences when produce was cultivated and marketed on a local scale, are not a feature of modern food stores, but seasons still hold good for home-grown produce.

Unlike store-cupboard (pantry) ingredients, the great characteristic of many vegetables is that they still have natural seasons. So, in addition to taking advantage of the multi-national displays in cosmopolitan supermarkets, it also pays to buy from local growers who offer freshly harvested produce. I think it is important to enjoy summer vegetables at their best during the season to which they traditionally belong and to savour winter produce in dishes

peas were among the first vegetables farmed in Thessaly and Macedonia. These legumes would have been very important to early societies as they grew easily to provide seeds, a starchy food that is high in protein and that dried well for long storage.

Many of our familiar vegetables were cultivated in historic times: the Egyptians grew onions, garlic, radishes, lettuce and broad (fava) beans; the Greeks and Romans

farmed produce that was native to their countries and also discovered a wider range of plants thanks to their contact with other cultures.

Not only did the Romans encounter the fruits of other lands, but their armies also introduced ingredients to the countries they invaded. In Britain, for example, at the beginning of the 1st century AD, beans, peas, leeks, parsnips and turnips were commonly grown.

Above: Spinach.

such as wholesome stews and broths, which are well suited to cooler weather.

NUTRITION

The total contribution of carbohydrate (starchy) foods and vegetables in a well-balanced diet may not be entirely understood, but the benefits and protective role they play in ensuring good health is widely recognized. Expert opinions agree on the fact that we should eat a high proportion of vegetables in our everyday diets.

Although the nutritional value of vegetables varies according to type, freshness, preparation and cooking method, they are a main source of many vitamins, especially vitamin C.

Some of the B-group vitamins are also found in vegetables, particularly in green vegetables and pulses. Carrots and dark green vegetables also include carotene, which is used by the body to manufacture vitamin A. Vegetable oils are a useful source of vitamin E.

Vegetables also contain calcium, iron, potassium and magnesium, as well as some trace elements that are required in small quantities.

Starchy vegetables such as potatoes, yams and sweet potatoes are an important source of energy-giving carbohydrate and they may also include useful quantities of fibre.

In a vegetarian diet, vegetables, particularly beans, peas, lentils and sprouting seeds, make a valuable contribution to the overall protein intake as well as supplying a good range of nutrients and fibre.

In the directory section of this book, where specific vegetables are a rich source of nutrients, a note is included under the relevant heading.

Almost all vegetables have the highest nutritional content when they are freshly picked. The vitamin content diminishes with staleness and exposure to sunlight. Use fresh vegetables as soon as possible after purchase and always avoid stale, limp specimens. The peel and the layer directly beneath it contain a high concentration of nutrients, so it is best to avoid peeling vegetables or to remove the thinnest layer for maximum nutrient retention.

Minerals and vitamins C and B are water soluble and they are lost by seepage into cooking water or the liquid over which vegetables are steamed. To minimize the loss of nutrients, do not cut up vegetables finely as this creates a greater surface area for seepage. Vitamin C is also destroyed by long cooking and by exposure to alkalines.

Raw and lightly cooked vegetables provide the best nutritional value and source of fibre. Any cooking liquid should, whenever possible, be used in stocks, gravies or sauces.

ABOUT THIS BOOK

Vegetables can play a starring role in a recipe or they may be combined to produce a harmony of flavours. Some of the best soups are examples of well-tuned mixtures – minestrone, for instance, is a blend of onions, carrots, tomatoes and cabbage, while a simple vegetable soup brings together a few ingredients. These, and many others, are loved for the sum of their parts rather than for the taste of individual vegetables.

In general, however, recipes in this book focus on a particular vegetable, so that their particular virtues can be appreciated to the full.

Above: Tomato and Basil Tart.
Left: Red, orange and green (bell) peppers.

This is not a vegetarian book; however, there are plenty of recipes that are vegetarian. In many instances, substituting vegetable stock for chicken stock will ensure that the recipe is acceptable.

The recipes are an eclectic mix of classic dishes from around the world and others I have devised over years of cooking; many are perennial favourites with my friends and family. The great thing about cooking with vegetables, however, is that once you have got the hang of using them, a recipe becomes unnecessary. You will discover how you most enjoy carrots, asparagus or less-common vegetables and will learn, as I have, to experiment in your own way. Good Luck!

ONIONS
AND
LEEKS

Onions

Shallots

Chives

Garlic

Leeks

ONIONS

There are bound to be vegetables you like better than others but a cook would be lost without onions. There are many classic recipes specifically for onion dishes so they can be appreciated in their own right. Onion tarts or French onion soup, for instance, have a sublime flavour and only onions are appropriate. But also, there is hardly a recipe where onions, or their cousins – garlic, leeks or shallots – are not used. Gently fried until soft, or fried more fiercely until golden brown, they add a unique, savoury flavour to dishes.

History

Onions, along with shallots, leeks, chives and garlic, belong to the *Allium* family which, including wild varieties, has some 325 members. All have the characteristic onion smell that is caused by volatile acids beneath the skin.

Archaeological and historical records show that onions have been eaten for thousands of years. They are believed to have originally come from the Middle East and their easy cultivation suggests that their use spread quickly. There are references to the onion in the Bible and it was widely eaten in Egypt. There was, we are told, an inscription on the Great Pyramid stating that the slaves who built the tomb ate their way through 1,600 talents worth of onions, radishes and garlic – presumably a lot, given that the Great Pyramid was made using more than two million 2$1/2$-tonne blocks of stone.

By the Middle Ages, onions were a common vegetable throughout Europe and would have been used in soups, stews and sauces when strong flavouring was preferred.

Varieties

As they keep well in a cool place, most people keep a handy stock of onions, usually a general purpose type that can be sautéed or browned. However, onions come in a variety of different colours and strengths, and for certain recipes particular onions are needed.

Right: Spanish (Bermuda) onions.
Far right top: Yellow onions.
Far right below: Red onions.

Spanish (Bermuda) Onions: Onions raised in warm areas are milder in taste than ones from cooler regions, and Spanish onions are among the mildest cultivated types. They are a beautiful pale copper colour and are noticeably larger than yellow onions. They have a delicate, sweet flavour that makes them ideal for serving raw in salads, thinly sliced, while their size makes them suitable for stuffing and baking whole.

Yellow Onions: These are the widely available onions you find everywhere and, though called yellow onions, their skins are more golden brown. They are the most pungent of all the onions and are a good, all-purpose variety. The smallest ones, referred to as baby (pearl), button or pickling onions, are excellent for pickling but can also be added whole to a casserole or sautéed in butter to make a vegetable accompaniment.

Red Onions: Sometimes called Italian onions, these have an attractive appearance and are now widely available from most good greengrocers and supermarkets. Below their ruby red skins the flesh is blushed with red. They have a mild, sweet flavour and are excellent thinly sliced and used raw in salads and *antipasti* dishes. They can also be caramelized and partnered with goat's cheese to make delicious tarts.

White Onions: These come in all sorts of interesting shapes and sizes – squat, round and oval, big and small. The very small white onions, with shimmery silver skins, are mild and best added whole to stews or served in a creamy sauce. Larger white onions can be mild or strong – there is no way of telling. Like yellow onions, white onions are extremely versatile whether used raw or cooked. The very small white onions, called Paris Silverskin, are the ones used for dry martinis and for commercial pickling.

Vidalia Onions: These popular American onions are a speciality of and named after a town in Georgia, USA. They are a large, pale yellow onion and are deliciously sweet and juicy. Used in salads, or roasted with meat or with other vegetables, they are superb.

Bermuda Onions: These are similar in size to Spanish onions but are rather more squat. They have a mild flavour and are good thinly sliced, fried until golden and served with steaks or burgers.

As well as the outer brown leaves, remove the next layer of onion, as it is often dry or damaged. Unless slicing onions for stir-fries, for which it is customary to slice the onion into wedges, always slice an onion through the rings, widthways. Make whole rings, or for half-rings, cut the onion in half lengthways through the root before slicing (*below*).

Spring Onions or Scallions: These are also true onions but harvested very young while their shoots are still green and fresh. They have a mild, delicate taste and both the small white bulb and the green tops can be used in salads, omelettes and stir-fries, or indeed any dish that requires a mild onion flavour.

Nutrition

As well as tasting good, onions are good for you. They contain vitamins B and C together with calcium, iron and potassium. Like garlic, they also contain cycloallin, an anticoagulant that helps protect against heart disease.

Buying and Storing

It used to be a common sight to see an onion seller travelling around on a bicycle with strings of onions hanging from every available support including his own neck.

Nowadays, strings of onions are hard to come by although, if you do find them in stores, they are a good way of buying and storing the vegetable.

Onions, more than almost any other vegetable, keep well provided they are stored in a cool, dry place, such as a larder or outhouse. Do not store them in the refrigerator as they will go soft, and never keep cut onions in the refrigerator – or anywhere else – unless you want onion-flavoured milk and an onion-scented home. Onions do not keep well once cut and it is worth buying onions in assorted sizes so that you do not end up having bits left over. Unused bits of onion can be added to stocks; otherwise it is best to dispose of them.

Preparing

Onions contain a substance called syn-propanethial-S-oxide that is released when they are cut and causes the eyes to water. There are various tricks that are supposed to prevent this, including cutting onions under running water, holding a piece of bread between your teeth or wearing goggles! It is known that eyes become less sensitive the more they are exposed to the compounds.

For finely chopped onion, slice again lengthways. Leaving the root intact at one end will make slicing onions easier, and you can simply discard it once you have finished.

Cooking

The volatile acids in onions are driven off during cooking, which is why cooked onion is never as strong as raw onion. The method of cooking, even the way of frying an onion, affects its eventual taste. Boiled or chopped onion added neat to soups or casseroles has a stronger, more raw taste. Frying or sautéing briefly, or sweating (frying in a little fat with the lid on) until soft and translucent gives a mild flavour. When fried until golden brown, onions develop a distinct flavour, both sweet and savoury, that is superb in curries and with grilled (broiled) meats and is essential for French onion soup.

Above far left: Vidalia onions.
Left: White onions.
Above left: Spring onions (scallions).

SHALLOTS

Shallots are not baby onions but a separate member of the onion family. They have a delicate flavour, less intense than most onions and they also dissolve easily into liquids, which is why they are favoured for sauces. Shallots grow in small, tight clusters so that when you break one open there may be two or three bunched together at the root.

Their size makes them convenient for a recipe where only a little onion is required or when a fine onion flavour is called for. Shallots are a pleasant, if maybe extravagant, alternative to onions, but where recipes specify shallots (especially sauce recipes), they should be used if possible.

Although classic cookery frequently calls for particular ingredients, the art of improvisation should not be ignored. For instance, Coq au Vin is traditionally made with walnut-size white onions, but when these are substituted with shallots, the result is delightful.

History

Shallots are probably as ancient as onions. Roman commentators wrote eloquently about the excellence of shallots in sauces.

Varieties

Shallots are small slender onions with long necks and golden, copper-coloured skins. There are a number of varieties, although there is unlikely to be a choice in the supermarkets. In any case, the differences are more in size and colour of skin than in flavour.

Buying and Storing

Like onions, shallots should be firm without any green shoots. They will keep well for several months in a cool, dry place.

Preparing and Cooking

Skin shallots in the same way as onions, i.e. top and tail them and then peel off the outer skin. Pull apart the bulbs. Slice them carefully and thinly using a sharp knife – shallots are so small, it is easy to slip and cut yourself. When cooking them whole, fry over a very gentle heat without browning too much.

CHIVES

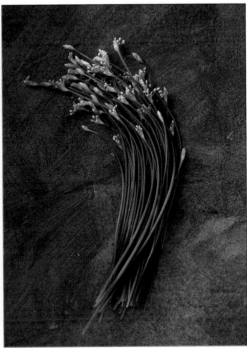

Chives: In culinary terms, chives are classed as a herb, but as members of the onion family they are worth mentioning here. As anyone who has grown them knows, chives are tufts of aromatic grass with pretty pale lilac flowers, which are also edible.

Preparing and Serving

Chives are often snipped with scissors and added to egg dishes, or used as a garnish for dips, salads and soups, adding a pleasant but faint onion flavour. Along with parsley, tarragon and chervil, they are an essential component of *fines herbes*.

Chives are also a delicious addition to soft cheeses – far nicer than store-bought cheeses containing chives, where the flavour virtually disappears. They can also be stirred into soft butter as an alternative to garlic butter. This can then be spread on to bread and baked like garlic bread.

If adding to cooked dishes, cook only very briefly, otherwise their flavour will be lost.

Chinese Chives: Chinese chives, sometimes called garlic chives, have a delicate garlic flavour, and if you see them for sale they are worth buying as they add a delicate onion flavour to stir-fries and other oriental dishes.

Preparing and Serving

Use them as you would chives – both the green and white parts are edible. They are also delicious served on their own as a vegetable accompaniment.

Buying and Storing

For both types of chives, look for plump, uniformly green specimens with no brown spots or signs of wilting. They can be stored for up to a week in the refrigerator. Unopened flowers on Chinese chives are an indication that the plant is young and therefore more tender than one with fully opened flowers.

Above left: Chives.
Above right: Chinese chives.

GARLIC

Garlic is an ingredient that almost anyone who does any cooking at all, and absolutely everyone who enjoys cooking, should not be without.

History

Garlic is known to have been first grown in around 3200BC. Inscriptions and models of garlic found in the pyramids of ancient Egypt testify to the fact that garlic was not only an important foodstuff but that it had ceremonial significance as well. The Greeks and Romans likewise believed garlic to have magical qualities. Warriors would eat it for strength before going into battle, gods were appeased with gifts of garlic, and cloves of garlic were fastened round the necks of babies to ward off evil. Hence, vampire mythology has ancient precedents.

The Greeks and Romans also used garlic for its therapeutic qualities. Not only was it thought to be an aphrodisiac but it was also believed to be good for eczema, toothache and snake bites.

Although garlic found its way all over Europe – vats of butter, strongly flavoured with garlic, that date back 200–300 years have been found by archaeologists working in Ireland – fundamentally, its popularity today derives from our liking for Mediterranean, Indian and Asian food, in which garlic plays a very important part.

Nutrition

As is often the case, what was once dismissed as an old wives' tale is, after thorough scientific inquiry, found to be true. Garlic is a case in point; most authorities accept that it has various therapeutic properties. The most significant of these is that it lowers blood cholesterol, thus helping prevent heart disease. In addition, raw garlic contains a powerful antibiotic and there is some evidence that it has a beneficial effect against cancer and strokes, and increases the absorption of vitamins. Many garlic enthusiasts take their garlic in tablet form, but true devotees prefer to consume it in its natural form, although this can result in bad breath.

Right: A string of pink-skinned garlic.

Varieties

There are numerous varieties of garlic, from the large 'elephant' garlic, to small tight bulbs. Their papery skin can be white, pink or purple. Colour makes no difference to taste but the particular attraction of the large purple bulbs is that they make a beautiful display in the kitchen.

As a general rule, the smaller the garlic bulb, the stronger it is likely to be. However, most garlic sold in stores is not classified in either shape or form (unless it is elephant garlic) and in practice you will simply pick up whatever you need, either loose, in bunches or on strings.

Garlic grown in a hot climate is likely to be the most pungent, and fresh new season's garlic has a subtle, mild flavour that is particularly good if it is to be used raw, for example, in salads and for dressings.

Above: Elephant garlic beside normal-size garlic bulbs.

Buying and Storing

Garlic bulbs should be firm and round with clear, papery skins. Avoid any that are beginning to sprout. Garlic bulbs keep well stored in a cool, dry place; if the air is damp they will sprout and if it is too warm the cloves will eventually turn to grey powder.

Preparing and Cooking

First break the garlic bulb into cloves and then remove the papery skin. You can blanch this off with hot water but using a fingernail or knife is just as effective and is quicker. When a garlic clove is split lengthways a shoot is revealed in the centre, which is sometimes green, and some people remove this whatever the colour. Cloves are the little segments that make up the bulb and most recipes call for one or more cloves of garlic. (Don't use a bulb when you just need a clove!)

Crush cloves either with the blade of a knife or use a garlic crusher. Crushed garlic cooks more evenly and distributes its flavour in food better than when it is used sliced or finely chopped (stir-fries are the exception). Prepare garlic according to the strength of flavour required: thinly sliced garlic is milder than chopped, which in turn is milder than crushed garlic and, of course, cooking mutes the pungency.

Garlic Breath

The taste and smell of garlic tends to linger on the breath and can be a problem to get rid of. Chewing parsley is a well-known remedy but is only moderately successful. Chewing the seeds of cardamom pods is also said to work but is rather unpleasant. The best suggestion is to eat garlic with your friends so that nobody notices!

LEEKS

Leeks are very versatile, having their own distinct, subtle flavour. They are excellent in pies and casseroles with other ingredients, braised in cream and served by themselves, or simmered in butter as an accompanying vegetable.

Leeks are also wonderful in soups and broths and have rightly earned the title, 'king of the soup onions'. Cock-a-leekie from Scotland and *Crème Vichyssoise*, invented by the chef of New York's Ritz-Carlton, are two classic leek soups, but many other soups call for leeks.

History

Leeks, like onions and garlic, have a long history. They were grown widely in ancient Egypt and were also eaten and enjoyed throughout the Greek and Roman period. In England, there is evidence that leeks were enjoyed during the Dark Ages. There is little mention of them during the Middle Ages, and history suggests that between the 16th and 18th centuries eating leeks was not considered fashionable.

However, while they may not have enjoyed a good reputation among the notoriously fickle aristocracy, the rural communities probably continued to eat leeks. They grow in all sorts of climates and are substantial enough to make a reasonable meal for a poor family. It was probably during this time that they were dubbed 'poor man's asparagus' – a name that says more about people's snobbery about food than it does about the vegetables themselves.

Many place names in England, such as Leckhampstead and Leighton Buzzard are derived from the word leek and, of course, the leek has been a national emblem of Wales for hundreds of years.

Varieties

There are many different varieties of leeks but among them there is little difference in flavour. Commercially grown leeks tend to be about 25cm/10in long and about 2cm/³⁄₄in in diameter. Leeks nurtured in home gardens can be left to grow to an enormous size but these may develop a woody centre, so are best picked when they are much smaller and more slender.

the first layer of white; then cut a slit from one end to the other through to the centre of the leek *(below)*. Wash under cold running water, pulling the sections apart so that the water rinses out any stubborn pieces of earth. If you slice the leeks – either slice thickly or thinly – place them in a colander and rinse thoroughly under cold water.

Cooking

Leeks can be steamed or boiled and then added to your recipe, or fry sliced leeks gently in butter for a minute or so and then cover with a lid to sweat so they cook without browning. Unlike onions, leeks shouldn't be allowed to brown as they become tough and unappetizing. They can be stir-fried, however, with a some garlic and ginger. If they begin to cook too fiercely, splash in a little stock and soy sauce and simmer until tender.

RAMP

Among the many wild onions and leeks, the Canadian ramp is perhaps the best known. Also called the wild leek, it looks a little like a spring onion (scallion), but has a stronger and more assertive garlic-onion flavour. Choose unblemished, clear white specimens with bright, fresh leaves and keep in a cool place, wrapped in a plastic bag to store.

Prepare and cook as you would spring onions, by trimming the root end and then slicing thinly. Use in cooking or in salads but remember the onion flavour is stronger, so use sparingly.

Buying and Storing

Buy leeks which look fresh and healthy. The white part should be firm and unblemished and the leaves green and lively. As leeks do not keep particularly well, it is best to buy them as and when you need them. If you need to store them, trim away the top of the leaves and keep them in the salad drawer of the refrigerator or in a cool place. After several days they will begin to shrivel.

Preparing

It is important to wash leeks thoroughly before cooking as earth and grit lodges itself between the white sections at the base. To prepare leeks, cut away the flags (leaves) and trim the base. Unless the leek is extremely fresh or home grown, you will probably have to remove

Left: Leeks.
Above: Ramp.

SHOOTS
AND
STEMS

ASPARAGUS

Asparagus is definitely a luxury vegetable. Its price, even in season, sets it apart from cabbages and cauliflowers, and it has a taste of luxury too. The spears, especially the thick, green spears, at their best in early summer, have an intense, rich flavour that is impossible to describe but easy to remember. If the gods eat, they will eat asparagus – served simply with a good Hollandaise!

History

The ancient Greeks are known to have enjoyed wild asparagus but it was not until the Roman period that we know it was cultivated. Even then asparagus was highly thought of; it is recorded that Julius Caesar liked to eat it with melted butter. There is little mention of asparagus being eaten in England until the 17th century. Mrs Beeton has 14 recipes for asparagus and from the prices quoted in her cookbook it is apparent that it was expensive even in Victorian times.

Nutrition

Asparagus provides vitamins A, B2 and C and is also a good source of potassium, iron and calcium. It is a well-known diuretic.

Varieties

There are many varieties of asparagus and many different ways of raising it too. Spanish and some Dutch asparagus is white with ivory tips; it is grown under mounds of soil and cut just as the tips begin to show before exposure to light makes them turn green. The purple variety is mostly grown in France, where the spears are cut once the tips are about 4cm/1 1/2 in above the ground. Consequently, the stalks are white and the tops tinged with green or purple. In contrast, English and American asparagus grows above the ground and the spears are entirely green. Arguments continue over which has the better flavour, most growers expressing a preference for their own asparagus!

Thin, short asparagus are called sprue and are excellent when briefly steamed or stir-fried and added to salads. In Italy, they are served by themselves, scattered with grated Parmesan cheese.

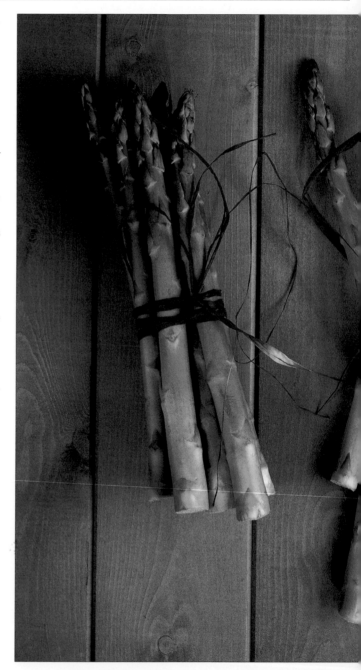

Preparing

Unless the asparagus comes straight from the garden, cut off the bottom of the stalk as it is usually hard and woody. If the bottom parts of the stem also feel hard, pare this away with a potato peeler *(below)*. However, if the asparagus is very fresh, this is not necessary, and sprue rarely needs trimming at all.

Buying and Storing

Asparagus has a relatively short growing season from late spring to early summer. Nowadays, it is available in the stores almost all year round but outside the season it will have been imported. It is still good, but it is expensive and will not have the flavour of home-produced asparagus, since it starts to lose its flavour once it is cut.

When buying asparagus, the tips should be tightly furled and fresh looking, and the stalks fresh and straight. If the stalks are badly scarred or droopy, it indicates that they have been hanging around for too long and it is not worth buying. Asparagus will keep for several days if necessary. Untie the bundles and store in the salad drawer of the refrigerator.

Cooking

The problem with cooking asparagus is that the stalks take longer to cook than the tender tips, which need to be only briefly steamed. Ideally, you should use an asparagus kettle. Place the asparagus spears with the tips upwards in the wire basket and then lower into a little boiling salted water in the kettle. Cover and cook until the stems are tender.

Alternatively, if you don't have an asparagus kettle, place the bundle upright in a deep pan of boiling salted water. (The bundle can be wedged into place with potatoes.) Cover with a dome of foil and cook for 5–10 minutes or until the spears are tender. The cooking time depends largely on the thickness and woodiness of the spears but take care not to overcook; the spears should still have a 'bite' to them.

Asparagus can also be roasted in a little olive oil. This cooking method intensifies the flavour and is gratifyingly simple. Serve with just a sprinkling of sea salt – it's quite delicious! If you are steaming asparagus, serve it simply with melted butter, which perfectly complements the luxurious nature of the vegetable.

Left: Asparagus.
Above: White asparagus.

GLOBE ARTICHOKES

Globe artichokes have an exquisite flavour and are a very sociable food to eat. They grow in abundance in Brittany, and during July and August farmers can frequently be seen selling them by the roadside. The globes are huge hearty specimens so they make a good buy.

History

It is not known for certain whether artichokes were eaten in antiquity. Although they are mentioned by writers, they could have been referring to the cardoon, which is the uncultivated form of artichoke. Cardoons grew wild in many southern European countries, and, as far as we know, cultivated artichokes first became a popular food in Italy, where they are still appreciated. However, Goethe did not share the Italians' liking for the vegetable and remarks in his book, *Travels Through Italy*, written in 1786–7 that "the peasants eat thistles", something he didn't care for at all.

Nowadays, artichokes are grown all over southern Europe and in California. People in Italy, France and Spain eat artichokes while the vegetable is still young, before the choke has formed and when the entire artichoke is edible. Unfortunately, such young delicacies are not usually exported but look out for them if you are in these countries.

Buying and Storing

It is only worth buying artichokes when they are in season, although they are available in supermarkets almost all year round. In winter, however, they are sad-looking specimens, small and rather dry, and are really not worth the bother of cooking. At their best, artichokes should be lively looking with a good bloom on their leaves, the inner leaves wrapped tightly round the choke and heart inside. Artichokes will keep for two or three days in the salad drawer of the refrigerator but are best eaten as soon as possible.

Preparing and Cooking

First twist off the stalk, which should also remove some of the fibres at the base, and then cut the base flat and pull away any small base leaves. If the leaves are very spiky, trim them with a pair of scissors if liked *(above)*, then rinse under running water. Cook in boiling water, acidulated with the juice of half a lemon. Large artichokes need to be simmered for 30–40 minutes until tender. To test if they are done, pull off one of the outer leaves. It should come away easily and the base of the leaf should be tender.

heart. Eat the tender, fleshy heart with a knife and fork, dipping it in the garlic butter or vinaigrette.

CARDOONS

This impressively large vegetable is closely related to the globe artichoke and has a superb flavour, a cross between artichokes and asparagus. Cultivated plants frequently grow to 2m/6ft in height and, once mature, cardoons, like celery, are blanched as they grow. This process involves wrapping the stalks with newspaper and black bags for several weeks, so that when harvested, in late autumn, before the frosts, the stalks are a pale green.

The cardoon is a popular vegetable in southern Europe but less commonly available elsewhere. In Spain, for instance, it is much appreciated and often appears on the table, poached and served with chestnuts or walnuts. Only the inner ribs and heart are generally used as the spiny leaves are inedible, although the root can also be eaten.

Artichokes and Drink

Artichokes contain a chemical called cynarin, which in many people affects the taste buds by enhancing sweet flavours. Among other things, this will spoil the taste of wine. Consequently, don't waste good wine with artichokes but drink iced water instead, which should taste pleasantly sweet.

Eating Artichokes

Artichokes are fun to eat. They have to be eaten with fingers, which does away with any pomp and ceremony, always a handicap for a good dinner party. Serve one artichoke between two, so that people can share the fun of pulling off the leaves and dipping them into garlic butter or vinaigrette. If you want to serve one each, serve them in succession.

The dipping sauces are an essential part of eating artichokes; people can either spoon a little on to their plates or give everyone a little bowl each. After dipping, draw the leaf through your teeth, eating the fleshy part and piling the remains of the leaf on your plate.

When most of the leaves have been eaten, a few thin pointed leaves remain in the centre, which can be pulled off altogether. Then pull or cut away the fine prickly choke and discard, to reveal the

Far left: Globe artichokes.
Top: Baby globe artichokes.
Above: Cardoons.

CELERY

Some people say that the act of eating celery has a slimming effect because chewing it uses up more calories than the vegetable itself contains. Although it may be insubstantial, celery nevertheless has a distinct and individual flavour, sharp and savoury, which makes it an excellent flavouring for soups and stuffings, as well as good on its own or in salads. The astringent flavour and crunchy texture of celery contrasts well with the other ingredients in salads such as Waldorf salad or walnut and avocado salad.

History

Celery has been eaten in this country for several hundred years, having been introduced from Italy where it was commonly eaten in salads.

Nutrition

Celery is very low in calories but contains potassium and calcium.

Varieties

Most greengrocers and supermarkets, depending on the time of year, sell both green and white celery and you would be excused for not knowing the difference. When celery is allowed to grow naturally, the stalks are green. However, by banking up earth against the shoots celery is blanched: the stalks are protected from sunlight and remain pale and white. Consequently, white celery is often 'dirty' – covered loosely in soil – while green celery will always be clean.

White celery, which is frost hardy, is only available in winter. It is more tender and less bitter than green celery and is generally considered superior. Celery is therefore thought of as a winter vegetable and is traditionally used at Christmas time, for stuffing and as a sauce to go with turkey or ham.

Buying and Storing

White celery is in season during the winter months. If possible, buy 'dirty' celery which hasn't been washed. It has a better flavour than the pristine but rather bland supermarket variety. Look for celery with green fresh-looking leaves and straight stems. If the leaves or any

outer stalks are missing, it is likely to be rather old, so worth avoiding. Celery will keep for several days in the salad drawer of the refrigerator. Limp celery can be revived by wrapping it in kitchen paper and standing it in a jar of water.

Preparing

Wash the celery if necessary and pull the stalks apart, trimming the base with a sharp knife. Cut into thick or thin slices according to the recipe. When served raw and whole, the coarse outer 'strings' should be removed from each stick by pulling them up from the base or using a vegetable peeler.

Cooking and Serving

Serve celery raw and finely sliced in salads, mixed with cream cheese or sour cream. Braised celery is tasty, either whole or sliced. Celery has a distinctive, savoury, astringent flavour so is excellent in soups or stuffings.

CELERIAC

Strictly speaking, celeriac is a root vegetable, being the root of certain kinds of celery. It is knobbly with a patchy brown/white skin and has a similar but less pronounced flavour than celery. Grated and eaten raw, it has a crunchy texture, but when cooked it is more akin to potatoes. Thin slices of potato and celeriac cooked *au gratin* with cream is a popular way of serving this vegetable.

Buying and Preparing

If possible, buy smallish bulbs of celeriac. The flesh discolours when exposed to light, so as soon as you have peeled, sliced, diced or grated the celeriac, plunge it into a bowl of acidulated water (water with lemon juice added).

Cooking

Celeriac can be used in soups and broths, or can be diced and boiled and eaten in potato salads.

Left: Green celery.
Above: White celery.
Right: Celeriac.

FIDDLEHEAD FERN

Sometimes called the ostrich fern, these shoots are a rich green colour and are normally about 5cm/2in long. They have an unusual flavour, something like a cross between asparagus and okra, and have a slightly chewy texture, which makes them a popular choice for oriental dishes.

Preparing and Cooking

To prepare and cook, trim the ends and then steam or simmer in a little water or sauté in butter until tender. Use in salads or serve as a first course with a Hollandaise sauce.

Right: Fiddlehead ferns.
Below left: Alfalfa sprouts.
Below right: Mung bean sprouts.

ORIENTAL SHOOTS

BAMBOO SHOOTS

In the Far East, edible bamboo shoots are sold fresh in the market. The young shoots are stripped of their brown outer skins and the insides are then eaten. Although fresh bamboo shoots can be found in oriental stores, the most readily available variety is sold in cans, but this undoubtedly spoils the flavour. Fresh bamboo shoots have a mild but distinct taste, faintly reminiscent of globe artichokes, while canned ones really taste of nothing at all. However, the texture, which, in Chinese cuisines particularly, is as important as the flavour, is not so impaired, and bamboo shoots have a pleasantly crunchy bite.

Preparing and Cooking

Peel away the outer skin and then cook in boiling water for about half an hour. They should feel firm, but not too hard. Once cooked, slice thinly and serve by themselves as a side dish, with garlic butter or a sauce, or add to stir-fries, spring rolls or any oriental dish where

you need a contrast of textures. Since canned bamboo shoots have been preserved in brine, always rinse well before using.

BEAN SPROUTS

Bean sprouts are rather a neglected vegetable, used almost carelessly for oriental dishes but otherwise passed by as being insipid and not very interesting. It's a reputation they don't deserve: not only do they have a lovely fresh flavour, but they are also good for you.

All sorts of seeds can be sprouted, but the bean family are favourites among the sprouted vegetables. The bean sprouts most commonly available in the stores are sprouted mung beans, but aduki beans, alfalfa, lentils and soybeans can all be sprouted and taste delicious.

Nutrition

Beans sprouts contain a significant amount of protein, Vitamin C and many of the B vitamins. They have an excellent flavour too, best appreciated eaten raw in salads or sandwiches, and for slimmers they are an ideal food, low in calories, yet with sufficient substance to be filling, and with a flavour and texture that can be enjoyed without a dressing.

Buying and Storing

Bean sprouts should only be bought when absolutely fresh. They don't keep for long and they will taste sour if past their best. The sprouts should be firm, not limp, and the tips should be green or yellow; avoid any that are beginning to turn brown.

Cooking

If stir-frying, add the bean sprouts at the last minute so they cook for the minimum period to keep plenty of crunch and retain their nutritional value. Most health food stores will have instructions on sprouting your own beans. Only buy seeds intended for sprouting.

PALM HEARTS

Fresh palm hearts are the buds of cabbage palm trees and are considered a delicacy in many parts of the world. They are available canned from oriental stores, but are most prized when fresh. These should be blanched before being cooked to eliminate any bitterness. They can be braised or sautéed and then served hot with a Hollandaise sauce, or cold with a simple vinaigrette.

WATER CHESTNUTS

Water chestnut is the common name for a number of aquatic herbs and their nut-like fruit, the best known and most popular variety being the Chinese water chestnut, sometimes known as the Chinese sedge. In China they are grown in exactly the same way as rice, the plants needing the same conditions of

high temperatures, shallow water and good soil. In spring, the corms are planted in paddy fields which are then flooded to a depth of 10cm/4in. These are drained in autumn, and the corms are harvested and stored over the winter.

Water chestnuts are much used in Chinese, Filipino, Vietnamese and Thai cooking and have a sweet crunchy flavour

with nutty overtones. They are edible cooked or raw and are excellent in all sorts of dishes, including a popular Thai dessert.

Above: Sprouting mung beans.
Below: clockwise from top left: canned water chestnuts, canned bamboo shoots, fresh water chestnuts, canned palm hearts.

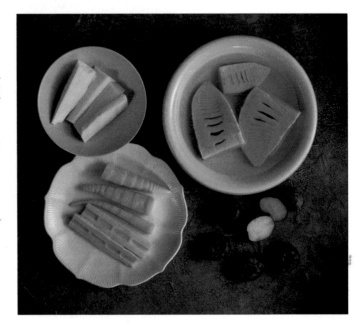

FENNEL

The vegetable fennel is closely related to the herb and spice of the same name. It is called variously Florence fennel, sweet fennel, *finocchio dulce* or Italian fennel.

 Like the herb, Florence fennel has the distinct flavour of anise, a taste that seems to go particularly well with fish, so the vegetable is often served with fish dishes while the herb or spice is commonly used in fish stocks, sauces or soups. The leaves are edible and can be used in soups and stocks as well as for garnishing.

History

Florence fennel has only been popular in Britain for the last 30 years, although it has a long history of cultivation, having been eaten by the ancient Egyptians, Greeks and Romans. In Italy, fennel has been grown and eaten for several centuries: many of the best fennel recipes come from Italy and other parts of the Mediterranean.

Buying and Storing

If possible, buy small tender bulbs. The bulbs should be clean and white with no bruises or blemishes and the feathery leaves should be green and lively. Fennel will keep for a day or two in the salad drawer of the refrigerator.

Preparing

Unless the bulbs are very young and tender, remove the first layer of skin, as it is likely to be tough (this can be used for a stock). Fennel can then be sliced into slivers by cutting downwards or into rings by cutting across the bulb. When used raw in salads, it needs to be cut into smaller pieces.

Cooking and Serving

Fennel can be served raw if it is thinly sliced and dressed with a light vinaigrette. In salads, its flavour contrasts well with apple, celery and other crunchy ingredients. Fennel is also excellent braised with onions, tomatoes and garlic or baked with cream and cheese for a heart winter dish.

Right: Florence fennel.
Far right: Marsh samphire.

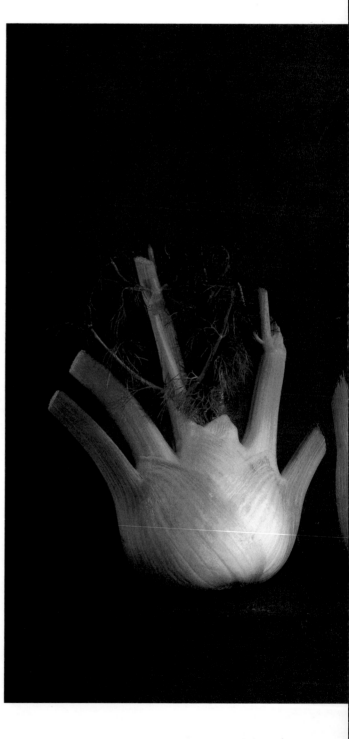

SAMPHIRE

There are two types of samphire. Marsh samphire grows in estuaries and salt marshes while rock samphire, which is sometimes called sea fennel, grows on rocky shores. The two are understandably confused since they are both connected with the sea, yet they are completely different plants.

The type likely to be sold by a fishmonger is marsh samphire. It is also known as glasswort and is sometimes called sea asparagus, as its shoots are similar to sprue, small asparagus shoots.

Although marsh samphire grows easily and is commonly found all over Europe and North America, it is not cultivated and is only available for a short time while it is in season, normally in late summer and early autumn.

Samphire has a distinctly salty, iodine flavour and a pleasant crisp texture. The taste is reminiscent of the sea and goes particularly well with fish and shellfish. However, samphire can be enjoyed simply steamed and dipped into melted butter.

Buying and Storing

When in season, good fishmongers get regular stocks of marsh samphire, and it should look bright and fresh. Buy it as you need it, as it will not keep for long.

Preparing and Cooking

If necessary, wash marsh samphire under cold running water. It is best steamed over a pan of boiling water for no more than 3 minutes. Alternatively, blanch it in boiling water for 3–5 minutes and then drain. Samphire can be eaten raw but blanching it removes some of the saltiness.

To eat samphire, draw the shoots through the teeth to peel the succulent part from the thin central core.

— THREE —
ROOTS

Potatoes

Parsnips

Jerusalem Artichokes

Turnips and Swedes

Carrots

Horseradish

Beetroot

Salsify and Scorzonera

Exotic Roots

Ginger and Galangal

POTATOES

History

The potato originates from South America. Most people learned at school that Sir Walter Raleigh brought the tubers to England from Virginia, but this never convinced historians as the potato was completely unknown in North America until the 18th century. They now believe that Sir Francis Drake was responsible. In 1586, after battling against the Spaniards in the Caribbean, Drake stopped to pick up provisions from Cartegena in northern Colombia – and these included tobacco and potato tubers. En route home, he stopped off at Roanoke Island, off the coast of Virginia. The first group of English colonists had been sponsored to settle there by Sir Walter Raleigh but by this time they had had enough. Drake brought them back to England, along with some of Raleigh's men and, of course, the provisions – including the potato tubers.

Potatoes apparently fascinated Queen Elizabeth and intrigued horticulturists, but they were not an overnight success among the people. The wealthy frequently reviled them as being flavourless and the food of the poor. People distrusted the fact that they reached maturity underground, believing them to be the work of the devil.

In Scotland, Presbyterian ministers darkly advised their congregations that there was no mention of potatoes in the Bible, and thus the eating of them was an ungodly act!

In spite of such a bad press, potatoes nevertheless were slowly recognized for their merit. By 1650 they were the staple food of Ireland, and elsewhere in Europe potatoes began to replace wheat as the most important crop, both for people and for livestock. In an early English cookbook, *Adam's Luxury and Eve's Cookery*, there are 20 different recipes for cooking and serving potatoes.

The first mention of potatoes in America is in 1719 in Londonderry, New Hampshire. They arrived not from the south, but via Irish settlers who brought their potatoes with them.

The current popularity of potatoes is probably thanks to a Frenchman called Antoine-Auguste Parmentier. A military pharmacist of the latter part of the 18th century, Parmentier recognized the virtues of the potato, both for its versatility and as an important food for the poor, and set out to improve its image. He persuaded Louis XVI to let him grow potatoes on royal land around the palace in Versailles in order to impress the fashion-conscious Parisians. He also produced a court dinner in which each course contained potatoes. Gradually, eating potatoes became chic, first among people in the French court and then in French Society. Today, if you see *Parmentier* in a recipe or on a menu, it means 'with potato'.

Nutrition

Potatoes are an important source of carbohydrate. Once deemed fattening, we now know that, on the contrary, potatoes can be an excellent part of a calorie-controlled diet – provided, of course, they are not fried in oil or mashed with too much butter. Potatoes are also a very good source of vitamin C, and during the winter potatoes are often the main source of this vitamin. They also contain potassium, iron and vitamin B.

Varieties

There are more than 400 varieties of potato but unless you are a gardener, you will find only some 15 varieties generally available. Thanks to labelling laws, packaged potatoes carry their names which makes it easier to learn to differentiate between the varieties and find out which potato is good for what.

New Potatoes

Carlingford: Available as a new potato or as main crop, Carlingford has a close white flesh.
Jersey Royal: Often the first new potato of the season, Jersey Royals have been shipped from Jersey for over a hundred years and have acquired an enviable reputation among everyone who enjoys good food. Boiled or steamed and then served with butter and a sprinkling of parsley, they cannot be beaten.

Jersey Royals are kidney-shaped, with yellow firm flesh and a distinctive flavour. Don't confuse Jersey Royals with Jersey Whites, which are actually Maris Pipers, grown in Jersey.
Maris Bard: A regularly shaped, slightly waxy potato with white flesh.
Maris Peer: This variety has dry firm flesh and a waxy texture and doesn't disintegrate when cooked – consequently, it is good in salads.

Main Crop Potatoes

Desirée: A potato with a pink skin and yellow soft-textured flesh. It is good for baking, frying, roasting and mashing.

Estima: A good all-rounder with yellow flesh and pale skin.

Golden Wonder: A russet-skinned potato that was the original favourite for making crisps (US potato chips). It has a distinctive flavour, and should you find them for sale, buy them at once for baked potatoes. They are also good boiled or roasted.

Kerr's Pink: A good cooking potato with pink skin and creamy flesh.

King Edward: Probably the best known of British potatoes, although not the best in flavour. King Edwards are creamy white in colour with a slightly floury texture.

Red King Edwards are virtually identical except for their red skin. Both are good roasted or baked. However, the flesh disintegrates when boiled, so while they are good for mashing, do not use King Edwards if you want to serve whole boiled potatoes.

Maris Piper: This is a widely grown variety of potato, popular with growers and cooks because it is good for all kinds of cooking methods – baking, deep-frying, roasting and mashing. It has a pale, smooth skin and creamy white flesh.

Left: Maris Bard potatoes.
Above: Kerr's pink (left) and Maris Piper (right) potatoes.
Right: Romano potatoes.

Pentland Dell: A long, oval-shaped potato with a floury texture that disintegrates when boiled. For this reason, it is popular for roasting as the outside becomes soft when par-boiled and then crisps up with the fat during roasting.

Romano: The Romano has a distinctive red skin with creamy flesh and is a good all-rounder, similar to Desirée.

Wilja: Introduced from Holland, this is a pale, yellow-fleshed potato with a good, sweet flavour and waxy texture.

Other Varieties

Although most of these varieties are also main crop, they are less widely available than those listed above but are increasingly sold in supermarkets. They are fabulous for salads but many are also excellent sautéed or simply boiled.

Cara: A large main crop potato, which is excellent baked or boiled but is a good all-rounder.

Finger Potatoes: Thumb-sized, long baby potatoes are sometimes called finger potatoes or fingerlings. Among the many varieties are the German Lady's Finger. Since they are new crop potatoes, they need simply be boiled and then served either in salads or with a little butter and a sprinkling of parsley.

La Ratte: A French potato with a smooth skin and waxy yellow flesh. It has a chestnut flavour and is good in salads.

Linzer Delikatess: These small, kidney-shaped potatoes look a little like Jersey Royals but have a pale smooth skin. They do not have much taste and are best in salads where their flavour can be enhanced with other ingredients.

Pink Fir Apple: This is an old English variety, with pink skin and a smooth yellow flesh. It is becoming increasingly popular and has a distinctive flavour.

Above left: Cara (left) and Estima (right) potatoes.
Left: Linzer Delikatess potatoes.
Above: Desirée (left) and King Edward (right) potatoes.
Right: Finger potatoes.

Purple Congo: If you want to startle your friends, serve some of these striking purple-blue potatoes. There are several varieties of blue potato, ranging from a pale lavender to a purple-black, but one of the most popular is the Purple Congo, which is a wonderful deep purple. They are best boiled and served simply with a little butter and do retain their colour when cooked.

Truffe de Chine: Another deep purple, almost black potato, of unknown origin but now grown in France. It has a nutty, slightly mealy flavour and is best served in a salad with a simple dressing. Like the Purple Congo, it retains its colour after being cooked.

Recommended Varieties for Cooking

Baking: As for roasting, use potatoes with a floury texture, such as Golden Wonder, Pentland Dell, King Edward and Maris Piper.

Boiling: Jersey Royal, Maris Bard and Maris Peer, or any of the Egyptian or Belgian new crop varieties. In addition, Pink Fir Apple, La Ratte and Linzer Delikatess are excellent.

Deep-frying: King Edward, Golden Wonder, Romano, Maris Piper and Desirée.

Mashing: Golden Wonder, Maris Piper, King Edward, Wilja, Romano and Pentland Dell.

Roasting: Pentland Dell, Golden Wonder, Maris Piper, King Edward, Desiree and Romano are among the best roasting potatoes. Ideally, use potatoes with a floury texture.

Salads: All the small, specialist potatoes, such as La Ratte, Pink Fir Apple and Linzer Delikatess as well as Finger Potatoes and small new potatoes.

Sautéing: Any waxy type of potato, such as Maris Bard, Maris Peer, any of the specialist potatoes, and Romano and Maris Piper.

Buying and Storing

Potatoes should always be stored in a dark, cool, dry place. If they are stored exposed to the light, green patches will develop which can be poisonous, and they will go mouldy if kept in the damp. When buying potatoes in bulk, it is best to buy them in paper sacks rather than plastic bags as humid conditions will cause them to go rotten. Similarly, if you buy potatoes in plastic bags, remove them when you get home and place them in a vegetable rack or in a paper bag, in a dark place.

Main crop potatoes will keep for several months in the right conditions but will gradually lose their nutritional value. New potatoes should be eaten within two or three days as they will go mouldy if stored for too long.

Preparing

Most of the minerals and vitamins present in potatoes are contained in or just below the skin. It is therefore better to eat potatoes in their skins. New potatoes need only be washed under running water; older potatoes need to be scrubbed.

If you peel potatoes, use a peeler that removes only the very top surface (*below left*) or, alternatively, for salads and cold dishes, boil the potatoes in their skins and peel when cool.

Cooking

Baking: Cook baked potatoes in a low oven for well browned and crunchy skins and fluffy flesh. Baked potatoes can be cooked more quickly in a microwave oven; for a crunchy texture to the skin place them in a hot oven for 10 minutes.

Boiling: It is impossible to generalize on how long to boil as it depends so much on the variety of potato. Try to cut potatoes to an even size (new potatoes should not need to be cut), salt the water if liked, cover and cook over a moderate heat. Don't boil potatoes too fiercely; old ones especially may disintegrate and leave you with a pan of starchy water.

Deep-frying: Home-cooked chips (French fries) are a treat worth giving the family instead of the convenient but otherwise disappointing oven chips. However, they are fatty and therefore not good for you when eaten in great quantities or too often.

To make them, cut the potatoes into even chips and place in a bowl of cold water for about 10 minutes before frying. Drain and then dry in an old dish towel before frying. Fry only as many chips as will comfortably sit in the fat. Halfway through cooking, drain them and allow the oil to come back to temperature before plunging the chips back in. This browns the chips and they don't soak up excessive amounts of oil. Be warned; the cooking smells from making chips tend to linger!

Mashing: Boil the potatoes until tender, drain thoroughly and then tip them back into the pan; mash with a little milk and

butter using a potato masher (*below right*), and season to taste with a little salt, if necessary, and pepper. Never use a food processor or liquidizer: the potatoes will turn into an inedible thick grey paste. You may lightly whisk potatoes with a fork after mashing to fluff them up but no more – for once modern machines have not improved on the basic utensil.

Roast Potatoes: The best roast potatoes are made using a floury textured potato such as Maris Piper or King Edward. Wash and cut them into even chunks and par-boil them in lightly salted water until they begin to go tender and the outside looks soft. Drain them through a sieve (strainer) or colander and then tip them back into the pan, put the lid on and shake the pan two or three times. This roughens up the surface of the potato. Place the potatoes in a dish of hot oil or fat, or round a joint of meat, and turn them over so that they are evenly coated. Roast them in the oven for 40–50 minutes until golden. Serve as soon as possible once cooked as the outsides become leathery if they are kept in a warm oven for too long.

Sautéing: There are various ways to sauté potatoes and no one way is better than another. For sautéed sliced potatoes, par-boil whole potatoes for 5–10 minutes until they begin to soften. Drain them thoroughly and then slice into thick rounds. Using sunflower oil or a mixture of sunflower and olive oil (not butter as it will burn), fry them in a large frying pan. Turn the potatoes occasionally and cook until evenly browned. For sautéed, diced potatoes, cut the potatoes into small cubes, blanch for 2 minutes and then drain well. Either fry them on the stove or cook them in a little oil in the oven; turn them once or twice to brown evenly.

Steaming: New potatoes are excellent steamed. Place them on a bed of mint in a steamer or a colander over a pan of boiling water for 15–20 minutes.

Above left: Purple Congo potatoes.
Below left: Truffe de Chine (left) and Pink Fir Apple (right) potatoes.

PARSNIPS

There's something very old-fashioned about parsnips. They conjure up images of cold winter evenings and warm comforting broths supped in front of a blazing wood fire. Nowadays parsnips are available all year through, but many people still feel they belong to winter, adding their characteristic flavour to soups and stews.

Parsnips are related to carrots and are similarly sweet but with a distinct earthy flavour that blends well with other root vegetables and is also enhanced with spices and garlic.

History

Parsnips have a long history. The Romans grew and cooked them to make broths and stews. When they conquered Gaul and Britain, the Romans discovered that root vegetables grown in northerly areas had a better flavour than those grown in the south – they may have been the first to decree that parsnips should be eaten after the first frost!

Throughout the Dark Ages and early Middle Ages, parsnips were the main starchy vegetable for ordinary people (the potato had yet to be introduced). Parsnips were not only easy to grow but were a welcome food to eat during the lean winter months. They were also valued for their sugar content. Sweet parsnip dishes such as jam and desserts became part of traditional English cooking, and they were also commonly used for making beer and wine. Parsnip wine is still one of the most popular of the country wines, with a beautiful golden colour and a rich sherry-like flavour.

Nutrition

Parsnips contain moderate amounts of vitamins A and C, along with some of the B vitamins. They are also a source of calcium, iron and potassium.

Buying and Storing

Parsnips are really a winter crop, although nowadays they are available all year round. Tradition has it that parsnips are best after the first frost, but many people like the very young tender parsnips available in the early summer. When buying parsnips, choose small or

medium specimens as the large ones tend to be rather fibrous. They should feel firm and be a pale ivory colour without any sprouting roots. Store parsnips in a cool place, ideally an airy larder or cool outhouse, where they will keep well for 8–10 days.

Preparing

Very small parsnips need little or no peeling; just trim the ends and cook according to your recipe. Medium and large parsnips need to be peeled. Larger parsnips also need to have the woody core removed; if it is cut out before cooking, the parsnips will cook more quickly and evenly.

Cooking

Roast parsnips are best par-boiled for a few minutes before being added to the roasting dish. Very young parsnips can be roasted whole but larger ones are best halved or quartered lengthways. Roast in butter or oil for about 40 minutes in an oven preheated to 200°C/400°F/Gas 6.

To boil parsnips, cut them into pieces about 5cm/2in long and boil for 15–20 minutes until tender. When boiled briefly like this, they keep their shape, but when added to a casserole or stew they eventually disintegrate. Don't worry if this happens; parsnips need plenty of cooking so that the flavour can blend with the other ingredients.

JERUSALEM ARTICHOKES

Jerusalem artichokes are related to the sunflower and have nothing to do with Jerusalem. One explanation for their name is that they were christened girasole, 'Jerusalem', because their yellow flowers turned towards the sun. The Italian name for the Jerusalem artichoke is *girasole articocco*.

These small knobbly tubers have a lovely distinct flavour and are good in Palestine soup, a popular classic recipe. They are also delicious baked or braised.

History

Jerusalem artichokes are thought to have come from the central United States and Canada, where they were cultivated by the American-Indians as long ago as the 15th century. However, many writers have alluded to the fact that they cause 'wind', which tempers their popularity.

Buying and Storing

Jerusalem artichokes are at their best during winter and early spring. They are invariably knobbly but if possible buy neat ones with the minimum of knobs to save waste. The skins should be pale brown without any dark or soft patches. If they are stored in a cool dark place they will keep well for up to 10 days.

Preparing

The white flesh of artichokes turns purplish brown when exposed to light, so when peeling or slicing them raw, place them in a bowl of acidulated water (water to which the juice of about half a lemon has been added). Because artichokes are so knobbly, it is often easier to boil them in acidulated water in their skins and peel them afterwards – the cooked skins should slip off easily.

Cooking

Jerusalem artichokes can be cooked in many of the ways in which you would cook potatoes or parsnips. They are excellent roasted, sautéed or dipped in batter and fried, but first par-boil them for 10–15 minutes until nearly tender. For creamed artichokes, mix with potatoes in equal amounts; this slightly blunts their flavour, making a tasty side dish that is not too overpowering.

Left: Parsnips.
Below: Jerusalem artichokes.

TURNIPS AND SWEDES (RUTABAGAS)

Turnips and swedes are both members of the cabbage family and are closely related to each other – so close that it is not surprising that their names are often confused. For instance, swedes are sometimes called Swedish turnips or swede-turnips and in Scotland, where they are thought of as turnips, they are called neeps.

Nowadays, the confusion is not so acute. Many greengrocers and supermarkets sell early or baby turnips or, better still, French turnips – *navets*.

Both are small and white, tinged either with green or in the case of *navets*, with pink or purple. Consequently, people are learning to tell their swedes from their turnips and also discovering what a delicious vegetable the turnip is.

History

Turnips have been cultivated for centuries, principally as an important livestock feed but also for humans. Although they were not considered the food of gourmets, they have been grown by poorer families

as a useful addition to the winter table. Swedes were known as turnip-rooted cabbages until the 1780s, when Sweden began exporting the vegetable to Britain and the shorter name resulted.

Until recently, turnips and swedes have not enjoyed a very high reputation among cooks in many parts of the world. This is partly because they are perceived as cattle food and partly because few people have taken the trouble to find acceptable ways of cooking them. Schools and other institutions tend to boil and then mash

them to a watery pulp, and for many people this is the only way they have eaten either vegetable.

The French, in contrast, have had far more respect for the turnip, at least. For centuries they have devised recipes for their delicate *navets*, roasting them, caramelizing them in sugar and butter or simply steaming and serving with butter. Young, tender turnips have also been popular all over the Mediterranean region for many years, and there are many dishes using turnips with fish, poultry, or teamed with tomatoes, onions and spinach.

Nutrition

Both turnips and swedes are a good source of calcium and potassium.

Varieties

French *navets*, small round, squashed-shaped turnips tinged with pink or purple, are increasingly available in greengrocers and supermarkets in the spring. Less common, but even more prized by the French, are the long carrot-shaped turnips, called *vertus*. English turnips are generally larger and are mainly green and white.

Both *navets* and *vertus* have the characteristic peppery flavour, but this is less pronounced in *navets,* which are generally sweeter.

Swedes have a more substantial, fuller-bodied flavour than turnips but at their best have a subtle, pleasant taste. The Marian is a yellow fleshed variety with a distinct 'swede' flavour. White-fleshed swedes, such as Merrick, have a more watery, turnip-like flavour.

Buying and Storing

Turnips: If possible, buy French *navets* or failing that, the smallest and youngest turnips, available in the stores from spring. They should be firm, smooth and unblemished, ideally with fresh green tops. Store in a cool dry place.
Swedes: Unlike turnips, swedes generally seem to come large. However, if possible, choose small swedes with smooth and unblemished skins as large ones are likely to be tough and fibrous. Store as for turnips.

Preparing and Cooking

Turnips: Young turnips should not need peeling; simply trim, then simmer or steam until tender. They are delicious raw, thinly sliced or grated into salads.

Peel older turnips (*below*) and then slice or dice before cooking. Remember, turnips are members of the cabbage family and older specimens particularly can show signs of that unpleasant cabbage rankness if overcooked. To avoid this, blanch turnips if they are to be served as a vegetable dish, or add sparingly to soups and casseroles, so that the rank flavour is dispersed.

Swedes: Peel to remove the skin and then cut into chunks (*below*). Swedes will disintegrate if overcooked, and they are unpleasantly raw-tasting if not cooked sufficiently. The only answer is to check frequently while they are cooking. Swedes are particularly good when teamed with other root vegetables in soups and casseroles, adding a pleasant, slightly nutty flavour.

Far left: Navets *and turnips.*
Below: Swedes *(rutabagas).*

CARROTS

After potatoes, carrots are without doubt
our best-known and best-loved root
vegetable. In the days when vegetables
were served merely as an accessory to
meat, carrots always made an appearance
– often overcooked but still eaten up
because, we were told, they helped you
to see in the dark.

Carrots have many different flavours,
depending on how they are cooked.
Young, new season carrots braised in
butter and a splash of water are intensely
flavoured and sweet; when steamed,
they are tender and melting. Carrots
grated into salads are fresh and clean-
tasting, while in casseroles they are
savoury with the characteristic carrot
flavour. In soups they are fragrant and
mild, and in cakes their flavour can
hardly be detected, yet their sweetness
adds richness.

History

Until the Middle Ages, carrots were
purple. The orange carrots came from
Holland, from where they were exported
in the 17th and 18th centuries. Although
purple and white carrots continued to be
eaten in France, nowadays they are
something of a rarity.

Nutrition

Carrots contain large amounts of
carotene and vitamin A, along with
useful amounts of vitamins B3, C and E.
To obtain the maximum amount of
carotene, carrots require cooking.
However, when eaten raw, they provide
good quantities of potassium, calcium,
iron and zinc, and these are reduced
when carrots are boiled. Whether eaten
raw or cooked, they are very nutritious
and versatile, being used in savoury as
well as sweet dishes.

The idea that carrots are good for your
night sight originated in the Second
World War. Early radar stations were
established along the south and east
coasts of England in 1939 to detect
aggressors in the air or at sea. The
Germans attributed this sudden
remarkable night vision to the British
habit of eating carrots. Indeed, the
vitamin A in carrots forms retinal, a lack
of which brings on night blindness.

Buying and Storing

Home-grown carrots are so much nicer than store-bought ones. Almost all vegetables have a better flavour if grown organically, but this is particularly true of carrots.

When buying carrots, look out for the very young, pencil thin ones, which are beautifully tender either eaten raw or steamed for just a few minutes. Young carrots are commonly sold with their feathery tops intact, which should be fresh and green. Older carrots should be firm and unblemished. Avoid tired-looking carrots as they will have little nutritional value.

Carrots should not be stored for too long. They will keep for several days if stored in a cool, airy place or in the salad drawer of the refrigerator.

Preparing

Preparation depends on the age of the carrots. The valuable nutrients lie either in or just beneath the skin, so if the carrots are young, simply wash them under cold running water. Medium carrots may need to be scraped and large carrots will need either scraping or peeling.

Cooking

Carrots are excellent cooked or raw. Children often like raw carrots as they have a very sweet flavour. They can be cut into julienne strips, with a dressing added, or grated into salads and coleslaw – their juices run and blend wonderfully with the dressing. Carrots can be cooked in almost any way you choose. As an accompaniment, cut them into julienne strips and braise in butter and cider, or cook in the minimum of stock and toss in butter and a sprinkling of caraway seeds.

Roasted carrots are delicious, with a melt-in-the-mouth sweetness. Par-boil large ones first, but younger carrots can be quickly blanched or added direct to the pan with a joint of meat.

HORSERADISH

Horseradish is grown for its pungent root, which is normally grated and mixed with cream or oil and vinegar and served with roast beef. Fresh horseradish is available in many supermarkets in the spring, and you can make your own horseradish sauce by simply peeling the root and then mixing 45ml/3 tbsp grated horseradish with 150m/^{1}/$_4$ pint/^{2}/$_3$ cup whipping cream and adding a little Dijon mustard, vinegar and sugar to taste. As well as being excellent with hot or cold beef, horseradish sauce is delicious with smoked trout or mackerel or spread thinly on sandwiches with a fine pâté.

Left: Carrots.
Right: Horseradish.

BEETROOT (BEET)

Experience of vinegar-sodden beetroot has doubtlessly put many people off beetroot. Those who love it know to buy their beetroot fresh, so that they can cook it themselves. It can be served in a number of different ways: baked and served with sour cream, braised in a creamy sauce, grated in a salad or used for the classic soup *borscht*.

History

Beetroot is closely related to sugar beet and mangelwurzels. As the demand for sugar increased over the centuries, when sugar could successfully be extracted from beet, its production became a big industry in Britain and Europe. Mangelwurzels were eaten in parts of Europe and in England in times of famine, although they were primarily grown as cattle fodder.

Beetroot, however, has probably been eaten since Roman times. By the mid-19th century it was clearly a popular and common vegetable, and Mrs Beeton in her famous cookbook has 11 recipes for it, including a beetroot and carrot jam and beetroot fritters.

Nutrition

Beetroot is an excellent provider of potassium. The leaves, which have the flavour of spinach, are high in vitamin A, iron and calcium.

Buying and Storing

If possible, buy small beetroots which have their whiskers intact and have at least 5cm/2in of stalk at the top; if they are too closely cropped they will bleed during cooking. Beetroots will keep for several weeks if stored in a cool place.

Preparing

To cook beetroot whole, first rinse under cold running water. Cut the stalks to about 2.5cm/1in above the beetroot and don't cut away the root or peel it – or the glorious deep red colour will bleed away. When serving cold in salads, or where the recipe calls for chopped or grated beetroot, peel away the skin with a potato peeler or sharp knife.

Cooking

To bake in the oven, place the cleaned beetroot in a dish with a tight-fitting lid, and add 60–75ml/4–5 tbsp of water. Lay a double layer of foil over the dish before covering with the lid, then bake in a low oven for 2–3 hours or until the beetroot is tender. Check occasionally to ensure the pan doesn't dry out and to see whether the beetroot is cooked. It is ready when the skin begins to wrinkle and can be easily rubbed away with your fingers.

Alternatively, simply wrap the beetroot in a double layer of foil and cook as above. To boil beetroot, prepare as above and simmer for about 1 1/2 hours.

BEET GREENS

The tops of several root vegetables are not only edible, but are also extremely nutritious. Beet greens are particularly good, being very high in vitamins A and C, and indeed have more iron and calcium than spinach itself. They are delicious, but not easily available unless you grow your own. If you are lucky enough to get some, boil the greens for a few minutes, then drain well and serve with butter or olive oil.

Left: Beetroot (beet).
Above right: Scorzonera.
Below right: Salsify.

SALSIFY AND SCORZONERA

These two root vegetables are related to each other as well as to members of the same family as dandelion and lettuce. All have long tapering roots.

Salsify has a white or pale brownish skin and scorzonera, sometimes called black salsify, has a black skin. They both have a pale creamy flesh and a fairly similar flavour reminiscent of artichokes and asparagus. Salsify is said to have the superior flavour and has been likened to oysters (it is sometimes referred to as the oyster plant), although many people fail to detect this.

Both salsify and scorzonera make an unusual and pleasant accompaniment, either creamed or fried in butter. They can also be also used in soups.

History

Salsify is native to the Mediterranean but now grows in most areas of Europe and North America. Scorzonera is a southern European plant.

Both roots are classified as herbs and, like many wild plants and herbs, their history is bound up with their use in medicines. The roots, together with their leaves and flowers, were used for the treatment of heartburn, loss of appetite and various liver diseases.

Buying and Storing

Choose specimens that are firm and smooth and, if possible, still with their tops on, which should look fresh and lively. Salsify will keep for several days stored in a cool dark place.

Preparing

Salsify and scorzonera are difficult to clean and peel. Either scrub the root under cold running water and then peel after cooking, or peel with a sharp stainless steel knife (*below*). As the flesh discolours quickly, place the trimmed pieces into acidulated water (water to which lemon juice has been added).

Cooking

Cut into short lengths and simmer for 20–30 minutes until tender. Drain well and sauté in butter, or serve with lemon juice, melted butter or chopped parsley.

Alternatively, they can be puréed for soups or mashed. Cooked and cooled salsify and scorzonera can be served in a mustard or garlic vinaigrette with a simple salad.

EXOTIC ROOTS

Throughout the tropical regions of the world all sorts of tubers are grown and used for a fabulous variety of dishes. Yams, sweet potatoes, cassava and taro, to name but a few, are for many people a staple food, not only cooked whole as a vegetable accompaniment, but ground or pounded for bread and cakes. There is an enormous variety of these tropical and subtropical tubers, and while they cannot be cultivated in a moderate climate, the more common tubers are now widely available in specialist stores and in most supermarkets.

SWEET POTATOES

Sweet potatoes are another one of those vegetables that once tasted, are never forgotten. They are, as the name suggests, sweet, but they also have a slightly spicy taste. It's this distinct sweet and savoury flavour which makes them such an excellent foil to many savoury dishes and

they are fittingly paired with meat dishes that need a touch of sweetness, such as turkey or pork.

History

Sweet potatoes are native to tropical America, but today they are grown all over the tropical world. They have been grown in South America from before the Inca civilizations and were introduced into Spain before the ordinary potato. They also have a long history of cultivation in Asia spreading from Polynesia to New Zealand in the fourteenth century.

They are an important staple food in the Caribbean and southern United States, and many famous recipes feature these vegetables. Candied sweet potatoes, for instance, are traditionally served with ham or turkey at Thanksgiving all over the United States, while Jamaica and the West Indies abound with sweet potato dishes, from the simple baked potato to

Caribbean pudding, a typically sweet and spicy dish with sweet potatoes, coconut, limes and cinnamon.

Sweet potatoes appear to have been introduced to England even earlier than regular potatoes. Henry VIII was said to have been very partial to them baked in a pie, believing they would improve his love life! If Henry VIII was eating sweet potatoes in the early/mid-16th century, then it's likely he received them via the Spanish, who, thanks to Christopher Columbus, were busy conquering the New World, thus experiencing a whole range of tropical vegetables and fruit.

Varieties

The skin colour ranges from white to pink to reddish brown. The red-skinned variety, which has a whitish flesh, is the one most commonly used in African and Caribbean cooking.

Buying and Storing

Choose small or medium ones if possible as larger specimens tend to be rather fibrous. They should be firm and evenly shaped; avoid those that seem withered, have damp patches or are sprouting. They will keep for several days in a cool place.

Preparing and Cooking

If baking, scrub the potatoes well and cook exactly as you would for ordinary potatoes. To boil, either cook in their skins and remove these after cooking, or peel and place in acidulated water (water to which lemon juice has been added). This prevents them turning brown and it's worth boiling them in a pan of lightly acidulated water for the same reason.

Sweet potatoes can be cooked in any of the ways you would cook ordinary potatoes – roast, boiled, mashed or baked. However, avoid using them in creamy or gratin-type dishes. They are both too sweet and too spicy for that.

It is preferable to roast or sauté them with onions and other savoury ingredients to bring out their flavour, or mash them and serve them American-style over chunks of chicken for a crusted chicken pie.

YAMS

Yams have been a staple food for many cultures for thousands of years. There are today almost countless varieties, of different shapes, sizes and colours and called different names by different people. Most varieties are thought to have been native to China, although they found their way to Africa at a very early period and became a basic food, being easy to grow in tropical and subtropical conditions, and containing the essential carbohydrate of all staple foods.

Although cush-cush or Indian yam was indigenous to America, most yams were introduced to the New World as a result of the slave trade in the 16th century. Today with such a huge variety of this popular vegetable available, there are innumerable recipes for yam, many probably not printed and published, but handed down by word of mouth from mother to daughter and making their appearance at mealtimes all over the hot regions of the world.

Varieties

The greater yam, as the name suggests, can grow to a huge size. A weight of 62kg/150lb has been recorded. The varieties you are likely to find in stores will be about the size of a small marrow (large zucchini), although smaller yams are also available such as the sweet yam, which looks like a large potato and is normally covered with whiskery roots. All sizes have a coarse brown skin and can be white or red-fleshed.

In Chinese stores, you may find the Chinese yam, which is a more elongated, club-like shape and is covered with fine whiskers.

Buying

Look out for firm specimens with unbroken skins. The flesh inside should be creamy and moist and if you buy from a grocery, the storekeeper may well cut open a yam so you can check that it is fresh. They can be stored for several weeks in a cool, dark place.

Preparing

Peel away the skin thickly to remove the outer skin and the layer underneath that contains the poison dioscorine. This in fact is destroyed during cooking, but discard the peel carefully. Place the peeled yam in salted water as it discolours easily.

Cooking

Yams, like potatoes, are used as the main starchy element in a meal, boiled and mashed, fried, sautéed or roasted. They tend to have an affinity with spicy sauces and are delicious cut into discs, fried and sprinkled with a little salt and cayenne pepper. African cooks frequently pound boiled yam to make a dough that is then served with spicy stews and soups.

TARO/EDDO

Like yams, taro is another hugely important tuber in tropical areas, and for thousands of years it has been a staple food for many people. It goes under many different names; in South-east Asia, South and Central America, all over Africa and in the Caribbean it is called variously eddo and dasheen.

There are two basic varieties of taro – a large barrel-shaped tuber and a smaller variety, which is often called eddo or dasheen. They are all a dark mahogany brown with a rather shaggy skin, looking like a cross between a beetroot (beet) and a swede (rutabaga).

Although they look very similar, taro belongs to a completely different family from yam and in flavour and texture is noticeably different. Boiled, it has a completely unique flavour, something like a floury water chestnut.

Buying and Storing

Try to buy small specimens as these have a better texture and flavour; the really small smooth bulbs are tiny attachments to the larger taro and are either called eddoes, or rather sweetly, 'sons of taro'. Stored in a cool, dark, dry place, they should keep well for several weeks.

Left: Sweet potatoes.
Above: Yams.

Preparing

Taros, like yams, contain a poison just under the skin which produces an allergic reaction. Consequently, either peel taros thickly, wearing rubber gloves, or cook in their skins. The toxins are completely eliminated by boiling, and the skins peel off easily.

Cooking

Taros soak up large quantities of liquid during cooking, and this can be turned to advantage by cooking in well-flavoured stock or with tomatoes and other vegetables. For this reason, they are excellent in soups and casseroles, adding bulk and flavour in a similar way to potatoes. They can also be steamed or boiled, deep-fried or puréed for fritters but must be served hot as they become sticky if allowed to cool.

CALLALOO

Callaloo are the leaves of the taro plant, poisonous if eaten raw, but used widely in Asian and Caribbean recipes. They are cooked thoroughly, then used for wrapping meat and vegetables. Callaloo can also be shredded and cooked together with pork, bacon, crab, prawns (shrimp), okra, chilli, onions and garlic, together with lime and coconut milk to make one of the Caribbean's most famous dishes, named after the leaves themselves, Callaloo.

JICAMA

Also known as the Mexican potato, this large root vegetable is a native of central America. It has a thin brown skin and white, crunchy flesh which has a sweet, nutty taste. It can be eaten cooked in the same way as potatoes or sliced and added raw to salads.

Buy specimens that are firm to the touch. Jicama in good condition will keep for about two weeks if stored in a plastic bag in the refrigerator.

Top: Taros (Eddoes).
Above: Jicama.
Left: Callaloo.

CASSAVA

This is another very popular West Indian root, used in numerous Caribbean dishes. It is native to Brazil, and found its way to the West Indies surprisingly via Africa, where it also became a popular vegetable. Known as cassava in the West Indies, it is called manioc or mandioc in Brazil, and juca or yucca is used in other parts of South America.

Cassava is used to make tapioca, and in South America a sauce and an intoxicating beverage are prepared from the juice. However, in Africa and the West Indies it is eaten as a vegetable either boiled, baked or fried, or cooked and pounded to a dough to make *fufu*, a traditional savoury African pudding.

Right: Cassava.
Below left: Ginger.
Below right: Galangal.

GINGER AND GALANGAL

GINGER

This is probably the world's most important and popular spice and is associated with a number of different cuisines – Chinese, Indian and Caribbean, to name but a few. It was known in Europe during the Roman period, but was still fairly rare until the spice routes opened up trade in the 16th and 17th centuries. Like many spices, ginger has the quality of enhancing and complementing both sweet and savoury food, adding a fragrant spiciness to all sorts of dishes. However, while ground ginger is best in recipes which will be baked, and stem ginger, where the ginger is preserved in syrup, tastes wonderful in desserts, for savoury dishes, use fresh root ginger.

Nowadays, the pale, knobbly roots of fresh ginger are widely available in supermarkets and whenever possible, buy just a small quantity, as you will not need a great deal and fresh ginger will not keep indefinitely.

To prepare, simply peel away the skin with a sharp knife and grate or thinly slice according to the recipe.

GREATER GALANGAL

Galangal looks similar to ginger except that the rhizome is thinner and the young shoots are bright pink. The roots should be prepared in the same way as ginger and can be used in curries and satay sauces. It has a very similar flavour to fresh root ginger.

— FOUR —
GREENS

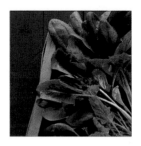

SPINACH

For many people, spinach is inextricably linked with Popeye, the cartoon character who used to eat huge amounts of spinach. It is a wonderfully versatile vegetable, popular worldwide, with nearly every cuisine featuring spinach somewhere in its repertoire. The Italians are particularly partial to spinach and have hundreds of dishes using the vegetable. The words *à la florentine* mean the dish contains spinach.

As well as being delicious on its own, chopped or puréed spinach can be mixed with a range of other ingredients with superb results. It has a particular affinity with dairy products and in the Middle East, feta or helim cheese is used to make *boreks* or other spinach pies. The Italians mix spinach with ricotta or Parmesan cheese for a huge range of recipes, and the English use eggs and sometimes cheese for a spinach soufflé.

History

Spinach was first cultivated in Persia several thousands of years ago. It came to Europe via the Arab world; the Moors introduced it to Spain, and Arabs in the Middle East took it to Greece. It first appeared in England in the 14th century, probably via Spain. It is mentioned in the first known English cookbook, where it is referred to as *spynoches*; which echoes the Spanish word for spinach which is *espinacas*. It quickly became a popular vegetable, probably because it is quick and easy to grow and similarly easy and quick to cook.

Nutrition

Spinach is an excellent source of vitamin C if eaten raw, as well as vitamins A and B, calcium, potassium and iron. Spinach was originally thought to provide far more iron than it actually does, but the iron is 'bound' up by oxalic acid in cooked spinach, which prevents the body absorbing anything but the smallest amounts. Even so, it is still an extremely healthy vegetable whether eaten cooked or raw.

Buying and Storing

Spinach grows all year round, so you should have no difficulty in buying it fresh. Frozen spinach is a poor substitute, mainly because it has so little flavour, so it is worth the effort to use the fresh product.

Spinach leaves should be green and lively; if they look tired and the stalks are floppy, look around until you find something in better condition. Spinach reduces significantly when cooked; about 450g/1lb will serve two people. Store it in the salad drawer of the refrigerator, where it will keep for 1–2 days.

Preparing

Wash well in a bowl of cold water and remove any tough or large stalks.

Cooking

Throw the leaves into a large pan with just the water that clings to the leaves and place over a low heat with a sprinkling of salt. Cover the pan so the spinach steams in its own liquid and shake the pan occasionally to prevent the spinach sticking to the bottom. It cooks in 4–6 minutes, wilting down to about an eighth of its former volume. Drain and press out the remaining liquid with the back of a spoon.

Spinach can be used in a variety of ways. It can be chopped and eaten with lots of butter, or similarly served with other spring vegetables such as baby

BRUSSELS SPROUTS

carrots or young broad (fava) beans. For frittatas, chop the spinach finely, stir in a little Parmesan cheese, a good sprinkling of salt and pepper and a dash of cream, if liked, and stir into the omelette before cooking. Alternatively, purée it for sauces or blend it for soups. Spinach is also delicious raw, served with chopped bacon or croûtons. A fresh spinach salad is very tasty as the leaves have just the right balance of flavour – sharp but not overpowering, and they are soft and hold dressings well.

Below: Spinach.
Below right: Brussels sprouts.

Brussels sprouts have a pronounced and sweet nutty flavour, quite unlike cabbage, although the two are closely related. They are traditionally served at Christmas with chestnuts and indeed have a definite affinity for certain nuts – particularly the sweet flavoured nuts, e.g. almonds pair well rather than hazelnuts or walnuts.

History

Brussels sprouts were cultivated in Flanders (now Belgium) during the Middle Ages. They are basically miniature cabbages that grow in a knobbly row on a long tough stalk. The Germans call sprouts *rosenkohl* – rose cabbage – a pretty and descriptive name as they look like small rosebuds.

Buying and Storing

Buy Brussels sprouts as fresh as possible as older ones are more likely to have that strong unpleasant 'cabbage' flavour. They should be small and hard with tightly wrapped leaves. Avoid any that are turning yellow or brown or have loose leaves. Brussels sprouts will keep for several days in a cool place such as a larder or salad drawer of a refrigerator, but it is far better to buy them as you need them.

Preparing

Cut away the bottom of the stalk and remove the outer leaves. Some people cut a cross through the bottom of the stalk although this is not really necessary. If you haven't been able to avoid buying big Brussels sprouts, cut them in half or into quarters, or slice them thinly for stir-frying.

Cooking

As with cabbage, either cook Brussels sprouts very briefly or braise slowly in the oven. Cook in small amounts of fast boiling water for about 3 minutes until just tender. To stir-fry Brussel sprouts, slice into three or four pieces and then fry in a little oil and butter – they taste great with onions and ginger.

CAULIFLOWER

Cauliflower is a member of the cabbage family, *Brassica oleracea*. Like all cabbages, cauliflower suffers terribly from overcooking. A properly cooked cauliflower has a pleasant fresh flavour but when overcooked it turns grey and becomes unpalatably soft, taking on a nasty rank flavour with an unpleasant aftertaste. Children often like raw cauliflower even though they may not connect it with the same vegetable served up at school.

History

Cauliflower is thought to have come originally from China and thence to the Middle East. The Moors introduced it to Spain in the 12th century and from there it found its way to England via established trading routes. The early cauliflower was the size of a tennis ball but they have gradually been cultivated to the enormous sizes we see today. Ironically, baby cauliflowers are now becoming more fashionable in restaurants and with gardeners.

Varieties

Green and purple cauliflowers are sometimes available in the stores. The purple variety was originally grown in Sardinia and Italy but is increasingly grown by other market gardeners. They look pretty and unusual but are otherwise similar to white cauliflowers.

Dwarf varieties of cauliflowers are now commonly available in stores, as well as baby white cauliflowers.

Romanescoes: These pretty green or white vegetables look like a cross between broccoli and cauliflower, but are more closely related to cauliflowers. They taste very much like cauliflowers, but since they are quite small, they are less likely to be overcooked and consequently retain their excellent flavour.

Broccoflower: A cross between broccoli and cauliflower, this looks like a pale green cauliflower. It has a mild flavour and should be cooked in the same way as you would cauliflower.

Right: Baby cauliflower.
Far right top: Romanescoes.
Far right bottom: Green cauliflower.

Nutrition

Cauliflower contains potassium, iron and zinc, although cooking reduces the amounts. It is also a good source of vitamins A and C.

Buying and Storing

In top condition, a cauliflower is a creamy white colour with the outer leaves curled round the flower. The head should be unblemished with no black or discoloured areas and the outer leaves should look fresh and crisp. Keep cauliflower in a cool place for no longer than 1–2 days; after that it will deteriorate and valuable nutrients will be lost.

Preparing

To cook a cauliflower whole, first trim away the coarse bottom leaves (leave the inner ones on, if liked). Very large cauliflowers are best halved or broken into florets, as the outside will overcook before the inside is tender. Some people trim away the stalk, but others like this part and only trim off the very thick stalk at the bottom of the plant.

Cooking

Cauliflowers are excellent steamed, either whole or in florets. Place in a steamer or colander over a pan of boiling water, cover and steam until just tender and immediately remove from the heat. The florets can then be fried in olive oil or butter for a few minutes to give a lightly browned finish.

When cooking a cauliflower whole, start testing it after 10 minutes; it should feel tender but still have plenty of 'bite' left in it. Cauliflower is a popular vegetable accompaniment, either served with just a little butter, or with a tomato or cheese sauce. It is also good stir-fried with onions and garlic together with a few tomatoes and capers.

Cauliflower is excellent in salads or used for crudités. Either use it raw or blanch it in boiling water for 1–2 minutes, then refresh under cold running water.

Small cauliflowers and romanescoes are intended to be cooked whole, and can be steamed or boiled, covered with a lid, in the minimum of water for 4–5 minutes, until just tender.

SPROUTING BROCCOLI AND CALABRESE

Varieties

Calabrese Broccoli: This is the vegetable we today commonly call broccoli, with large beautiful, blue-green heads on succulent stalks. It is named after the Italian province of Calabria where this variety was first developed.

Purple Sprouting Broccoli: The original variety – it has long thin stalks with small flowerheads that are normally purple but can be white or green. Heads, stalks and tender leaves are all edible. The purple heads turn green when cooked but the others keep their colour. Purple sprouting broccoli is more seasonal than the easily available calabrese; it is usually available from late winter onwards.

Buying and Storing

If possible, buy loose broccoli rather than the pre-wrapped bundles, because it is easier to check that it is fresh and also because wrapped vegetables tend to deteriorate more quickly.

Purple sprouting broccoli can also be sold loose or prepacked. Check that the stalk, flowerhead and leaves all look fresh and that the flowerlets are tightly closed and bright green. Neither type will keep for long.

Broccoli or calabrese is a relatively modern vegetable and is one of the most popular. It is quick and easy to prepare with little or no waste and similarly easy to cook. It is attractive, whether served raw or cooked, and you can buy it in the quantity you require, unlike cauliflower or cabbage.

History

Before calabrese came into our stores, people bought and ate purple sprouting broccoli. This is basically an 'untidy' version of calabrese, with long shoots and clusters of flowerheads at the end – the broccoli we know today has neat tidy heads. The stalks of purple sprouting broccoli have a faint asparagus flavour.

The Romans cooked purple sprouting broccoli in wine or served it with sauces and it is still a popular vegetable today in Italy, cooked in the oven with anchovies and onions or served with pasta in a garlic and tomato sauce.

Preparing and Cooking

Trim the ends and remove any discoloured leaves.

Calabrese Broccoli: Break into even pieces, dividing the stem and flowerhead lengthways if they are thick. Cook in a little boiling water for 4–5 minutes until just tender and then drain. Do not steam this variety of broccoli as its vibrant green colour tends to turn grey.

Purple Sprouting Broccoli: Either steam in long, even lengths in a steamer or, if you have an asparagus kettle, cook as you would asparagus. Alternatively, tie the stems loosely together and stand in a little water – if necessary, wedge it in with a potato or rolled up piece of foil. Cover with a dome of foil and steam for 4–5 minutes until tender.

Serving

Serve both varieties simply with butter and lemon juice or with a Hollandaise or Béarnaise sauce as an accompaniment. They are also excellent stir-fried.

Above far left: Purple cauliflower.
Below far left: Purple sprouting broccoli.
Above: Calabrese broccoli.
Below: Turnip tops.

TURNIP TOPS

Turnip tops, like beet greens, are both delicious and nutritious. They are not widely available but if you are able to buy some or if you grow your own, slice them *(below)* and boil or steam for a few minutes, then drain and serve with butter.

CABBAGE

Cabbage, sliced and cooked, can be one of two things: deliciously crisp, with a mild pleasant flavour – or overcooked and horrible! Cabbage and other brassicas contain the chemical hydrogen sulphide, which is activated during cooking at about the point the vegetable starts to soften. It eventually disappears, but during the in-between time, cabbage acquires its characteristic rank smell and flavour. So, either cook cabbage briefly, or cook it long and slow, preferably with other ingredients so that flavours can mingle.

History

Cabbage has a long and varied history. However, because there are many varieties of cabbage under the general heading of 'brassica', it is difficult to be sure whether the variety the Greeks and Romans enjoyed is the same as today's round cabbage, or something more akin to kale or even Chinese cabbage.

The round cabbages we know today were an important food during the Dark Ages, and by the Middle Ages they were in abundance, as you will see if you study the paintings of that period. These commonly show kitchen tables or baskets at market positively groaning with fruit and vegetables, and cabbages in all their shapes and sizes were often featured.

Medieval recipes suggest cooking cabbages with leeks, onions and herbs. In the days when all except the very wealthy cooked everything in one pot, it is fair to assume that cabbages were cooked long and slow until fairly recently.

Varieties

Savoy Cabbage: This is a variety of green cabbage with crimped or curly leaves. It has a mild flavour and is particularly tender, thus needing less cooking than other varieties.

Spring Greens (collards): These have fresh loose heads with a pale yellow-green heart. They are available in spring and are delicious simply sliced, steamed and served with butter.

Right: Savoy cabbage.
Above far right: Green cabbage.
Below far right: Spring greens (collards).

Green Cabbage: The early green, or spring, cabbages are dark green, loose leafed and have a slightly pointed head. They have little or no heart as they are picked before this has had time to develop. Nevertheless, they are a very good cabbage and all but the very outside leaves should be tender. As the season progresses, larger, firmer and more pale green cabbages are available. These are a little tougher than the spring cabbages and need longer cooking.

Red Cabbage: A beautifully coloured cabbage with smooth firm leaves. The colour fades during cooking unless a little vinegar is added to the water. Red cabbage can be pickled or stewed with spices and flavourings.

White Cabbage: Sometimes called Dutch cabbages, white cabbages have smooth firm pale green leaves. They are available throughout the winter and are good cooked or raw. To cook, slice them thinly, then boil or steam and serve with butter. To serve raw, slice thinly and use in a coleslaw.

Buying and Storing

Cabbages should be fresh-looking and unblemished. When buying, avoid any with wilted leaves or those that look or feel puffy. Savoys and spring greens will keep in a cool place for several days; firmer cabbages will keep happily for much longer.

Preparing

Remove the outer leaves, if necessary, and then cut into quarters. Remove the stalk and then slice or shred according to your recipe or to taste.

Cooking

For green or white cabbages, place the shredded leaves in a pan with a knob (pat) of butter and a couple of tablespoons of water to prevent burning. Cover and cook over a medium heat until the leaves are tender, occasionally shaking the pan or stirring.

Red cabbage is cooked quite differently and is commonly sautéed in oil or butter and then braised in a low oven for up to 1½ hours with apples, currants, onions, vinegar, wine, sugar and spices.

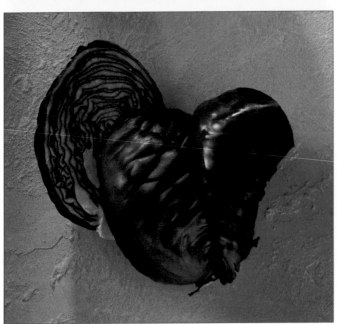

KALE AND CURLY KALE

Kale is the name used for a variety of green leafed vegetable of the brassica family. Most kales have thick stems and robust leaves that do not form a head. Many kales have curly leaves, which are the variety most commonly eaten. Large coarse-leafed kales are grown for cattle and sheep feeds.

History

Kale is thought to be one of the first cultivated brassicas. Colewort, the wild ancestor, still grows along the coasts of western Europe.

Varieties

Collards: Collards, or collard greens, are a popular green vegetable in the southern United States. They are grown in summer and autumn for harvesting in the spring and are a good source of vitamin A.
Curly Kale: With its crimped, curly leaves, this is the most commonly available kale, although even this can be quite hard to come by. If you are a big fan and don't grow your own, try farm stores in early spring.
Purple or Silver Kale: This is an ornamental variety, and is grown almost exclusively for display.

Preparing and Cooking

Kale is probably the strongest tasting of the brassicas and is best cooked simply, paired with a bland-flavoured vegetable, such as potatoes. To prepare, break the leaves from the stalk and then cut out any thick stalk from the leaf. This can then be rolled and sliced or cooked whole. Boil the leaves in a little salted water for 3–5 minutes until tender. Owing to its robust nature, kale is frequently teamed with fairly hot spices and is consequently popular in many Indian dishes.

Above far left: White cabbage.
Below far left: Red cabbage.
Left: Collards.
Above: Curly kale.

GARDEN AND WILD LEAVES

VINE LEAVES

All leaves from vines that produce grapes can be eaten when young. They make an ideal wrapping for various meats and vegetables as they are surprisingly strong and of course edible. Most countries that produce wine will have dishes where vine leaves appear. *Dolmades*, commonly eaten in Greece and the Middle East is perhaps the best known dish, but in France, Spain and Italy, there are recipes using vine leaves to wrap small birds, such as quail or snipe.

Vine leaves have a faintly lemon/cabbage flavour which can be detected at its best in a good *dolma*. The leaves need to be cooked briefly before using, so that they are pliable and don't crack or break as you wrap the food. Bring to the boil and simmer for about 1 minute. The leaves should then be drained, separated and cooled until you are ready to use them.

DANDELION

Any child who has picked dandelions for his or her rabbits or guinea pigs and has watched them gobble them up greedily will know that this weed, though hated by the gardener in the family, has something going for it. Some gardeners, of course, are very partial to dandelion themselves and raise the plant carefully so that the leaves are fresh and tender for a salad, and in France dandelions can often be seen for sale at markets for use in various dishes.

Look in any book of herbal remedies, and dandelions will feature prominently. They are a well-known diuretic, their French name – *pissenlits* (piss-a-bed) – attesting to this in no uncertain terms.

Although it's gratifying to pick your own vegetables for free, it is generally recommended, if you like dandelions, that you buy the domestic seeds and grow your own. These are likely to be the juiciest and least bitter plants. If you do pick your own, do so well away from the roadside and wash the leaves carefully.

Dandelion leaves can be added to salads or used in *pissenlits au lard*, where whole young dandelion plants are dressed in vinaigrette and then covered in finely chopped pieces of salt pork or bacon and bacon fat.

SORREL

Sorrel is not always available commercially, although it is in France and is greatly prized. However, it grows wild in cool soils or you could grow it in your own garden. Young leaves are delicious in salads, or, later in the year, use it in soups or sauces to accompany fish. It has a sharp, distinct, lemon flavour and is commonly teamed with eggs and cream.

ORACHE

Although not related to spinach, this beautiful red or golden-leaved plant is called mountain spinach and its large leaves can be treated like spinach.

GOOD KING HENRY AND FAT HEN

These are both members of the goosefoot family and were popular vegetables in Tudor times. Today, Good King Henry has all but disappeared, and Fat Hen only grows wild as a weed. Both were superseded by spinach, which they are said to resemble in taste, although Fat Hen is milder.

NETTLES

Wild food enthusiasts get very excited about nettles as food, perhaps because they are plentiful and free and maybe because they take pleasure in eating something that everyone else avoids. Of course, once cooked, the sting completely disappears. They should be picked when they are very young and are good used in soups.

Above far left: Fresh vine leaves.
Above left: Dandelion.
Below left: Sorrel.
Right: Good King Henry.
Below: Nettles.

CHINESE GREENS

CHINESE CABBAGE/LEAVES (PE-TSAI)

Chinese cabbage, also called Napa cabbage, has pale green, crinkly leaves with long, wide, white ribs. Its shape is a little like a very fat head of celery, which gives rise to another of its alternative names, celery cabbage. It is pleasantly crunchy with a faint cabbage flavour and since it is available all year round, it makes a useful winter salad component. Chinese cabbage is also very good stir-fried with a tasty sauce. It is an essential ingredient of many oriental recipes.

Buying and Storing

For some reason, Chinese leaves almost always look fresh and perky when on sale in the supermarket, which probably indicates that they travel well and are transported quickly. Avoid any with discoloured or damaged stems. The leaves should be pale green and straight without blemishes or bruises. They will keep for up to six days in the salad drawer of the refrigerator.

Preparing

Remove the outside leaves and slice as much as you need for a particular dish, then rinse the sliced cabbage in a sieve (strainer) or colander.

Many Chinese greens are members of the brassica family. If you go into a popular and reasonably large Chinese supermarket, you'll be astonished at the varieties of green vegetables for sale. Discovering the name of these vegetables, on the other hand, can be a bit of a hit-and-miss undertaking, as the storekeepers, although always well intentioned, rarely know the English name, if indeed there is one.

CHINESE MUSTARD GREENS

Mustard greens are worth buying if you can, as they are very good to eat. The plant is a member of the cabbage family, but is grown in Europe solely for its mustard seed. In India and Asia it has long been grown for its oil seed, but the Chinese developed the plant for its leaves as well. These are deep green and slightly puckered-looking and have a definite mustard flavour, which can be quite fiery.

If you grow your own, then you'll be able to enjoy the young leaves, which can be added to lettuce to spice up salads. Older leaves are best stir-fried and then dressed with a light Chinese sauce. They are also good cooked with onion and garlic and served as a side dish to accompany pork or bacon.

Preparing and Cooking

Break apart the stalks, rinse, then cut both stalks and leaves into thick or thin slices. These can then be stir-fried with garlic and onions, or cooked and served as you would Swiss chard. It has a pleasant flavour, milder than mustard greens, yet with more bite than the bland Chinese cabbage.

CHINESE BROCCOLI

This is another leafy vegetable, but with slender heads of flowers that look a little like our own broccoli, except that the flowers are usually white or yellow. Once the thicker stalks are trimmed, the greens can be sliced and cooked and served in the same way as Chinese mustard greens.

Far left: Chinese mustard greens.
Left: Chinese leaves (Chinese cabbage).
Above: Chinese broccoli.
Below: Pak choi (bok choy).

Cooking and Serving

If adding to salads, combine Chinese cabbage with something fairly forceful, such as endive or rocket (arugula), and add a well-flavoured dressing. If adding to a stir-fry, cook with garlic, ginger and other fairly strong flavours. While the faint cabbage flavour will be lost, you will still get the pleasant crunchy 'bite' of the stalk, and the leaves will carry the sauce.

PAK CHOI (BOK CHOY)

If you frequent your local Chinese supermarket, you will almost certainly have come across *pak choi*. In English it should correctly be called Chinese celery cabbage and its thick stalks, joined at the end in a small root, are vaguely celery-like. Its leaves, on the other hand, are generally large and spoon shaped. There are many different species of this vegetable, and smaller specimens look more like the tops of radish and have small slim stalks. Consequently the vegetable can be known by all sorts of picturesque names, such as 'horse's ear' and 'horse's tail'. There is no rule for discovering exactly what you are buying, but the important thing is to choose a fresh plant whatever its size: look for fresh green leaves and crisp stalks.

KOHLRABI

Kohlrabi looks like a cross between a cabbage and a turnip and is often classified as a root vegetable, though it grows above ground. It is a member of the brassica family, but, unlike cabbages, it is the bulbous stalk that is edible rather than the flowering heads.

There are two varieties of kohlrabi: one is purple and the other pale green. They both have the same mild and fresh tasting flavour, not dissimilar to water chestnuts. It is neither as peppery as turnip nor as distinctive as cabbage, but it is easy to see why people think it a little like both. It can be served as an alternative to carrots or turnips.

History

Although kohlrabi is not a very popular vegetable in Britain, it is commonly eaten in other parts of Europe, as well as in China, India and Asia. In Kashmir, where it is grown extensively, there are many recipes – the bulbs are often finely sliced and eaten in salads and the greens are cooked in mustard oil with garlic and chillies.

Buying and Storing

Kohlrabi is best when small and young, since larger specimens tend to be coarse and fibrous. It keeps well for 7–10 days if stored in a cool place.

Preparing

Peel the skin with a knife and then cook whole or slice.

Cooking

Very small kohlrabi are tender and can be cooked whole. However, if they are any bigger than 5cm/2in in diameter, they can be stuffed. To do this, hollow out the centre a little before cooking in boiling water and then stuff with fried onions and tomatoes, for instance. For sliced kohlrabi, cook in boiling water or a steamer until just tender and serve with butter or a creamy sauce. They can also be cooked long and slow in gratin dishes, with, for example, potatoes, as a variation of *Gratin Dauphinois*. Alternatively, par-boil them, then place in an ovenproof dish and bake in the oven covered with a cheese sauce.

SWISS CHARD

Swiss chard is one of those vegetables that needs plenty of water when growing, which explains why it is a popular garden vegetable in many places that have a high rainfall. Gardeners are very fond of Swiss chard, not only because it is delicious to eat but also because it is so very striking.

Swiss chard is often likened to spinach. The leaves have similarities, although they are not related and chard is on an altogether larger scale. Swiss chard leaves are large and fleshy with distinctive white ribs, and the flavour is stronger and more robust than spinach. It is popular in France where it is baked with rice, eggs and milk in *tians*, and cooked in a celebrated pastry from Nice – *tourte de blettes* – which is a sweet tart filled with raisins, pinenuts, apples and Swiss chard bound together with eggs. It is also often combined with eggs in frittatas and tortillas.

Swiss chard is a member of the beet family and is called by several names on this theme, including seakale beet and spinach beet.

Ruby or rhubarb chard has striking red ribs and leaf beet is often cultivated as a decorative plant, but they both have the same flavour, and unlike sugar beet and beetroot (beet), they are cultivated only for their leaves.

Buying and Storing

Heads of chard should be fresh and bright green; avoid those with withered leaves or flabby stems. It keeps better than spinach but should be eaten within a couple of days.

Preparing

Some people buy or grow chard for the white stems alone and discard the leaves (or give them to pet guinea pigs), but this is a waste of a delicious vegetable. The leaf needs to be separated from the ribs, and this can be done roughly with a sharp knife (*right*) or more precisely using scissors. The ribs can then be sliced. Either shred the leaves, or blanch them and use them to wrap little parcels of fragrant rice or other food. If the chard is young and small, the ribs do not need to be removed.

Cooking

For pies, frittatas and gratins, the leaves and ribs can be cooked together. Gently sauté the ribs in a pan with a little butter and oil and then add the leaves a minute or so later, so they don't overcook. Alternatively, the ribs can be simmered in a little water until tender and the leaves added a few minutes later or steamed over the top.

Above far left: Kohlrabi.
Left: Purple kohlrabi.
Above: Swiss chard.

BEANS,
PEAS
AND
SEEDS

BROAD (FAVA) BEANS

One of the delights of having a garden is discovering how truly delicious some vegetables are when garden fresh. This seems particularly true of broad beans, which have a superb sweet flavour that sadly can never be reproduced in the frozen product. If you're lucky enough to grow or be given fresh broad beans, don't worry about recipes; just cook them until tender and serve with butter. It will be a revelation! However, if you are not one of those lucky few, don't dismiss broad beans, as they are still a wonderfully versatile vegetable. They can be used in soups or casseroles, and, since they have a mealy texture, they also purée well.

History

People have been eating broad beans almost since time began. A variety of wild broad bean grew all over southern Europe, North Africa and Asia, and they would have been a useful food for early man. There is archaeological evidence that by Neolithic times broad beans were being farmed, making them one of the first foods to be cultivated.

Broad beans will grow in most climates and most soils. They were a staple food for people throughout the Dark Ages and the Middle Ages, grown for feeding people and livestock until being replaced by the potato in the 17th and 18th centuries. Broad beans were an important source of protein for the poor, and because they dry well, they would have provided nourishing meals for families until the next growing season.

Nutrition

Beans are high in protein and carbohydrates and are also a good source of vitamins A, B1 and B2. They also provide potassium and iron as well as several other minerals.

Buying and Storing

Buy beans as fresh as possible. The pods should preferably be small and tender. Use as soon as possible.

Preparing

Very young beans in tender pods, no more than 7.5cm/3in in length, can be eaten pod and all; top and tail, and then slice roughly. Usually, however, you will need to shell the beans. Elderly beans are often better skinned after they are cooked to rid them of the strong, bitter flavour that puts many people off this vegetable.

Cooking

Plunge shelled beans (or in their pods if very young) into rapidly boiling water and cook until just tender. They can also be par-boiled and then finished off braised in butter. For a simple broad bean purée, blend the cooked beans with garlic cooked in butter, cream and a pinch of fresh herbs, such as savory or thyme.

LIMA BEANS

These are popular in the US, named after the capital of Peru, and are sold mainly shelled. They are an essential ingredient in the American-Indian dish *succotash*. Lima beans should be cooked in a little boiling water until tender. Elderly beans need skinning after they are cooked. The dried bean, also known as the butter bean, can be large or small. These large beans tend to become mushy when cooked so are best used in soups or purées.

Above: Broad (fava) beans.
Below: Lima beans.
Right: Runner (green) beans.

RUNNER (GREEN) BEANS

The runner bean is native to South America, where it has been cultivated for more than 2000 years and there is archaeological evidence of its existence much earlier than that.

It is a popular vegetable to grow. Most home vegetable gardeners have a patch of runner beans – they are easy to grow and, like all legumes, their roots contain bacteria that help renew nitrogen supplies in the soil.

They have a more robust flavour and texture than French (green) beans and are distinct from green beans in several ways: they are generally much larger with long, flattened pods; their skin is rough textured, although in young beans this softens during cooking; and they contain purple beans within the pods, unlike green beans whose beans are mostly white or pale green. Nevertheless, runner beans belong to the same family as all the green beans.

Buying and Storing

Always buy young beans as the pods of larger beans are likely to be tough. The pods should feel firm and fresh; if you can see the outline of the bean inside the pod it is likely to be fibrous – although you could leave the beans to dry out and use the dried beans later in the season. Ideally, the beans inside should be no larger than your small fingernail.

Use as soon as possible after buying; they do not store well.

Preparing

Runner beans need to be topped and tailed and may also need stringing. Carefully put your knife through the top of the bean without cutting right through, and then pull downwards; if a thick thread comes away, the beans need stringing, so do the same on the other side. The beans can then be sliced either using a sharp knife or a slicer.

Slice through lengthways, not diagonally, so that you will be able to serve the beans with just a little skin and lots of succulent flesh.

Cooking

Plunge the beans into boiling salted water and cook until al dente.

PEAS

Fresh peas are wonderful – try tasting them raw, straight from the pod. Unfortunately, the season for garden peas is short, and frozen peas, which are the next best thing, never quite come up to the mark. If you grow your own peas, for three or four weeks in early summer, you can eat like kings; otherwise you can buy them from a good greengrocer, who may be able to keep you supplied all through the early summer.

History

Peas have an even longer history than broad (fava) beans, with archaeological evidence showing they were cultivated as long ago as 5700BC. High in protein and carbohydrate, they would have been another important staple food and were eaten fresh or dried for soups or potage.

Pease porridge is mentioned in a Greek play written in 5BC. Pease pudding, probably something similar, made with split peas with onion and herbs, is an old-fashioned but still very popular dish, especially in the north of England, traditionally eaten with ham and pork.

One of the first recipes for peas, however, comes from *Le Cuisinier Français*, which was translated into English in the middle of the 17th century and gives a recipe for *petits pois à la française* (peas cooked with small hearted lettuces) – still a popular recipe today.

Varieties

Mangetouts (snow peas): These are eaten whole and have a delicate flavour, providing they are not overcooked. Unfortunately, they are easy to overcook and the texture then becomes rather slippery. Alternatively, blanch or stir-fry them. They are also good raw in salads.

Petits Pois (baby peas): These are not, as you might expect, immature peas but are a dwarf variety. Gardeners grow their own, but they are not available fresh in the stores as they are mainly grown commercially for canning or freezing.

Snow Peas, Sugar Peas, Sugar Snaps: These have the distinct fresh flavour of raw peas and are more plump and have more snap than mangetouts.

Buying and Storing

Only buy fresh peas; if they are old they are bound to be disappointing and you would be better off buying them frozen. In top condition, the pods are bright green and lively looking; the more withered the pod, the longer they have been hanging around. It is possible to surreptitiously sample peas on occasions, to check if they are fresh (greengrocers don't seem to mind if you buy some). Use fresh peas as soon as possible.

Preparing

Shelling peas can be very relaxing. Press open the pods and use your thumb to push out the peas *(below)*. Mangetouts and sugar snaps just need to be topped and tailed *(below right)*.

Left: Peas.
Above right: Sugar snap peas.

Cooking

Cook peas with a sprig of mint in a pan of rapidly boiling water or in a covered steamer until tender. Alternatively, melt butter in a flameproof casserole, add the peas and then cover and sweat over a gentle heat for 4–5 minutes. Cook mangetouts and sugar snaps in any of these ways but for a shorter time.

GREEN BEANS

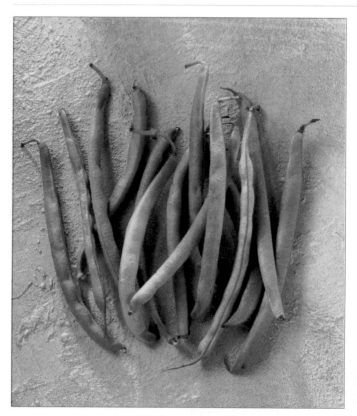

Whether you call beans French beans, wax beans, haricot (navy) or green beans, they all belong to a large and varied family.

History

The bean is a New World vegetable that had been cultivated for thousands of years by native people in both the north and south of the continent, which accounts for its wide diversity.

Varieties

One variety or another is available all year round and so they are one of the most convenient fresh green vegetables.
French (green) Beans: This name encompasses a range of green beans, including the snap bean and bobby bean. They are mostly fat and fleshy and when fresh, should be firm so that they break in half with a snapping sound.

Haricots Verts: These are considered the best French beans and are delicate and

slim in shape. They should be eaten when very young, no more than 6–7.5cm/2½–3in in length.
Thai Beans: These long beans are similar to French beans and can be prepared and cooked in the same way.
Yellow Wax Beans: This is also a French bean and has a mild, slightly buttery taste.

Buying and Storing

Whatever variety, beans should be bright and crisp. Avoid wilted ones, or those with overly mature pods that feel spongy when lightly squeezed. They do not keep well, so use as soon as possible after buying or picking.

Preparing

To top and tail the beans: gather them together in one hand and then slice away the top 5mm/¼in *(below)*, then do the same at the other end. If necessary, pull off any stringy bits.

Cooking

Plunge beans into rapidly boiling salted water and cook until al dente. When overcooked, beans have a flabby texture and also lose much of their flavour. Drain and toss them in butter or serve in a sauce with shallots and bacon. For salads, cook until just tender and then refresh under cold water. They are excellent with a garlicky vinaigrette. Serve with carrots or other root vegetables and savour the contrast in flavours.

Above left: Bobby beans.
Below left: Yellow wax beans.
Right: Haricots verts.
Below: Thai beans.

CORN

Fresh corn, eaten on the cob with salt and a little butter is deliciously sweet. Some gardeners who grow it have a pan ready on the boil, so that when they cut the corn it goes into the pan in only the time it takes to race up from the garden to the kitchen. Buying it from the supermarket is inevitably a bit hit-or-miss, although if purchased in season, corn can be very good indeed.

History

In 1492, as Christopher Columbus disembarked on the island now called Cuba, he was met by American Indians offering two gifts of hospitality – one was tobacco and the other something the Indians called *maïs*. The English word for staple food was then corn, so that when Columbus and his crew saw that maize was the staple food for the Indians, it was dubbed 'Indian corn'.

Corn originated in South America and had enormous significance to the native Indians of the whole continent, who were said to have lived and died by corn. They referred to it as their 'first mother and father, the source of life'. By far their most important food, corn was used in many other ways as well. They used the plant for their shelters and for fences, and they wore it and decorated their bodies with it.

The Aztecs had corn planting ceremonies that included human sacrifices, and other tribes had similar customs to appease the god 'corn'. Countless myths and legends have been woven around corn, each tribe telling a slightly different story, but each on the same theme of planting and harvesting corn. For anthropologists and historians, they make compelling study.

Nutrition

Corn is a good carbohydrate food and is rich in vitamins A, B and C. It contains protein, but less so than other cereals. It is also a good source of potassium, magnesium, phosphorus and iron.

Varieties

There are five main varieties of corn – popcorn, sweet corn, dent corn, flint corn and flour corn. Dent corn is the most commonly grown worldwide, for

animal feeds and oil, and the corn we eat on the cobs is sweet corn. Baby corn cobs are picked when immature and are cooked and eaten whole.

Buying and Storing

As soon as corn is picked, its sugar begins to turn to starch and therefore the sooner it goes into the pot, the better. Wherever possible, buy locally grown corn.

Look for husks that are clean and green and tassels which are golden, with no sign of matting. The corn itself should look plump and yellow. Avoid cobs with pale or white kernels or those with older shrivelled kernels, which will undoubtedly be disappointing.

Preparing

Strip away the husks. To use the corn kernels for recipes, carefully cut downwards using a sharp knife from top to bottom *(left)*.

Cooking

Cook corn on the cob in plenty of boiling salted water until tender. Timing depends on the size of the cobs but 10–15 minutes will normally be enough. Serve them with sea salt and butter, but if the cobs are really sweet, leave out the butter. Stir-fry baby corn cobs briefly and serve in oriental dishes.

Far left: Corn cobs.
Below: Baby corn cobs.

OKRA

History

Okra originated in Africa. In the 16th century, when African people were enslaved by the Spanish and shipped to the New World, they took with them the few things they could, including the plants and seeds from home – dried peas, yams, ackee – and okra. This lantern-shaped pod containing rows of seeds oozes a sticky mucilaginous liquid when cooked, and it was popular not only for its subtle flavour but also for thickening soups and stews.

The plant thrived in the tropical climate and by the early 19th century, when the slave trade was finally abolished, okra was an important part of the cuisine of the Caribbean and the southern United States. In and around New Orleans, the Creoles, the American-born descendants of European-born settlers, adopted a popular native American-Indian dish called *gumbo*. An essential quality of this famous dish was its thick gluey consistency. The Indians used filé powder (the dry pounded leaves of the sassafras tree), but okra was welcomed as a more satisfactory alternative.

Gumbos are now the hallmark of Creole cooking, and in some parts of America, the word 'gumbo' is an alternative word for okra itself.

Buying and Storing

Choose young, small pods as older ones are likely to be fibrous. They should be green, firm and slightly springy when squeezed. Avoid any that are shrivelled or bruised. They will keep for a few days in the salad drawer of the refrigerator.

Preparing

When cooking whole, trim the top but don't expose the seeds inside or the viscous liquid will ooze into the rest of the dish. If, however, this is what you want, slice thickly or thinly according to the recipe *(right)*. If you want to eliminate some of this liquid, first soak the whole pods in acidulated water (water to which lemon juice has been added) for about an hour.

Cooking

The pods can be steamed, boiled or lightly fried, and then added to or used with other ingredients. If cooked whole, okra is not mucilaginous but is pleasantly tender. Whether cooked whole or sliced, use garlic, ginger or chilli to perk up the flavour, or cook Indian-style, with onions, tomatoes and spices.

Above: Okra.

DRIED BEANS AND PEAS

Dried beans feature in traditional cuisines all over the world, from Mexican refried beans to Italy's *pasta e fagioli*. They are nutritious, providing a good source of protein when combined with rice, and are a great store-cupboard (pantry) standby.

Black-eyed Beans (peas): Sometimes called black-eyed peas, these small cream-coloured beans have a black spot or eye. When cooked, they have a tender, creamy texture and a mildly smoky flavour. Black-eyed beans are widely used in Indian cooking.

Chana Dhal: Chana dhal is very similar to yellow split peas but smaller in size and with a slightly sweeter taste. It is used in a variety of vegetable dishes.

Chickpeas: These round beige-coloured pulses have a strong, nutty flavour when cooked. As well as being used for curries, chickpeas are also ground into a flour which is widely used in many Indian dishes such as *pakoras* and *bhajees*.

Flageolet (small cannellini) Beans: Small oval beans that are white or pale green in colour. They have a mild, refreshing flavour and feature in classic French dishes.

Green Lentils: Also known as continental lentils, these have quite a strong flavour and retain their shape during cooking. They are very versatile and are used in a number of dishes.

Haricot (navy) Beans: Small, white oval beans that come in different varieties. Haricot beans are ideal for Indian cooking because not only do they retain their shape but they also absorb the flavours of the spices.

Kidney Beans: One of the most popular types of bean, these are dark red/brown, kidney-shaped beans with a strong flavour.

Mung Beans: These are small, round green beans with a slightly sweet flavour and creamy texture. When sprouted they produce the familiar beansprouts.

Red Split Lentils: A readily available lentil that can be used for making dhal. Use instead of toovar dhal.

Toovar Dhal: A dull orange-coloured split pea with a very distinctive earthy flavour. Toovar dhal is available plain and in an oily variety.

Soaking and Cooking Tips

Most dried beans and peas, but not lentils, need to be soaked overnight before cooking. Wash the beans thoroughly and remove any small stones and damaged beans. Put into a large bowl and cover with plenty of cold water. When cooking, allow double the volume of water to beans and boil for 10 minutes. This initial boiling period is essential to remove any harmful toxins. Drain, rinse and cook in fresh water. The cooking time for all pulses varies depending on the type and their freshness. Beans and peas can be cooked in a pressure cooker to save time. Lentils, on the whole, do not need soaking. They should be washed in several changes of cold water before being cooked.

Left: Clockwise from bottom right: Mung beans, flageolet (small cannellini) beans, chickpeas, haricot (navy) beans, black-eyed beans (peas), kidney beans. Above: Clockwise from top: Red split lentils, green lentils, toovar dhal, chana dhal.

— SIX —

SQUASHES

Courgettes

Marrows and Summer Squashes

Pumpkins and Winter Squashes

Exotic Gourds

Cucumbers

COURGETTES (ZUCCHINI)

Courgettes are the best loved of all the squashes as they are so versatile. They are quick and easy to cook and are succulent and tender with a delicate, unassuming flavour. Unlike other squashes, they are available year round.

Vegetables taste best when eaten immediately after they have been picked, and this particularly applies to courgettes. They have a long season and are good to grow since the more you cut, the more the plants produce. Left unchecked, they turn into marrows (large zucchini).

Varieties

The courgette is classified as a summer squash, *cucurbita pepo*, along with marrows and pattypan squashes.

Courgettes: Sometimes called zucchini, courgettes are basically immature marrows. The word is a diminutive of the French *courge*, meaning marrow, and similarly zucchini means miniature *zucca*, Italian for gourd. Courgettes have a deep green skin, with firm pale flesh. The seeds and pith found in marrows have yet to form but are visible in more mature courgettes. Conversely, the prized baby courgettes have no suggestion of seeds or pith and the flesh is completely firm.

Yellow Courgettes: These are bright yellow and somewhat straighter than green courgettes. They have a slightly firmer flesh than green courgettes but are otherwise similar.

Pattypan Squashes: These little squashes look like tiny custard squashes. They can be pale green, yellow or white and have a slightly firmer texture than courgettes, but a similar flavour. They can be sliced and grilled (broiled) in the same way as courgettes but, to make the most of their size and shape, steam them whole.

Summer Crooknecks: Pale yellow with curves at the neck and a bumpy skin, crooknecks are prepared and cooked in the same way as courgettes.

Italian Courgettes: These very long, thin courgettes are grown in Italy. They are treated like ordinary courgettes but are strictly a bottle gourd.

Buying and Storing

Courgettes should be firm with a glossy, healthy looking skin. Avoid any that feel squashy or generally look limp, as they will be dry and not worth using. Choose small courgettes whenever possible and buy in small quantities as needed.

Preparing

The tiny young courgettes need no preparation at all, and if they still have their flowers, so much the better. Other courgettes should be topped and tailed and then prepared according to the recipe, either sliced or slit for stuffing.

Cooking

Baby courgettes require little or no cooking. Steam them whole or just blanch them. Sliced larger courgettes can be steamed or boiled but take care that they do not overcook as they go soggy very quickly. Alternatively, grill (broil), roast or fry them. Try dipping slices in a light batter and then shallow-frying in a blend of olive and sunflower oil. To roast, place them in a ovenproof dish, scatter with crushed garlic and a few torn basil leaves and sprinkle with olive oil; then bake in a very hot oven until tender and light golden brown, turning the slices occasionally.

Top left: Pattypan squashes.
Far left: Baby courgettes (zucchini).
Left: Yellow courgettes (zucchini).
Right: Italian courgettes (zucchini) beside white and green courgettes.

MARROWS (LARGE ZUCCHINI) AND SUMMER SQUASHES

Vegetable marrow is classified as a summer squash yet it is rather the poor relation of squashes. Most of the edible flesh is water and at best it is a rather bland vegetable, with a slightly sweet flavour. At worst, it is insipid and if cooked to a mush it is completely tasteless.

Marrows can be stuffed, although it involves a lot of energy expended for very little reward; but marrow cooked over a low heat in butter with no added water (so that it steams in its own juice) brings out the best in it.

History

Marrows, like all the summer and winter squashes, are native to America. Squashes were eaten by native American-Indians, traditionally with corn and beans, and in an Iroquois myth the three vegetables are represented as inseparable sisters. Although the early explorers would almost certainly have come into contact with them, they were not brought back home, and vegetable marrow was not known in England until the 19th century. Once introduced, however, it quickly became very popular. Mrs Beeton gives eight recipes for vegetable marrow and observes that 'it is now extensively used'. No mention at all is made of courgettes (zucchini), which of course are simply immature marrows.

Varieties

The word 'marrow' as a general term tends to refer to the summer squashes. At the end of summer and in the early autumn a good variety of the large summer squashes is available.

Vegetable Marrows: This is the proper name for the large prize marrows, beloved of harvest festivals and country fairs. Buy small specimens whenever possible.

Spaghetti Squashes/Marrows: Long and pale yellow, like all marrows these squashes can grow to enormous sizes, but buy small specimens for convenience as well as flavour. They earned their name from the resemblance of the cooked flesh to spaghetti.

To boil a spaghetti squash, first pierce the end, so that the heat can reach the middle, then cook for about 25 minutes or until the skin feels tender. Cut the squash in half lengthways, remove the seeds, and then fork the strands of flesh out on to a plate. It has a fragrant, almost honey and lemon flavour and tastes good with garlic butter or pesto.

Custard Marrows: These are pretty, pale green squashes with scalloped edges and a similar flavour to courgettes. If possible, buy small specimens, about 10cm/4in across. Boil these whole until tender, then cut a slice off the tops, scoop out the seeds and serve with a knob (pat) of butter.

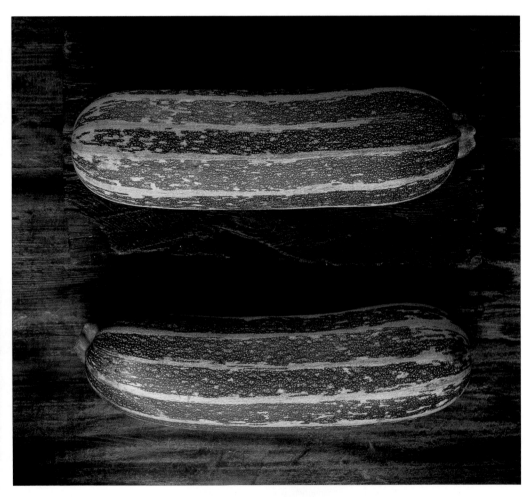

Buying and Storing

Buy vegetables that have clear, unblemished flesh and avoid any with soft or brown patches. Vegetable marrows and spaghetti squashes will keep for several months provided they are kept in a cool, dark place. Custard marrows will keep up to a week.

Preparing

Wash the skin. For sautéing or steaming, or if the skin is tough, peel it away. For braised marrow, cut into chunks and discard the seeds and pith (*right*). For

stuffing, cut into slices or cut lengthways and discard the seeds and pith.

Cooking

Place chunks of marrow in a heavy pan with a little butter, cover and cook until tender. It can then be livened up with garlic, herbs or tomatoes. For stuffed marrow, blanch first, stuff, then cover or wrap it in foil to cook.

Above: Vegetable marrows (large zucchini).
Far left: Spaghetti squashes.
Left: Custard marrows (large zucchini).

PUMPKINS AND WINTER SQUASHES

Pumpkins are the most famous of the winter squashes; aesthetically they are one of nature's most pleasing vegetables for their huge size, their colour and the smoothness of their skin. They originally came from America and, from a culinary point of view, they have their home there.

The name squash comes from America and as well as pumpkins, the family includes acorn, butternut and turban squashes to name but a few. There are simply hundreds of different squashes, including Sweet Dumpling, Queensland Blue (from Australia), Calabaza, Cushaw and Golden Nugget.

History

The tradition of eating pumpkin at Thanksgiving came from when the Pilgrim Fathers, who had settled in New England, proclaimed a day of thanksgiving and prayer for the harvest. The early tradition was to serve the pumpkin with its head and seeds removed, the cavity filled with milk, honey and spices, and baked until tender. The custom of eating pumpkin at Thanksgiving has remained but it is now served in a different way: puréed pumpkin, either fresh or tinned, is used to make tarts.

Varieties

There is a huge number of varieties of winter squashes and, confusingly, many are known by several different names. However, from a cooking point of view, most are interchangeable although it is best to taste dishes as you cook them, as seasoning may differ from one to the other. In general, they all have a floury and slightly fibrous flesh and a mild, almost bland flavour tinged with sweetness. Because of this blandness, they harmonize well with other ingredients.

Acorn Squashes: These are small and heart-shaped with a beautiful deep green or orange skin, or a mixture of the two. Peel, then use as for pumpkins or bake whole, then split and serve with butter.

Butternut Squashes: Perfectly pear-shaped, these are a buttery colour. Use in soups or in any pumpkin recipe.

Delicata Squashes: This pretty pale yellow squash has a succulent yellow flesh,

tasting like a cross between sweet potato and butternut squash.

English Pumpkins: These have a softer flesh than the American variety and are good for soups or, if puréed, combined with potatoes or other root vegetables.

Hubbard Squashes: These large winter squashes have a thick, bumpy, hard shell which can range in colour from bright orange to dark green. If they are exceptionally large, they are sometimes sold in halves or large wedges. They have a grainy texture and are best mashed with butter and seasoning.

Kabocha Squashes: Attractive bright green squashes with a pale orange flesh.

They are similar in flavour and texture to acorn squashes and can be prepared and cooked in the same way.

Onion Squashes: Round, yellow or pale orange, onion squashes have a mild flavour, less sweet than pumpkin but still with a slightly fruity or honey taste. They are good in risottos or in most pumpkin recipes, but taste for flavour – you may need to add extra seasoning or sugar.

Above: Clockwise from right: A pumpkin hybrid, kabocha squash, acorn squash.
Right: Clockwise from top right: Hybrid squash, two golden acorn squashes, two small and one large pumpkin.

Pumpkins: Large, bright yellow or orange squashes, with a deep orange flesh. They have a sweet, slightly honeyed, flavour and are very much a taste North Americans and Australians grow up with. However, they are not to everyone's liking and some people find them rather cloying and sickly. Pumpkin soup, pumpkin bread and pumpkin pie are part of the American tradition, as are faces carved from the shell at Hallowe'en, and this practice has spread to many parts of the world.

Buying and Storing

All winter squashes may be stored for long periods. Buy firm, unblemished vegetables with clear, smooth skins.

Preparing

For larger squashes, or for those being used for soups or purées, peel and cut into pieces, removing the seeds (*left*).

Cooking

Boil in a little water for about 20 minutes until tender, then mash and serve with butter and plenty of salt and pepper. Smaller squashes can be baked whole in their skins, then halved, seeded and served with butter and maple syrup. Pumpkin and other squashes can also be lightly sautéed in butter before adding stock, cream or chopped tomatoes.

EXOTIC GOURDS

While the squashes are native to America, most gourds originated in the Old World – from Africa, India and the Far East. However, over the millennia, seeds crossed water and, over the centuries, people crossed continents so that squashes and gourds are now common all over the world. Both belong to the family *Cucurbitacea*, and both are characterized by their rapid-growing vines.

Bottle Gourds: Bottle gourds are still a familiar sight in Africa, where they are principally grown not for their fruit, but for their dried shells. The gourds can grow to enormous sizes and the shells are used for water bottles, cups and musical instruments. The young fruit can be eaten, but it is extremely bitter and is normally only added to highly flavoured stews, such as curries.

Chayotes: The chayote (pronounced chow-chow) is a popular gourd in all sorts of regions of the world and can be found in just about any ethnic supermarket, be it Chinese, African, Indian or Caribbean. In each it is known by a different name, christophine being the Caribbean term, but choko, shu-shu and chinchayote are among its many other names used elsewhere. Unlike most gourds, it originated in Mexico but was widely grown throughout the tropics after the invasions of the Spanish.

It is a pear-shaped fruit with a large central stone (pit) and has a cream-coloured or green skin. It has a bland flavour, similar to marrow (large zucchini), and a slightly firmer texture something like pumpkin. It is commonly used in Caribbean cooking, primarily as a side dish or in soufflés. Alternatively it can be used raw in salads.

Chinese Bitter Melons: These are a common vegetable in all parts of Asia and go by myriad names, including bitter gourd and bitter cucumber. They are popular throughout Asia, eaten when very young, but are extremely bitter and rarely eaten in the West. They are easily recognized as they have warty, spiny skins that are white when young but will probably have ripened to a dark green by the time they appear in the stores.

Most recipes from China suggest halving the gourd, removing the pulp and then slicing the flesh before boiling it for several minutes to remove their bitterness. They can then be added to stir-fries or other oriental dishes.

Far left: Sweet dumpling.
Left: Pumpkin.
Top right: Chinese bitter melon.
Middle right: Loofah.
Below: Chayote.

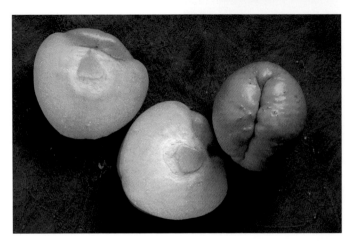

Smooth and Angled Loofahs: The smooth loofah must be one of the strangest plants. When young it can be eaten, although it is not much valued. However, the plant is grown almost exclusively for sponges, used everywhere as a back rub in the bath. The ripe loofahs are picked and, once the skin has been stripped off and the seeds shaken out, allowed to dry. The plant then gradually dries to a fibrous skeleton and thence to bathrooms everywhere – so now you know!

Angled or ribbed loofahs are more commonly eaten but again are only edible when young as they become unpleasantly bitter when mature. They taste something like courgettes (zucchini) and are best cooked in a similar way – fried in butter or cooked with tomatoes, garlic and oil.

CUCUMBERS

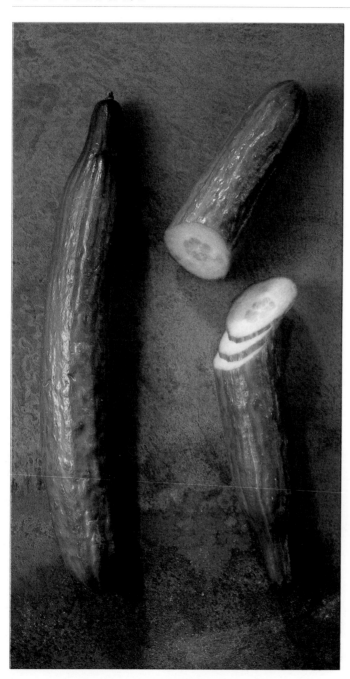

The Chinese say food should be enjoyed for its texture as well as flavour; cucumbers have a unique texture and refreshing cool taste. A traditional British afternoon tea with cucumber sandwiches, sliced cucumber between wafer thin brown buttered bread, provides a delight of contrasts – the soft bread, the smooth butter and the cool crisp cucumber.

Varieties

English Cucumbers: These are the cucumbers the English are most familiar with. They have fewer seeds and thinner skin than the ridged cucumber.
Gherkins: These are tiny cucumbers with bumpy, almost warty skins and are mostly pickled in vinegar and eaten with cold meats or chopped into mayonnaise.
Kirbys: Small cucumbers, available in the United States and used for pickling.
Ridged Cucumbers: These are smaller than most cucumbers with more seeds and a thick, bumpy skin. You can buy them all over France but otherwise they tend to be available only in specialist greengrocers. The waxed ones need to be peeled before eating but most ridged cucumbers on the Continent are unwaxed and good without peeling.

Buying and Storing

Cucumbers should be firm from top to bottom. They are often sold pre-wrapped in plastic and can be stored in the salad drawer of the refrigerator for up to a week. Remove the plastic packaging once you've 'started' a cucumber. Discard once it begins to go soggy.

Preparing

Whether you peel a cucumber or not is a matter of personal preference, but wash it if you don't intend to peel it. Some producers use wax coatings to give a glossy finish and these cucumbers must be peeled. If you are in doubt, buy organic cucumbers. Special citrus peelers can remove strips of peel to give an attractive striped effect when sliced.

Left: Cucumbers.
Above right: Ridged cucumbers.
Above far right: Baby cucumbers.
Below right: Kirbys.

Serving

Thinly sliced cucumber is most frequently served with a light dressing or sour cream. In Greece cucumber is an essential part of a Greek country salad, *horiatiki salata*, cut into thick chunks and served with tomatoes, (bell) peppers and feta cheese and dressed simply with olive oil and a little wine vinegar.

Iced cucumber soup is delicious, and cucumber can also be puréed with yogurt, garlic and herbs and served with sour cream stirred in.

Cooking

Cucumbers are normally served raw, but are surprisingly good cooked. Cut the cucumber into wedges, remove the seeds and then simmer for a few minutes until tender. Once drained, return the cucumber to the pan and stir in a little cream and seasoning, then serve as a vegetable accompaniment.

FRUIT

TOMATOES

Next to onions, tomatoes are one of the most important ingredients in the kitchen. In Mediterranean cooking, they are fundamental. Along with garlic and olive oil, they form the basis of so many Italian, Spanish and Provençal recipes that it is hard to find many dishes in which they are not included.

History

Tomatoes are related to potatoes, aubergines (eggplants) and sweet (bell) and chilli peppers, and all are members of the nightshade family. Some very poisonous members of this family may well have deterred our ancestors from taking to tomatoes. Indeed, the leaves of tomato plants are highly toxic and can result in very bad stomach aches if consumed.

Tomatoes are native to western South America. By the time of the Spanish invasions in the 16th century, they were widely cultivated throughout the whole of South America and Mexico. Hernán Cortés, conqueror of the Aztecs, sent the first tomato plants, a yellow variety, to Spain (no doubt along with the plundered Aztec gold).

However, people did not instinctively take to this 'golden apple' when it was introduced in the West. English horticulturists mostly grew them as ornamental plants to adorn their gardens and had little positive to say about them as food. Spain is recorded as the first country to use tomatoes in cooking, stewing them with oil and seasoning. Italy followed suit, but elsewhere they were treated with suspicion.

The first red tomatoes arrived in Europe in the 18th century, brought to Italy by two Jesuit priests. They were gradually accepted in northern Europe where, by the mid-19th century, they were grown extensively, eaten raw, cooked or used for pickles.

Above right: Red and yellow cherry tomatoes.
Below right: Yellow pear tomatoes.
Opposite above: Round or salad tomatoes on the vine.
Opposite below: Beefsteak tomatoes.

Varieties

There are countless varieties of tomatoes, ranging from the huge beefsteak ones that measure 10cm/4in across, to tiny cherry tomatoes, not much bigger than a thumb nail. They come in all shapes too – elongated, plum-shaped or slightly squarish and even pear-shaped.

Beefsteak Tomatoes: Large, ridged and deep red or orange in colour, these have a good flavour so are good in salads.

Canned Tomatoes: Keep a store of canned tomatoes, especially in the winter when fresh ones tend to taste insipid. Tomatoes are one of the few vegetables that take well to canning, but steer clear of any that are flavoured with garlic or herbs. It is far better to add flavouring yourself.

Cherry Tomatoes: These small, dainty tomatoes were once the prized treasures of gardeners but are now widely available in supermarkets and food stores. Although more expensive than round tomatoes, they have a delightful sweet

flavour and are worth paying the extra money for serving in salads or for cooking whole.

Plum Tomatoes: Richly flavoured with fewer seeds than regular tomatoes, these Italian-grown tomatoes are usually recommended for cooking, although they can be used in salads.

Round or Salad Tomatoes: These are the common tomatoes found in greengrocers and supermarkets. They vary in size according to the exact type and season. Sun-ripened tomatoes have the best flavour, although for year-round availability the fruit is often picked and ripened off the plant. These tomatoes are versatile in everyday cooking. Adding a pinch of sugar and taking care to season the dish well helps to overcome any weakness in flavour.

Sun-Dried Tomatoes: This is one of the fashionable foods of the late 1980s and early 1990s. They add an evocative flavour to many Mediterranean dishes but don't use them too indiscriminately.

Tomato Purée (paste): This is good for adding an intense tomato flavour, but use carefully or the flavour will be overpowering. Tubes have screw tops

and are better than cans as, once they are opened, they can be kept for up to 4–6 weeks in the refrigerator.
Yellow Tomatoes: These are exactly like red tomatoes – they may be round, plum or cherry-sized – except they are yellow.

Buying and Storing

Ideally, tomatoes should be allowed to ripen slowly on the plant so that their flavour can develop. Consequently, home-grown tomatoes are best, followed by those grown and sold locally. When buying from a supermarket or greengrocer, look at the leafy green tops; the fresher they look the better. Buy locally grown beefsteak or cherry tomatoes for salads and plum tomatoes for rich sauces. Paler tomatoes or those tinged with green will redden if kept in a brown paper bag or the salad drawer of the refrigerator, but if you intend to use tomatoes straight away, buy bright red specimens. Overripe tomatoes, where the skin has split and they seem to be bursting with juice, are excellent in soups. Check for any sign of mould or decay, as this will spoil all your efforts.

Preparing

Slice tomatoes across rather than downwards for salads and pizza toppings. For wedges, cut downwards; halve or quarter and cut into two or three depending on the size of the tomato.

Cooking

Among the many classic tomato dishes is tomato soup, cooked to a delicate orange colour with stock or milk, or simmered with vegetables, garlic and basil. Recipes *à la provençale* indicate that tomatoes are in the dish; in Provençal cooking and Italian dishes, tomatoes are used with fish, meat and vegetables, in sauces and stuffings, with pasta and in superb salads. The Italian *tri colore salata* is a combination of large tomatoes, mozzarella and basil (the three colours of the Italian flag). The natural astringency of tomatoes means that, in salads, they need only be sprinkled with a fruity olive oil.

Chopped Tomatoes

Chopped tomatoes add a depth of flavour to all sorts of meat and vegetarian dishes. Ideally, even in fairly rustic meals, the tomatoes should be peeled, since the skin can be irritating to eat once cooked. Some sauces also recommend seeding tomatoes, in which case cut the tomato into halves and scoop out the seeds before chopping (*above*).

Skinning Tomatoes

Cut a cross in the tops of the tomatoes, then place in a bowl and pour over boiling water. Leave for a minute (*above*), then use a sharp knife to peel away the skin, which should come away easily. Do a few at a time (five at most) otherwise they will begin to cook while soaking; boil the kettle for the next batch when you have finished peeling. The water must be boiling.

AUBERGINES (EGGPLANTS)

Many varieties of aubergines are cultivated and cooked all over the world. In Europe, Asia or America, they feature in a multitude of different dishes.

History

Although aubergines are a member of the nightshade family and thus related to potatoes, tomatoes and (bell) peppers, they were not discovered in the New World. The first mention of their cultivation is in China in 5BC, and they are thought to have been eaten in India long before that. The Moors introduced the aubergine to Spain some 1,200 years ago and it was grown in Andalucia. It is likely that they also introduced it to Italy, and possibly from there to other southern and eastern parts of Europe.

In spite of their popularity in Europe, aubergines did not become popular in Britain or the United States until very recently; although previous generations of food writers knew about them, they gave only the occasional recipe for cooking with them.

Above left: Plum tomatoes.
Top: Aubergines (eggplants).
Above: Baby aubergines (eggplants).
Left: Japanese aubergines (eggplants).

Meanwhile, in the southern and eastern
parts of Europe, aubergines (eggplants)
had become extremely well liked, and
today they are one of the most popular
vegetables in the Mediterranean. Indeed,
Italy, Greece and Turkey claim to have
100 ways of cooking them. In the Middle
East, aubergines are also a central part
of their cuisine.

Varieties

There are many different varieties of
aubergines, differing in colour, size
and shape according to their country
of origin. Small ivory-white and plump
aubergines look like large eggs (hence
their name in the States: eggplant).
Pretty striped aubergines may be either
purple or pink and flecked with white
irregular stripes. The Japanese or Asian
aubergine is straight and very narrow,
ranging in colour from a pretty variegated
purple and white to a solid purple. It has
a tender, slightly sweet flesh. Most
aubergines, however, are either glossy
purple or almost black and can be
long and slim or fat like zeppelins.

All aubergines have a similar flavour and texture; they taste bland yet slightly smoky when cooked, and the flesh is spongy to touch when raw, but soft after cooking.

Buying and Storing

Aubergines should feel heavy for their size and firm to the touch, with glossy, unblemished skins. They will keep well in the salad drawer of the refrigerator for up to two weeks.

Preparing

When frying aubergines for any dish where they need slicing (e.g. ratatouille), it is a good idea to salt the slices first in order to draw out some of their moisture, otherwise, they absorb large quantities of oil during cooking (they absorb copious amounts anyway, but salting reduces this slightly). Salting also used to be advised to reduce their bitterness but today's varieties are rarely bitter. To salt aubergines, cut into slices, about 1cm/¹/₂ in thick for fried slices, *(top right)* or segments *(above right)* and sprinkle generously with salt. Leave them to drain in a colander for about one hour, then rinse well and gently squeeze out the moisture from each slice or carefully pat dry with a piece of kitchen paper.

Cooking

Aubergine slices can be fried in olive oil, as they are or first coated in batter – both popular Italian and Greek appetizers.For moussaka, *parmigiana* and other dishes where aubergines are layered with other ingredients, fry the slices briefly in olive oil. This gives them a tasty crust, while the inside stays soft.

To make a purée, such as for Poor Man's Caviar, first prick the aubergine all over with a fork and then roast in a moderately hot oven for about 30 minutes until tender. Scoop out the flesh and mix with spring onions (scallions), lemon juice and olive oil. One of the most famous aubergine dishes is *Imam Bayaldi* – 'the Iman fainted' – fried aubergines stuffed with onions, garlic, tomato, spices and lots of olive oil.

Above left: White aubergines (eggplants).
Below left: Striped aubergines (eggplants).
Above: Thai aubergines (eggplants),
including white, yellow and pea types.

(BELL) PEPPERS

In spite of their name, peppers have nothing to do with the spice pepper used as a seasoning, although early explorers may have been mistaken in thinking the fruit of the shrubby plant looked like the spice they were seeking. It is thanks to this 400-year-old mistake that the name 'pepper' has stuck.

History

The journeys Christopher Columbus and the conquistadors made were partly to find the spices Marco Polo had found a hundred years earlier in the Far East. Instead of the Orient, however, Columbus discovered the Americas, and instead of spices, he found maize, potatoes and tomatoes. He would have noted, though, that the American-Indians flavoured their food with ground peppers, and since it was hot, like pepper, perhaps wishful thinking coloured his objectivity. In any case, he returned with the new vegetables, describing them as peppers and advertising them as more pungent than those from Caucasus.

Varieties

Peppers and chillies are both members of the capsicum family. To distinguish between them, peppers are called sweet peppers, bell peppers and even bullnose peppers and come in a variety of colours – red, green, yellow, white, orange and a dark purple-black.

The colour of the pepper tells you something about its flavour. Green peppers are the least mature and have a fresh 'raw' flavour. Red peppers are ripened green peppers and are distinctly sweeter. Yellow/orange peppers taste more or less like red peppers, although perhaps slightly less sweet and if you have a fine palate you may be able to detect a difference. Black peppers have a similar flavour to green peppers but when cooked are a bit disappointing as they turn green; so if you buy them for their dramatic colour, they are best used in salads.

In Greece and other parts of southern Europe, longer, slimmer peppers are often available and these have a more pronounced sweet and pungent flavour than the bell-shaped peppers found elsewhere – although this may be because they are locally picked and therefore absolutely fresh. Whichever is the case, they are quite delicious.

Buying and Storing

Peppers should look glossy and sprightly and feel hard and crisp; avoid any that look wrinkled or have damp soft patches. They will keep for a few days at the bottom of the refrigerator.

Preparing

To prepare stuffed peppers, cut off the top and then cut away the inner core and pith, and shake out the seeds. The seeds and core are easily removed when halving, quartering or slicing.

Cooking

There are countless ways of cooking peppers. Sliced, they can be fried with onions and garlic in olive oil and then braised with tomatoes and herbs. This is the basic ratatouille; other vegetables, such as courgettes and aubergines (eggplants), can of course be added.

Peppers can be roasted, either with ratatouille ingredients or with only onions and garlic. Cut into large pieces, place in a roasting pan and sprinkle with olive oil, torn basil and seasoning. Roast in a very hot oven (220°C/425°F/Gas 7) for about 30 minutes, turning occasionally. Grilled (broiled) peppers are another superb dish. Once grilled they can be skinned to reveal a soft texture and added to salads.

Above far left: Red, green and orange (bell) peppers.
Below far left: Yellow (bell) peppers.
Above left: White (bell) peppers.
Above right: Purple (bell) peppers.

Skinning Peppers

Cut the pepper into quarters lengthways and grill (broil), skin side up (*above*), until the skin is charred and blistered. Place the pieces immediately into a plastic bag (you will need tongs or a fork as they will be hot) and close the top of the bag with a tie or a loose knot. Leave for a few minutes and then remove from the bag and the skin will peel off easily.

CHILLIES

Some people apparently become so addicted to the taste of hot food that they carry little jars of chopped dried chillies around with them and scatter them over every meal. Although this is a bit extreme, it is chillies more than any other ingredient that spice up our mealtimes.

Varieties

Chillies are the most important seasoning in the world after salt. Unlike (bell) peppers, to which they are closely related, the different varieties of chilli can have widely different heat values – from the 'just about bearable' to the 'knock your head off' variety.

Anaheim Chilli: A long, thin chilli with a blunt end, named after the Californian city. It can be red or green and has a mild, sweet taste.

Ancho Chilli/Pepper: These look like tiny peppers. They are mild enough that it is possible to taste the underlying sweetness beneath the heat.

Birdseye or Bird Chilli: These small red chillies are fiery hot. Also known as pequin chillies.

Cayenne Pepper: This is made from the dried, ground seeds and pods of chillies. The name comes from the capital of French Guiana, north of Brazil, although the cayenne chilli does not grow there any longer and the pepper is made from chillies grown all over the world.

Early Jalapeño: A popular American chilli, which starts dark green and gradually turns to red.

Habañero: Often called Scotch Bonnet, this is the hottest of all chillies and is small and can be green, red or yellow. Colour is no real guide to its heat properties, so don't be fooled into thinking that green ones are mild. They are all *very* hot. The habañero comes from Mexico and is frequently used in Mexican and Caribbean dishes.

Hot Gold Spike: This chilli is a large, pale, yellow-green fruit grown in the south-western United States. Be warned, it is very hot!

Above: Birdseye chillies.
Left: Habañero chillies (in and below bowl) and Yellow wax peppers.

Preparing

The capsaicin in chillies is most concentrated in the pith inside the pod and this, together with the seeds, should be cut away (*below*) unless you want maximum heat. Capsaicin irritates the skin and especially the eyes, so take care when preparing chillies. Either wear gloves or wash your hands thoroughly after handling chillies.If you rub your eyes, even if you have washed your hands carefully, it will be painful.

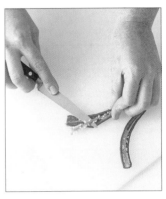

Poblano: A small, dark green chilli, served whole in Spain either roasted or grilled (broiled). They are mostly mild but you can get the rogue fiery one, so beware if eating them whole.

Red Chilli: These are long, rather wrinkled chillies that are green at first and then gradually ripen to red.They are of variable hotness and, because they are so long and thin, are rather fiddly to prepare.

Serrano Chilli: A long, red and extremely hot chilli.

Tabasco: A sauce made with chillies, salt and vinegar and first made in New Orleans. It is a fiery sauce, popular in Creole, Caribbean and Mexican cooking – or indeed in any dish requiring last minute heat.

Yellow Wax Pepper: Pale yellow to green, these can vary from mild to hot.

Buying and Storing

Some fresh chillies look wrinkled even in their prime and therefore this is not a good guide to their freshness. They should, however, be unblemished, and avoid any that are soft or bruised.

The substance that makes the chilli hot is a volatile oil called capsaicin. This differs not only from one type to another but also from plant to plant, depending on growing conditions; the more the plant has to struggle to survive in terms of light, water, soil, etc, the more capsaicin will be produced. It is therefore impossible to tell how hot a chilli will be before tasting, although some types are naturally hotter than others. The belief that green chillies are milder than red ones does not necessarily follow; generally red chillies will have ripened for longer in the sun with the result that they will only be sweeter for all that sunshine.

Chillies can be stored in a plastic bag, to prevent them contaminating other foods, in the refrigerator for a few days.

Cooking

In Mexican cooking chillies play a vital, and almost central role. It is difficult to think of any savoury Mexican dish that does not contain either fresh chillies or some form of processed chilli, whether canned, dried or ground. Other cuisines, however, are equally enthusiastic about chillies. They are essential in curries and similar dishes from India and the Far East, and in Caribbean and Creole food they are also used extensively.

If you have developed a tolerance for really hot food, then there is no reason why you shouldn't add as many as you wish. In general, however, use chillies discreetly, if for no better reason than you can't take the heat away if you make a mistake.

Above: Ancho chillies (left) and Anaheim chillies (on board).

PLANTAINS AND GREEN BANANAS

While bananas are well and truly fruit, eaten almost exclusively as a dessert or by themselves as fruit, plantains can reasonably be considered among the vegetable fraternity as they have a definite savoury flavour, are normally eaten as a first or main course and can only be eaten once cooked.

Varieties

Plantains: Also known as cooking bananas, these have a coarser flesh and more savoury flavour than sweet bananas. While superficially they look exactly like bananas, they are, on closer inspection, altogether larger and heavier looking. They can vary in colour from the unripe fruit, which is green, through yellow to a mottled black colour, which is when the fruit is completely ripe.

Green Bananas: Only certain types of green bananas are used in African and Caribbean cooking, and the 'greenish' bananas you find in most western supermarkets are normally eating bananas, just waiting to ripen. If you need green bananas for a recipe, look out for them in West Indian or African stores.

Preparing

Plantains: These are inedible raw and must be cooked before eating. Unless very ripe, the skin can be tricky to remove. With yellow and green plantains, cut the fruit into short lengths, then slit the skin along the natural ridge of each piece of plantain. Gently ease the skin away from the flesh and pull the skin until it peels off completely (*below*).

Once peeled, plantains can be sliced horizontally or into lengths then roasted or fried. Like bananas, plantains will discolour if exposed to the air so, if not using immediately, sprinkle with lemon juice or place in a bowl of salted water.

Green Bananas: These should be prepared in a similar way. As with plantains, green bananas should not be eaten raw and are usually boiled, either in their skins or not, according to the recipe.

If making green banana crisps (US chips), use a potato peeler to produce the thinnest slices (*left*).

If cooking plantains or green bananas in their skins, slit the skin lengthways along the sides and place in a pan of salted water. Bring to the boil, simmer gently for about 20 minutes until tender and then cool. The peel can then easily be removed before slicing.

Cooking and Serving

Plantains and green bananas both have an excellent flavour. In many African and Caribbean recipes they are roasted or fried and then served simply with salt. However, if boiled, they can be sliced and served in a simple salad with a few

sliced onions, or added to something far more elaborate like a gado gado salad, with mango, avocado, lettuce and prawns (shrimp).

Plantains also make a delicious soup, where they are often teamed with corn. After frying an onion and a little garlic, add two sliced and peeled plantains, together with tomatoes, if liked. Fry gently for a few minutes and then add vegetable stock to cover and one or two sliced chillies, together with about 175g/6oz corn. Simmer gently together until the plantain is tender.

Above left: Plantains.
Below left: Green bananas.
Below: Canned ackee.

ACKEE

Ackee is a tropical fruit that is used in a variety of savoury dishes, mainly of Caribbean origin, where the fruit is very popular. The fruit itself is bright red and, when ripe, bursts open to reveal three large black seeds and a soft, creamy flesh resembling scrambled eggs. It has a slightly lemony flavour and is traditionally served with saltfish to make one of Jamaica's national dishes. Only buy ripe fruit as, when under-ripe, certain parts of the fruit are toxic.

However, unless you are visiting the Caribbean you are probably only likely to find ackee in cans, and indeed most recipes call for canned ackee, which is a good substitute for the fresh fruit.

Jamaican cooks also use ackee to add a subtle flavour to a variety of vegetable and bean dishes. The canned ackee needs very little cooking, and should be added to dishes in the last few minutes of cooking to heat it through rather than cook it. Take care when stirring into a dish as it breaks up very easily.

AVOCADOS

The avocado has been known by many names – butter pear and alligator pear to name but two. It earned the title butter pear clearly because of its consistency, but alligator pear was the original Spanish name. Although you would be forgiven for thinking this was due to its knobbly skin (among some varieties anyway), the name in fact derives from the Spanish, which was based on the Aztec word, *ahuacatl*.

History

The avocado is a New World fruit, native to Mexico, but while it would have been 'discovered' by the Old World explorers, it didn't become a popular food in Europe until the middle of the 20th century, when modern transport meant that growers in California, who started farming avocados in the middle of the 19th century, could market this fruit worldwide. Avocados are now also exported to the rest of the world by South Africa and Australia.

Nutrition

The avocado is high in protein and carbohydrate. It is one of the few fruits that contains fat, and it is also rich in potassium, Vitamin C, some B vitamins and Vitamin E. Its rich oils, particularly its Vitamin E content, mean that it is not only useful as food, but for skin and hair care too, something the Aztecs and Incas were aware of a thousand years ago. The cosmetic industry may have been in its infancy, but it still knew a good thing when it saw it.

Because of their valuable protein and vitamin content, avocados are a popular food for babies. They are easily blended, and small children generally enjoy their creamy texture and pleasant flavour.

Varieties

There are four varieties: Hass, the purple-black small knobbly avocado, the Ettinger and Fuerte, which are pear-shaped and have smooth green skin, and the Nabal, which is rounder in shape. The black-coloured Hass has golden-yellow flesh, while green avocados have pale green to yellow flesh.

Buying and Storing

The big problem in buying avocados is that they're never ripe when you want them to be. How often do you see shoppers standing by the avocado shelves, feeling around for that rare creature, the perfectly ripe avocado? Most times they all feel as hard as rocks; that or else they're hopelessly soft and squashy and clearly past their best. The proper and sensible thing to do is buy fruit a few days before you need it. An unripe avocado will ripen in between four to seven days at room temperature. Once it is ripe, it will keep well in the refrigerator for a few days, but you still need to plan well in advance if you want to be sure of the perfect avocado.

The alternative is to hope for the best and keep feeling around until you find a ripe fruit. A perfect avocado should have a clean, unblemished skin without any brown or black patches. If ripe, it should 'give' slightly if squeezed gently in the hand, but not so much that it actually feels soft. Over-ripe avocados are really not worth bothering with, however persuasive and generous the offer from the man on the market. The flesh will be unattractively brown and stringy and the bits of good flesh you do manage to salvage will be soft and pulpy. Good for a dip, but nothing much else.

Preparing

Although they are simple fruits, avocados can be tricky to prepare. Once peeled, you are left with a slippery object that is then almost impossible to remove from the stone (pit).

If you intend to eat the avocados in halves, it's fairly simple to just prise out the stone once halved. If you want to slice the fruit, use this tip I learnt from my chef friend. The only thing you need is a very sharp knife. Cut the avocado in half, remove the stone and then, with the skin still on, cut through the flesh and the skin to make slices. It is then relatively simple to strip off the peel.

Use prepared avocadoes immediately, or sprinkle the flesh with lemon juice if you are preparing them slightly ahead as the flesh discolours very quickly once exposed to the air.

Cooking

Most popular raw, avocados can also be baked, grilled (broiled) or used in sautéed and sauced dishes.

Serving Ideas

As well as prawns (shrimp) or vinaigrette, a half avocado can hold a mixture of chopped tomatoes and cucumber, a mild garlic cheese dip or a sour cream potato salad. Slices of avocado are delicious served with sliced tomatoes and mozzarella, sprinkled simply with olive oil, lemon juice and plenty of black pepper. Avocado can be chopped and added to a salad, or puréed for a rich dressing.

In Mexico, where avocados grow in abundance, there are countless avocado recipes. Guacamole is perhaps the best known, but they are also eaten in soups and stews and commonly used to garnish tacos and enchiladas.

BREADFRUIT

Breadfruit is the common name for a tropical tree that grows on the islands of the South Pacific ocean. The fruit of the tree is about the size of a small melon with a rough rind and a pale, mealy flesh.

Preparing

The fruit should be peeled and the core removed.

Cooking

Breadfruit can be treated like potatoes: the flesh may be boiled, baked or fried and eaten as an accompaniment. It is a staple food for the people of the Pacific islands who bake the flesh, or dry and grind it for biscuits (cookies), bread and desserts. It has a sweet flavour and soft texture when ripe.

Left: Clockwise from the right: Fuerte, Hass and Nabal avocados.
Right: Breadfruit.

SALAD
VEGETABLES

Lettuce

Rocket

Chicory and Radicchio

Radishes

Watercress

Mustard and Cress

LETTUCE

One aspect of lettuce that sets it apart from any other vegetable is that you can only buy it in one form – fresh.

History

Lettuce has been cultivated for thousands of years. In Egyptian times it was sacred to the god Min, and tubs of lettuce were ceremoniously carried before this fertility god. It was then considered a powerful aphrodisiac, yet for the Greeks and the Romans lettuce was thought to have quite the opposite effect, making one sleepy and generally soporific. Chemists today confirm that lettuce contains a hypnotic similar to opium, and in herbal remedies lettuce is recommended for insomniacs.

Varieties

There are hundreds of different varieties of lettuce. Today, an increasing variety is available in the stores so that the salad bowl can be wealth of colour and texture.

Round Lettuces

Sometimes called head or cabbage lettuces, round lettuces have cabbage-like heads and include:
Butterheads: These are the classic lettuces seen in kitchen gardens. They have a pale heart and floppy, loosely packed leaves. They have a pleasant flavour as long as they are fresh.
Crispheads: Crisp lettuces, such as Iceberg, have an excellent crunchy texture and will keep their vitality long after butterheads have faded and died.
Looseheads: These are non-hearting lettuce with loose leaves and include lollo rosso and lollo biondo, oakleaf lettuce and Red Salad Bowl. Although they are not particularly remarkable for their flavour, they look superb.

Cos Lettuces

The cos is the only lettuce that would have been known in antiquity. It is known by two names: cos, derived from the Greek island where it was found by

Above: Butterhead (round) lettuce.
Right: Lollo rosso lettuce.
Above far right: Cos lettuce.
Below far right: Lamb's lettuce.
Below extreme right: Little Gem (Bibb).

the Romans; and romaine, the name used by the French after it was introduced to France from Rome. There are two types of cos lettuce, both of which have long, erect heads.

Cos: Considered the most delicious lettuce, this has a firm texture and a faintly nutty texture. It is the correct lettuce for Caesar Salad, one of the classic salads.

Little Gem (Bibb): In appearance Little Gems look like something between a baby cos and a tightly furled butterhead. They have firm hearts and are enjoyed for their distinct flavour. Like other lettuce hearts, they cope well with being cooked.

LAMB'S LETTUCE OR CORN SALAD

This popular winter leaf does not actually belong to the lettuce family (it is related to Fuller's teasel), but as it makes a lovely addition to salads, this seems a good place to include it. Called *mâche* in France, it has spoon-shaped leaves and an excellent nutty flavour that marries well with other salad vegetables.

Nutrition

As well as containing vitamins A, C and
E, lettuce provides potassium, iron
and calcium and traces of other minerals.

Buying and Storing

The best lettuce is that fresh from the
garden. The next best thing is to buy
lettuce from a farm store or pick-your-
own farms (although if fertilizers and
pesticides are used, their flavour will
be disappointing compared to the
organic product). Nowadays, lettuce is
frequently sold ready shredded and
packed with herbs etc, an acceptable
and convenient form of buying lettuce.
Whether you buy lettuce prepacked or
from the shelf, it must be fresh. Soil and
bugs can be washed off but those with
limp or yellow leaves are of no use.
Eat lettuce as soon as possible after
purchasing; in the meantime keep it in
a cool dark place, such as the salad
drawer of the refrigerator.

Making Salads

Salads can be made using only one
lettuce or a mixture of many. There are
no rules but, when mixing salads,
choose leaves to give contrast in texture
and colour as well as flavour. Fresh herbs,
such as parsley, coriander (cilantro) and
basil add an extra dimension.

Tear rather than cut the leaves of
loose-leafed lettuce; icebergs and other
large lettuces are commonly sliced or
shredded. Eat as soon as possible
after preparing.

Dressings should be well-flavoured
with a hint of sharpness but never too
astringent. Make them in a blender, a
screw top jar or in a large bowl so that
the ingredients can be thoroughly
blended. Always use the best possible
oils and vinegars, in roughly the
proportion of five oil to one vinegar or
lemon juice. Use half good olive oil and
half sunflower oil, or for a more fragrant
dressing, a combination of walnut oil and
sunflower oil. A pinch of salt and pepper
is essential, French mustard is optional
and a little sugar will blunt the flavour.

Add the dressing to the salad when
you're ready to serve – never before,
as it will make the leaves wilt.

ROCKET (ARUGULA)

Rocket has a wonderful peppery flavour and is excellent in a mixed green salad. It has distinctive small, bright green dandelion-shaped leaves. The Greeks and Romans commonly ate rocket in mixed salads, apparently to help counterbalance the dampening effect lettuce had on the libido – rocket's aphrodisiac properties in antiquity are well catalogued. It used to be sown around the statues of Priapus, the mythological Greek god of fertility and protector of gardens and herbs and son of Aphrodite and Dionysus.

Buying and Storing

Rocket is to be found either among the salads or fresh herbs in supermarkets, but it is extremely easy to grow in the garden or in pots on a windowsill. Buy fresh green leaves and use soon after purchasing. If necessary, the leaves can be kept immersed in cold water.

Preparing and Serving

Discard any discoloured leaves. Add rocket to plain green salads, or grind with garlic, pine nuts and olive oil for a dressing for pasta.

Since it has such a striking flavour, a little rocket goes a long way, making it an excellent leaf for garnishing. It tastes superb contrasted with grilled (broiled) goat's cheese, or one or two leaves can be added to sandwiches, or loosely packed into pitta bread pockets along with tomatoes, avocado, peanuts and bean sprouts. It can also be blitzed with toasted walnuts to make a wonderful pesto.

Above left: Oak Leaf lettuce.
Below left: Frisée lettuce.
Below: Rocket (arugula).

Chicory (Belgian endive) AND Radicchio

Chicory, radicchio, endive (US chicory) and escarole are all related to each other and when they are tasted together you can easily detect their family resemblance. Their names are occasionally interchanged: chicory is often referred to as Belgian or French endive and French and Belgian *chicorée* is the English curly endive.

CHICORY

During the late 18th century, chicory was grown in Europe for its root, and this was added to coffee. A Belgian, M. Brezier, discovered that the white leaves could be eaten, a fact he kept secret during his lifetime; but after his death chicory became a popular vegetable, first in Belgium and later elsewhere in Europe. Its Flemish name is *witloof*, meaning 'white leaf', and its characteristic pale leaf is due to its being grown in darkness; the paler it is, the less bitter its flavour.

Chicory can be eaten raw but is often cooked, either baked, stir-fried or poached. To eat raw, separate the leaves and serve with fruit, such as oranges or grapefruit, which counteract chicory's slight bitterness.

RADICCHIO

This is one of many varieties developed from wild chicory. It looks like a small lettuce with deep wine-red leaves and striking cream ribs and owes its splendid foliage to careful shading. If it is grown completely in the dark the leaves are marbled pink, and those that have been exposed to some light can be patched with a green or copper colour. Its flavour tends to be bitter but contrasts well with green salads. Radicchio can be stir-fried or poached, although the leaves turn dark green when cooked.

FRISÉE LETTUCE AND ESCAROLE

These are robust salad ingredients in both flavour and texture. The curly-leaved frisée lettuce looks like a green frizzy mop and the escarole is broad-leaved, but both have a distinct bitter flavour. Serve mixed with each other and a well-flavoured dressing. This dampens down the bitter flavour but gives the salad a pleasant 'bite'.

Preparing

To prepare chicory, take out the core at the base with a sharp knife (*left*) and discard any wilted or damaged leaves. Rinse thoroughly, then dry the leaves.

Above: Chicory (Belgian endive).
Above right: Radicchio.
Below right: Escarole.

Preparing Salad Leaves

Pull the leaves away from the stalk, discarding any wilted or damaged leaves.

Wash the leaves in plenty of cold water, swirling gently to make sure all dirt and any insects are washed away.

Place the washed leaves in a soft dish towel and then gently pat dry.

Place in a dry dish towel in a plastic bag. Chill in the refrigerator for about 1 hour.

RADISHES

Radishes have a peppery flavour that can almost be felt in the nostrils as you bite into one. Their pungency depends not only on the varieties but also on the soil in which they are grown. Freshly harvested radishes have the most pronounced flavour and crisp texture.

Varieties

Radishes were loved throughout antiquity and consequently there are many varieties worldwide. Both the small red types and the large white radishes are internationally popular.

Red Radishes: These small red orbs have many pretty names, such as Cherry Belle and Scarlet Globe, but are mostly sold simply as radish. They are available all year round, have a deep pink skin, sometimes paler or white at the roots and a firm white flesh. Their peppery flavour is milder in the spring and they are almost always eaten raw. Finely sliced and sandwiched in bread and butter, they make an interesting *hors d'oeuvre*.

French Breakfast Radishes: These are red and white and slightly more elongated than the red radish. They tend to be milder than English radishes and are popular in France either eaten on their own or served with other raw vegetables as *crudités*.

Daikon (mooli) Radishes: Sometimes known as the oriental radish, the daikon is a smooth-skinned, long, white radish. Those bought in the stores have a mild flavour, less peppery than the red radish – perhaps because they lose their flavour after long storage (daikons straight from the garden are hot and peppery). They can be eaten raw or pickled, or added to stir-fries.

Buying and Storing

Buy red radishes that are firm with crisp leaves. If at all possible, buy moolis or daikons that still have their leaves; this is a good indication of their freshness as they wilt quickly. The leaves should be green and lively and the skins clear with no bruises or blemishes. They can be stored in the refrigerator for a few days.

Preparing and Serving

Red radishes need only to be washed. They can then be sliced or eaten whole by themselves or in salads. You can make a feature of them by slicing them into a salad of, say, oranges and walnuts, perhaps with a scattering of rocket (arugula) and dressed with a walnut oil vinaigrette.

To use moolis in a stir-fry, cut into slices and add to the dish for the last few minutes of cooking. They add not only flavour but also a wonderfully juicy and crunchy texture.

Left: Red radishes.
Above: French breakfast radishes.
Right: Daikon (mooli) radishes.

WATERCRESS

Watercress is perhaps the most robustly flavoured of all the salad ingredients and a handful of watercress is all you need to perk up a rather dull green salad. It has a distinctive 'raw' flavour, both peppery and slightly pungent and this, together with its bright green leaves, make it a popular garnish.

Watercress, as the name suggests, grows in water. It needs fast flowing clean water to thrive and is really only successful around freshwater springs on chalk hills. The first watercress beds were cultivated in Europe but the vegetable is now grown worldwide.

WINTER CRESS

Winter cress or land cress is often grown as an alternative to watercress, when flowing water is not available. It looks like a robust form of watercress and indeed has a similar if even more assertive flavour, with a distinct peppery taste. Use as you would use watercress, either in salads or in soups.

Nutrition

Watercress is extremely rich in vitamins A, B2, C, D and E. It is also rich in calcium, potassium and iron and provides significant quantities of sulphur and chloride.

Buying and Storing

Only buy fresh-looking watercress – the darker and larger the leaves the better. Avoid any with wilted or yellow leaves. It will keep for several days in the refrigerator or better still, submerged in a bowl, or arranged in a jar of cold water, and kept in a cool place.

Preparing and Cooking

Discard any yellow leaves and remove thick stalks, which will be too coarse for salads or soups. Small sprigs can be added to salads.

For using in soups and purées, either blend watercress raw or cook it briefly in stock, milk or water. Cooking inevitably destroys some of the nutrients but cooked watercress has a less harsh flavour, while still retaining its characteristic peppery taste, meaning that it will appeal to more people.

MUSTARD AND CRESS (FINE CURLED CRESS)

Mustard and cress are often grown together, to provide spicy greenery as a garnish or for salads. They are available all year round.

Mustard seedlings germinate 3–4 days sooner than the cress, so if you buy mustard and cress from the market or supermarket, or grow your own on the windowsill, initially the punnets will only show mustard seedlings.

History

Cress has been grown for thousands of years, known first to the Persians. There is a story that the Persians would always eat cress before they baked bread, and there are other references in antiquity to people eating cress with bread.

Serving

Today mustard and cress are often enjoyed in sandwiches, either served simply on buttered bread, or with avocado or cucumber added. Cress probably wouldn't be substantial enough as a salad in itself, but, with its faint spicy flavour, it can perk up a plain green salad, and it is also excellent in a tomato salad, dressed simply with olive oil and tarragon vinegar.

Above left: Watercress.
Below left: Winter cress.
Above right: Mustard seedlings.
Right: Cress seedlings.

NINE

MUSHROOMS

Button Mushrooms

Field Mushrooms

Woodland Mushrooms

*Wild Mushrooms
and Other Fungi*

BUTTON (WHITE) MUSHROOMS

There is nothing like fried mushrooms on toast for breakfast, served sizzling hot straight from the pan. Once cooked, mushrooms, especially fried ones, go soft and flabby quickly; they still taste alright but the pleasure is not so great.

History

In the past, mushrooms have had a firm association with the supernatural and even today their connection with the mysterious side of life hasn't completely disappeared. Fairy rings – circles of mushrooms – inexplicably appear overnight in woods and fields and thunder is still thought to bring forth fresh crops of mushrooms.

Many types of mushrooms and fungi are either poisonous or hallucinogenic, and in the past their poisons have been distilled for various murderous reasons.

The use of the term mushroom to mean edible species, and toadstool to mean those considered poisonous, has no scientific basis, and there is no simple rule for distinguishing between the two. Picking wild mushrooms is not safe unless you are confident about identifying edible types. In France, during the autumn, people take the wild mushrooms they have gathered to the local pharmacy for identification.

Varieties

Button/White Mushrooms: Cultivated mushrooms are widely available in stores and are sold when very young and tiny as button mushrooms. The slightly larger ones are known as closed cap, while larger ones still are open capped or open cup mushrooms. They have ivory or white caps with pinky/beige gills which darken as they mature. All have a pleasant unassuming flavour.

Chestnut Mushrooms: These have a thicker stem and a darker, pale brown cap. They have a more pronounced 'mushroomy' flavour and a meatier texture than white mushrooms.

Buying and Storing

It is easy to see whether or not button mushrooms are fresh – their caps will be clean and white, without bruises or blemishes. The longer they stay on the shelves, the darker and more discoloured the caps become, while the gills underneath turn from pink to brown.

If possible, use the paper bags provided in many supermarkets when buying mushrooms. Mushrooms in plastic bags sweat in their own heat, eventually turning slippery and unappetizing. If you have no choice or you buy mushrooms in plastic-wrapped cartons, transfer loose to the bottom of the refrigerator as soon as possible. They will keep only for a day or two.

Preparing

Mushrooms should not be washed but wiped with a damp cloth or a piece of kitchen paper (*below*). This is partly because you don't want to increase their water content, and also because they should be fried as dry as possible.

Unless the skins are very discoloured, it should not be necessary to peel them, although you probably will need to trim the very base of the stem.

Cooking

Mushrooms are largely composed of water and shrink noticeably during cooking. They also take up a lot of fat as they cook so it is best to use butter or a good olive oil for frying. Fry mushrooms briskly over a moderately high heat so that as they shrink the water evaporates and they don't stew in their own juice. For the same reason do not fry too many mushrooms at once in the same pan.

Most of the recipes in this book use fried mushrooms as their base and they are completely interchangeable – so if you can't get wild mushrooms or chestnut mushrooms for instance, button mushrooms can be used instead.

Above: Button (white) mushrooms.
Top right: Flat mushrooms.
Far right: Field (portobello) mushrooms.
Right: Chestnut mushrooms (top) and open capped or cup mushrooms.

FIELD (PORTOBELLO) MUSHROOMS

Field mushrooms are the wild relatives of the cultivated mushroom and when cooked have a wonderful aroma. Flat mushrooms, although indistinguishable from field mushrooms in appearance, have probably been cultivated and are also excellent. Connoisseurs say that only wild mushrooms have any flavour but many would argue against this. However, if you know where to find field mushrooms, keep the secret to yourself (most mushroom devotees seem to know this) and count yourself lucky!

Buying and Storing

Field mushrooms are sometimes available during the autumn in farm stores. Since they are likely to have been picked recently, they should be fresh unless obviously wilting. Unless you intend to stuff them, don't worry if they are broken in places as you will be slicing them anyway. Use as soon as possible after purchase.

Preparing

As with cultivated mushrooms, trim the stalk bottoms if necessary and wipe the caps with a damp cloth. Slice according to the recipe.

Cooking

For true field mushrooms, you need do nothing more complicated than simply fry them in butter or olive oil with a suggestion of garlic if liked. However, like flat mushrooms, field mushrooms can be used for stuffing, in soups or indeed any mushroom recipe. They are darker than button mushrooms and will colour soups and sauces brown, but the flavour will be extremely good.

When stuffing mushrooms, gently fry the caps on both sides for a few minutes. The stalks can be chopped and added to the stuffing or can be used for soups or stocks.

WOODLAND MUSHROOMS

Varieties

Ceps: Popular in France, where they are known as *cèpes* and in Italy where they are called *porcini*, these meaty, bun-shaped mushrooms have a fine almost suede-like texture and a good flavour. Instead of gills they have a spongy texture beneath the cap and unless they are very young it is best to scrape this away as it goes soggy when cooked. Ceps are excellent fried in oil or butter over a brisk heat to evaporate the liquid and then added to omelettes.

Alternatively, an Italian way of cooking is to remove the stalk and the spongy tubes, and brush the tops with olive oil. Grill (broil) for about 10 minutes under a moderate grill (broiler) and then turn them over and pour olive oil and a little garlic into the centre. Grill for a further 5 minutes and then serve sprinkled with seasoning and parsley.

Chanterelles: Frilly, trumpet-shaped chanterelles are delicate mushrooms that range in colour from cream to a vivid yellow. Later, winter chanterelles, have greyish-lilac gills on the underside of their dark caps. Chanterelles have a delicate, slightly fruity flavour and a firm, almost rubbery texture. They are difficult to clean as their tiny gills tend to trap grit and earth. Rinse them gently under cold running water and then shake dry. Fry in butter over a gentle heat to start with so they exude their liquid and then increase the heat to boil it off. They are delicious with scrambled eggs, or served by themselves with finely cut toast.

Horn of Plenty/Black Trumpets: Taking its name from its shape, this mushroom ranges in colour from mid-brown to black. As it is hollow, it will need to be brushed well to clean or, if a large specimen, sliced in half. It is versatile, but goes particularly well with fish.

Hedgehog Fungus: This mushroom is difficult to find either on sale or on the woodland floor, but it has great culinary value and is much sought after. Small, young specimens can be cooked whole or sliced, or even used raw in salads. More mature mushrooms may be bitter and are best cooked with butter and herbs. They go well with both meat and fish.

Morels: These are the first mushrooms of the year, appearing not in autumn but in spring. In Scandinavia they are called the 'truffles of the north' and are considered among the great edible fungi. They are cone-shaped with a crinkled spongy cap but are hollow inside. You will need to wash them well under running water as insects tend to creep into their dark crevices. Morels need longer cooking than most mushrooms: sauté them in butter, add a squeeze of lemon and then cover and simmer for up to an hour until tender. The juices can then be thickened with cream or egg yolks.

Dried Mushrooms: Most wild mushrooms are available dried. To reconstitute, soak in warm water for about 20–30 minutes; in the case of morels when they are added to stews, soak for about 10 minutes. Dried wild mushrooms, particularly ceps, have an intense flavour.

Left: Clockwise from the top: Hedgehog fungus, horn of plenty, chanterelles.
Above right: Dried mushrooms.
Above left: Morels.
Right: Winter chanterelles.

WILD MUSHROOMS <u>AND</u> OTHER FUNGI

Mushroom gathering, a seasonal event throughout Eastern Europe, Italy and France, is increasingly popular in Britain. The French are particularly enthusiastic: in autumn whole families drive to secret locations to comb the ground for prizes such as shaggy ink caps or ceps. Wild mushrooms are sold in supermarkets.

OYSTER MUSHROOMS

These ear-shaped fungi grow on rotting wood. Cap, gills and stem are all the same colour, which can be greyish brown, pink or yellow. They are now widely cultivated, although they are generally thought of as wild mushrooms. Delicious both in flavour and texture, they are softer than the button (white) mushroom when cooked but seem more substantial, having more 'bite' to them.

Buying and Storing

Fresh specimens are erect and lively looking with clear gills and smooth caps. They are often sold packed in plastic

boxes under cellophane wrappings and will wilt and go soggy if left on the shelf for too long. Once purchased, remove them from the plastic packaging and use as soon as possible.

Preparing

Oyster mushrooms rarely need trimming at all but if they are large, tear rather than cut them into pieces. In very large specimens the stems can be tough and should be discarded.

Cooking

Fry in butter until tender – they take less time to cook than white mushrooms. Do not overcook oyster mushrooms as the flavour will be lost and the soft texture will become more rubbery.

Left: Pink and yellow oyster mushrooms.
Above: Grey oyster mushrooms.

ENOKITAKI MUSHROOMS

This is another Japanese mushroom. The wild variety is orangy-brown with shiny caps but outside Japan, you will probably only be able to find the cultivated variety, which are similarly fine, with pin-sized heads, but are pale coloured with snowy white caps. They have a fine, sweet and almost fruity flavour. In Japanese cookery they are added to salads or used as a garnish for soups or hot dishes. Since they become tough if overcooked, add enokitaki mushrooms at the very last minute of cooking.

SHIITAKE MUSHROOMS

These Japanese fungi are now commonly available in supermarkets. They are among a variety of tree mushrooms (called *take* in Japan, the *shii* being the hardwood tree from which they are harvested). They have a meaty, slightly acid flavour and a distinct slippery texture. Shiitake mushrooms, though once only available in oriental stores, are now widely available in most large supermarkets. Unlike button mushrooms that can be flash-fried, shiitake need to be cooked through, although even this only takes 3–5 minutes. Add them to stir-fries for a delicious flavour and texture. Alternatively, fry them in oil until tender. Sprinkle with sesame oil and then serve with a little soy sauce.

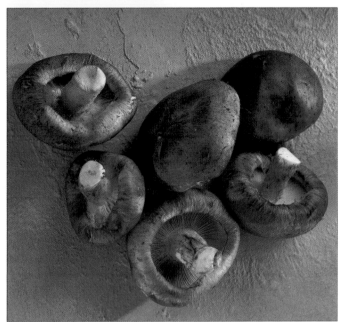

Above: Enokitaki mushrooms.
Right: Shiitake mushrooms.

COOKING
WITH
VEGETABLES

ONION AND LEEK RECIPES

BAKED ONIONS STUFFED WITH FETA

TANGY FETA CHEESE, CRUNCHY PINE NUTS AND FRESH-TASTING CORIANDER ARE COMBINED TO MAKE A DELECTABLE STUFFING IN THIS SIMPLE YET ELEGANT RECIPE.

SERVES FOUR

INGREDIENTS
  4 large red onions
  15ml/1 tbsp olive oil
  25g/1oz pine nuts
  115g/4oz feta cheese, crumbled
  25g/1oz/½ cup fresh white breadcrumbs
  15ml/1 tbsp chopped fresh
    coriander (cilantro)
  salt and freshly ground black pepper

1 Preheat the oven to 180°C/350°F/ Gas 4 and grease a shallow ovenproof dish. Peel the onions and cut a thin slice from the tops and bases. Cook in boiling water 10–12 minutes until just tender. Drain on kitchen paper and leave to cool.

2 Using a small knife or your fingers, remove the inner sections of the onions, leaving about two or three outer rings. Finely chop the inner sections and place the shells in an ovenproof dish.

3 Heat the oil in a medium frying pan and fry the onions for 4–5 minutes until golden, then add the pine nuts and stir-fry for a few minutes.

4 Place the feta cheese in a small bowl and stir in the onions and pine nuts, the breadcrumbs and chopped fresh coriander. Season well with salt and pepper and then spoon the mixture into the onion shells.

5 Cover loosely with foil and bake in the oven for about 30 minutes removing the foil for the last 10 minutes.

6 Serve as an appetizer or as a light lunch with warm olive bread.

ONION TARTS WITH GOAT'S CHEESE

A VARIATION OF A CLASSIC FRENCH DISH, TARTE À L'OIGNON, *THIS DISH USES YOUNG GOAT'S CHEESE INSTEAD OF CREAM. THIS RECIPE MAKES EITHER EIGHT INDIVIDUAL TARTS OR ONE LARGE 23CM/9IN TART.*

SERVES EIGHT

INGREDIENTS
For the pastry
  175g/6oz/1½ cups plain
    (all-purpose) flour
  65g/2½oz/scant 6 tbsp butter
  25g/1oz/¼ cup grated goat's cheddar
    or Cheddar cheese
For the filling
  15–25ml/1–1½ tbsp olive or
    sunflower oil
  3 onions, finely sliced
  175g/6oz young goat's cheese
  2 eggs, beaten
  15ml/1 tbsp single (light) cream
  50g/2oz/½ cup grated goat's cheddar
  15ml/1 tbsp chopped fresh tarragon
  salt and freshly ground black pepper

1 To make the pastry, sift the flour into a bowl and rub in the butter until the mixture resembles fine breadcrumbs. Stir in the grated cheese and add enough cold water to make a dough. Knead lightly, put in a plastic bag and chill. Preheat the oven to 190°C/375°F/Gas 5.

2 Roll out the dough on a lightly floured surface, and then cut into eight rounds using a 11.5cm/4½in pastry cutter, and line eight 10cm/4in patty tins (muffin pans). Prick the bases and bake in the oven for 10–15 minutes until firm but not browned. Reduce the oven temperature to 180°C/350°F/Gas 4.

3 Heat the olive or sunflower oil in a large frying pan and fry the onions over a low heat for 20–25 minutes until they are a deep golden brown. Stir occasionally to prevent them burning.

4 Beat the goat's cheese with the eggs, cream, goat's cheddar and tarragon. Season with salt and pepper and then stir in the fried onions.

5 Pour the mixture into the part-baked pastry cases and bake in the oven for 20–25 minutes until golden. Serve warm or cold with a green salad.

Stuffed: Energy 250kcal/1037kJ; Protein 9g; Carbohydrate 23g, of which sugars 14g; Fat 14g, of which saturates 5g; Cholesterol 20mg; Calcium 172mg; Fibre 4g; Sodium 454mg.
Tarts: Energy 251kcal/1048kJ; Protein 8g; Carbohydrate 23g, of which sugars 5g; Fat 15g, of which saturates 8g; Cholesterol 88mg; Calcium 149mg; Fibre 2g; Sodium 151mg.

CLASSIC FRENCH ONION SOUP

WHEN FRENCH ONION SOUP IS MADE SLOWLY AND CAREFULLY, THE ONIONS ALMOST CARAMELIZE TO A DEEP MAHOGANY COLOUR. IT HAS A SUPERB FLAVOUR AND IS A PERFECT WINTER SUPPER DISH.

SERVES FOUR

INGREDIENTS
4 large onions
30ml/2 tbsp sunflower or olive oil,
   or 15ml/1 tbsp of each
25g/1oz/2 tbsp butter
900ml/1½ pints/3¾ cups beef stock
4 slices French bread
50g/2oz/½ cup grated Gruyère or
   Cheddar cheese
salt and freshly ground black pepper

1 Peel and quarter the onions and slice or chop them into 5mm/¼in pieces. Heat the oil and butter gently together in a deep, heavy pan, preferably with a medium base so that the onions form a thick layer.

3 When the onions are a rich mahogany brown, add the beef stock and a little seasoning. Simmer, partially covered, for 30 minutes, then taste and adjust the seasoning according to taste.

4 Preheat the grill (broiler) and toast the bread. Spoon the soup into four ovenproof serving dishes and place a piece of bread in each. Sprinkle with the cheese and grill (broil) until golden.

2 Fry the onions briskly for a few minutes, stirring constantly, and then reduce the heat and cook gently for 45–60 minutes. At first, the onions need to be stirred only occasionally but as they begin to colour, stir frequently. The colour of the onions gradually turns golden and then more rapidly to brown, so take care to stir constantly at this stage so they do not burn on the base.

Energy 303kcal/1262kJ; Protein 8g; Carbohydrate 30g, of which sugars 14g; Fat 18g, of which saturates 7g; Cholesterol 25mg; Calcium 193mg; Fibre 5g; Sodium 538mg.

THAI NOODLES <u>WITH</u> CHINESE CHIVES

THIS RECIPE REQUIRES A LITTLE PREPARATION, BUT THE COOKING TIME IS VERY FAST. EVERYTHING IS COOKED SPEEDILY IN A HOT WOK AND SHOULD BE EATEN IMMEDIATELY.

SERVES FOUR

INGREDIENTS

350g/12oz dried rice noodles
1cm/½in fresh root ginger, grated
30ml/2 tbsp light soy sauce
45ml/3 tbsp vegetable oil
225g/8oz Quorn, cut into small cubes
2 garlic cloves, crushed
1 large onion, cut into thin wedges
115g/4oz fried tofu, thinly sliced
1 green chilli, seeded
  and finely sliced
175g/6oz beansprouts
115g/4oz Chinese chives, cut into
  5cm/2in lengths
50g/2oz/½ cup ground roasted peanuts
30ml/2 tbsp dark soy sauce
30ml/2 tbsp chopped fresh
  coriander (cilantro)
1 lemon, cut into wedges

1 Place the noodles in a bowl, cover with warm water and soak for 20–30 minutes, then drain. Blend together the ginger, soy sauce and 15ml/1 tbsp of the oil in a bowl. Stir in the Quorn and set aside for 10 minutes. Drain, reserving the marinade.

2 Heat 15ml/1 tbsp of the oil in a frying pan and fry the garlic for a few seconds. Add the Quorn and stir-fry for 3–4 minutes. Then transfer to a plate and set aside.

5 When hot, spoon on to serving plates and garnish with the remaining ground peanuts, coriander and lemon wedges.

VARIATION
Quorn makes this a vegetarian meal, however thinly sliced pork or chicken could be used instead. Stir-fry it initially for 4–5 minutes.

3 Heat the remaining oil in the wok or frying pan and stir-fry the onion for 3–4 minutes until softened and tinged with brown. Add the tofu and chilli, stir-fry briefly and then add the noodles. Stir-fry for 4–5 minutes.

4 Stir in the beansprouts, Chinese chives and most of the ground peanuts, reserving a little for the garnish. Stir well, then add the cooked Quorn, the dark soy sauce and the reserved marinade. Toss to combine thoroughly.

Energy 584kcal/2435kJ; Protein 19.7g; Carbohydrate 82.9g, of which sugars 7.5g; Fat 18.2g, of which saturates 2.6g; Cholesterol 0mg; Calcium 242mg; Fibre 5.8g; Sodium 984mg.

GARLIC MUSHROOMS

GARLIC AND MUSHROOMS MAKE A WONDERFUL COMBINATION. THEY MUST BE SERVED PIPING HOT, SO IF POSSIBLE USE A BALTI PAN OR CAST IRON FRYING PAN AND DON'T STAND ON CEREMONY – SERVE THE MUSHROOMS STRAIGHT FROM THE PAN SO THEY DON'T GET A CHANCE TO COOL DOWN.

SERVES FOUR

INGREDIENTS
    30ml/2 tbsp sunflower oil
    25g/1oz/2 tbsp butter
    5 spring onions (scallions), thinly sliced
    3 garlic cloves, crushed
    450g/1lb button (white) mushrooms
    40g/1½oz/½ cup fresh breadcrumbs
    15ml/1 tbsp chopped fresh parsley
    30ml/2 tbsp lemon juice
    salt and freshly ground black pepper

1 Heat the oil and butter in a balti pan, wok or cast iron frying pan. Add the spring onions and garlic and stir-fry over a medium heat for 1–2 minutes.

2 Add the whole button mushrooms and fry over a high heat for 4–5 minutes, stirring and tossing with a large wide spatula or wooden spoon, all the time.

3 Stir in the breadcrumbs, parsley, lemon juice and seasoning. Stir-fry for a few minutes until the lemon juice has virtually evaporated and then serve.

ROAST GARLIC WITH CROÛTONS

YOUR GUESTS WILL BE ASTONISHED TO BE SERVED A WHOLE ROAST GARLIC FOR AN APPETIZER. ROAST GARLIC HAS A HEAVENLY FLAVOUR AND IS SO IRRESISTIBLE THAT THEY WILL FORGIVE YOU THE NEXT DAY!

SERVES FOUR

INGREDIENTS
    2 garlic bulbs
    45ml/3 tbsp olive oil
    45ml/3 tbsp water
    a sprig of rosemary
    a sprig of thyme
    1 bay leaf
    sea salt and freshly ground
      black pepper
To serve
    slices of French bread
    olive or sunflower oil, for frying
    175g/6oz young goat's cheese or soft
      cream cheese
    10ml/2 tsp chopped fresh herbs, e.g.
      marjoram, parsley and chives

1 Preheat the oven to 190°C/375°F/ Gas 5. Place the garlic bulbs in a small ovenproof dish and pour over the oil and water. Add the rosemary, thyme and bay leaf and sprinkle with salt and pepper. Cover with foil and bake in the oven for 30 minutes.

2 Remove the foil, baste the garlic heads with the juices from the dish and bake for a further 15–20 minutes until they feel soft when pressed.

3 Heat a little oil in a frying pan and fry the French bread on both sides until golden.

4 Blend the cheese with the mixed herbs and place in a serving dish.

5 Cut each garlic bulb in half and open out slightly. Serve the garlic on small plates with the croûtons and soft cheese. Each garlic clove should be squeezed out of its papery shell, spread over a croûton and eaten with the cheese.

Mushrooms: Energy 410kcal/1695kJ; Protein 6g; Carbohydrate 11g, of which sugars 1g; Fat 38g, of which saturates 23g; Cholesterol 151mg; Calcium 64mg; Fibre 4g; Sodium 390mg.
Garlic: Energy 126kcal/519kJ; Protein 2g; Carbohydrate 4g, of which sugars 0g; Fat 11g, of which saturates 2g; Cholesterol 0mg; Calcium 5mg; Fibre 1g; Sodium 1mg.

LEEK SOUFFLÉ

SOME PEOPLE THINK OF A SOUFFLÉ AS A DINNER PARTY DISH, AND A RATHER TRICKY ONE AT THAT.
HOWEVER, OTHERS FREQUENTLY SERVE THEM FOR FAMILY MEALS BECAUSE THEY ARE QUICK AND EASY
TO MAKE, AND PROVE TO BE VERY POPULAR AND SATISFYING.

SERVES TWO TO THREE

INGREDIENTS
    15ml/1 tbsp sunflower oil
    40g/1½oz/3 tbsp butter
    2 leeks, thinly sliced
    about 300ml/½ pint/1¼ cups milk
    25g/1oz/¼ cup plain (all-purpose) flour
    4 eggs, separated
    75g/3oz/¾ cup grated Gruyère or
        Emmenthal cheese
    salt and freshly ground black pepper

1 Preheat the oven to 180°C/350°F Gas 4 and butter a large soufflé dish. Heat the oil and 15g/½oz/1 tbsp of the butter in a small pan or flameproof casserole and fry the leeks over a gentle heat for 4–5 minutes until soft but not brown, stirring occasionally.

2 Stir in the milk and bring to the boil. Cover and simmer for 4–5 minutes until the leeks are tender. Strain the liquid through into a measuring jug (cup).

3 Melt the remaining butter in a pan, stir in the flour and cook for 1 minute. Remove pan from the heat. Make up the reserved liquid with milk to 300ml/ ½ pint/1¼ cups. Gradually stir the milk into the pan to make a smooth sauce. Return to the heat and bring to the boil, stirring. When thickened, remove from the heat. Cool slightly and then beat in the egg yolks, cheese and the leeks.

4 Whisk the egg whites until stiff and, using a large metal spoon, fold into the leek and egg mixture. Pour into the prepared soufflé dish and bake in the oven for about 30 minutes until golden and puffy. Serve immediately.

Energy 477kcal/1979kJ; Protein 22g; Carbohydrate 13g, of which sugars 6g; Fat 37g, of which saturates 18g; Cholesterol 376mg; Calcium 436mg; Fibre 2g; Sodium 407mg.

LEEKS IN EGG AND LEMON SAUCE

THE COMBINATION OF EGGS AND LEMON IN SAUCES AND SOUPS IS COMMONLY FOUND IN RECIPES FROM GREECE, TURKEY AND THE MIDDLE EAST. THIS SAUCE HAS A DELICIOUS FRESH TASTE AND BRINGS OUT THE BEST IN THE LEEKS. BE SURE TO USE TENDER BABY LEEKS FOR THIS RECIPE.

SERVES FOUR

INGREDIENTS

    675g/1½lb baby leeks
    15ml/1 tbsp cornflour (cornstarch)
    10ml/2 tsp sugar
    2 egg yolks
    juice of 1½ lemons
    salt

1 Trim the leeks, slit them from top to bottom and rinse very well under cold water to remove any dirt.

2 Place the leeks in a large pan, preferably so they lie flat on the base, cover with water and add a little salt. Bring to the boil, cover the pan with a lid and simmer for 4–5 minutes until the leeks are just tender.

3 Carefully remove the leeks using a slotted spoon, drain well and arrange in a shallow serving dish. Reserve 200ml/ 7fl oz/scant 1 cup of the cooking liquid.

4 Blend the cornflour with the cooled cooking liquid and place in a small pan. Bring to the boil, stirring all the time, and cook over a gentle heat until the sauce thickens slightly. Stir in the sugar, then remove the pan from the heat and allow to cool slightly.

5 Beat the egg yolks thoroughly with the lemon juice and stir gradually into the cooled sauce. Cook over a very low heat, stirring all the time, until the sauce is fairly thick. Be careful not to overheat the sauce or it may curdle. As soon as it has thickened remove the pan from the heat and continue stirring for a minute. Taste and add salt or sugar as necessary. Cool slightly.

6 Stir the cooled sauce with a wooden spoon to incorporate that skin that may have formed on the surface. Pour the sauce over the leeks, then cover and chill for at least 2 hours before serving.

Energy 92kcal/389kJ; Protein 4g; Carbohydrate 11g, of which sugars 7g; Fat 4g, of which saturates 1g; Cholesterol 17mg; Calcium 27mg; Fibre 4.7g; Sodium 108mg.

TAGLIATELLE WITH LEEKS AND PROSCIUTTO

LEEKS ARE A VERY VERSATILE VEGETABLE. THEIR DELICATE, MILDLY ONIONY FLAVOUR MAKES THEM IDEAL TO USE IN STIR-FRIES, RISOTTOS, EGG DISHES, SOUPS AND SAUCES. IF USING OLDER LEEKS, MAKE SURE THEY HAVE NOT DEVELOPED A WOODY CORE.

SERVES FOUR

INGREDIENTS
5 leeks
40g/1½oz/3 tbsp butter or margarine
225g/8oz tagliatelle, preferably
    green and white
20ml/4 tsp dry sherry
30ml/2 tbsp lemon juice
10ml/2 tsp chopped fresh basil
115–150g/4–5oz prosciutto,
    torn into strips
175g/6oz/¾ cup fromage frais or
    Greek (US strained plain) yogurt
salt and freshly ground black pepper
fresh basil leaves, to garnish
Parmesan cheese, to serve

4 Stir the sherry, lemon juice, basil and seasoning into the leek mixture and cook for 1–2 minutes so that the flavours can blend together. Add the prosciutto and fromage frais or yogurt, stir and cook for about 1–2 minutes until heated through.

5 Drain the pasta and place in a warmed serving dish. Pour the leek and prosciutto mixture on top and mix lightly together. Garnish each serving with basil leaves and serve with shavings of Parmesan cheese.

1 Trim the leeks and then cut a slit from top to bottom, rinse well under cold water and cut into thin slices.

2 Melt the butter or margarine in a pan or flameproof casserole, add the leeks and fry over a gentle heat for 3–4 minutes, until tender but not too soft.

3 Add the tagliatelle to a large pan of boiling water and cook according to the instructions on the packet (about 3–5 minutes for fresh pasta; 8 minutes for dried pasta).

Energy 426kcal/1793kJ; Protein 21g; Carbohydrate 49g, of which sugars 7g; Fat 18g, of which saturates 9g; Cholesterol 25mg; Calcium 106mg; Fibre 7g; Sodium 723mg.

BAKED LEEKS WITH CHEESE AND YOGURT TOPPING

LIKE ALL VEGETABLES, THE FRESHER LEEKS ARE, THE BETTER THEIR FLAVOUR, AND THE FRESHEST SPECIMENS AVAILABLE SHOULD BE USED FOR THIS DISH. SMALL, YOUNG LEEKS ARE AROUND AT THE BEGINNING OF THE SEASON AND ARE PERFECT TO USE HERE.

SERVES FOUR

INGREDIENTS
    8 small leeks, about 675g/1½lb
    2 small (US medium) eggs or 1 large
       (US extra large) egg, beaten
    150g/5oz fresh goat's cheese
    85ml/3fl oz/⅓ cup natural
       (plain) yogurt
    50g/2oz/½ cup grated Parmesan cheese
    25g/1oz/½ cup fresh breadcrumbs
    salt and freshly ground black pepper

1 Preheat the oven to 180°C/350°F/
Gas 4 and butter a shallow ovenproof
dish. Trim the leeks, cut a slit from top to
bottom and rinse well under cold water.

2 Place the leeks in a pan of water,
bring to the boil and simmer gently for
6–8 minutes until just tender. Remove
and drain well using a slotted spoon, and
arrange in the prepared dish.

3 Beat the eggs with the goat's cheese,
yogurt and half the Parmesan cheese,
and season well with salt and pepper.

4 Pour the cheese and yogurt mixture
over the leeks. Mix the breadcrumbs and
remaining Parmesan cheese together
and sprinkle over the sauce. Bake in the
oven for 35–40 minutes until the top is
crisp and golden brown.

Energy 299kcal/1246kJ; Protein 18g; Carbohydrate 9g, of which sugars 5g; Fat 22g, of which saturates 13g; Cholesterol 126mg; Calcium 265mg; Fibre 3g; Sodium 433mg.

CHICKEN WITH SHALLOTS

THIS WARMING DISH IS IDEAL FOR A COLD WINTER'S DAY.

SERVES FOUR

INGREDIENTS
1 small chicken, about 1.3kg/3lb,
   or 4 chicken pieces
seasoned plain (all-purpose) flour
30ml/2 tbsp sunflower oil
25g/1oz/2 tbsp butter
115g/4oz/²⁄₃ cup chopped unsmoked
   streaky (fatty) bacon
2 garlic cloves
450ml/¾ pint/1¾ cups red wine
1 bay leaf
2 thyme sprigs
250g/9oz shallots
115g/4oz button (white) mushrooms,
   halved if large
10ml/2 tsp plain (all-purpose) flour
salt and freshly ground black pepper

1 Preheat the oven to 180°C/350°F/
Gas 4. Trim the chicken and cut into four
or eight pieces. Place a little seasoned
flour in a large plastic bag, add the
chicken pieces and shake to coat evenly.

2 Heat half the oil and half the butter in
a large casserole and fry the bacon and
garlic for 3–4 minutes. Add the chicken
and fry until browned. Add the wine, bay
leaf and thyme and bring to the boil.
Cover and cook in the oven for 1 hour.

3 Peel the shallots and boil them in
salted water for 10 minutes. Heat the
remaining oil in a small frying pan and
fry the shallots for 3–4 minutes until
beginning to brown. Add the mushrooms
and fry for a further 2–3 minutes.

4 Stir the shallots and mushrooms into
the casserole with the chicken and cook
for a further 8–10 minutes. Using a fork,
blend the flour with the remaining butter
to make a thick paste.

5 Transfer the chicken, shallots and
mushrooms to a serving dish and keep
warm. Bring the liquid to the boil and
then add pieces of the flour paste, stirring
after each addition. When the sauce is
thick, either pour over the chicken or return
the chicken to the casserole and serve.

GLAZED SHALLOTS

SERVE THESE ONIONS WITH ROASTED MEAT OR A VEGETABLE DISH.

SERVES FOUR

INGREDIENTS
15ml/1 tbsp olive oil
25g/1oz/2 tbsp butter
350–400g/12–14oz shallots, peeled
15ml/1 tbsp sugar
about 175ml/6fl oz/¾ cup water
salt and freshly ground black pepper

1 Heat the oil and butter in a heavy pan
and gently fry the shallots for 5–6 minutes
until patches of brown begin to appear.
Stir occasionally.

2 Sprinkle the shallots with the sugar
and cook, stirring, for 1 minute. Add
enough water to just cover the shallots
and then cover and simmer over a low
heat for about 25–35 minutes until tender,
adding a little extra water if necessary,
then remove the lid and continue
simmering gently until the liquid has
reduced to a thin syrup. Stir occasionally.
Season with salt, if liked.

3 Spoon the shallots into a serving dish
and pour over the syrup. Sprinkle with
black pepper.

Chicken: Energy 537kcal/2227kJ; Protein 34.3g; Carbohydrate 11g, of which sugars 3.6g; Fat 36.8g, of which saturates
14.4g; Cholesterol 189mg; Calcium 47mg; Fibre 2.4g; Sodium 229mg.

Glazed: Energy 96kcal/399kJ; Protein 1.3g; Carbohydrate 5.4g, of which sugars 5.4g; Fat 7.5g, of which saturates 1.1g;
Cholesterol 0mg; Calcium 22mg; Fibre 1.2g; Sodium 9mg.

SHOOT AND STEM RECIPES

ASPARAGUS TART WITH RICOTTA

THIS ELEGANT SUMMER TART IS IDEAL FOR A LIGHT LUNCH AND THE COMBINATION OF CRUMBLY PASTRY, CREAMY FILLING AND TENDER ASPARAGUS IS TRULY DIVINE.

SERVES FOUR

INGREDIENTS
For the pastry
175g/6oz/1½ cups plain
(all-purpose) flour
75g/3oz/6 tbsp butter or margarine
a pinch of salt
For the filling
225g/8oz asparagus
2 eggs, beaten
225g/8oz1 cup ricotta cheese
30ml/2 tbsp thick natural (plain) yogurt
40g/1½oz/½ cup grated Parmesan cheese
salt and freshly ground black pepper

1 Preheat the oven to 200°C/400°F/ Gas 6. Rub the fat into the flour and salt until the mixture resembles breadcrumbs.

2 Stir in enough cold water to form a smooth dough and knead lightly on a floured surface.

3 Roll out the pastry and line a 23cm/9in flan ring. Press firmly into the ring and prick with a fork. Bake for 10 minutes until the pastry is pale but firm. Remove from the oven and reduce the temperature to 180°C/350°F/Gas 4.

4 To make the filling, trim the asparagus if necessary. Cut 5cm/2in from the tops and chop the remaining stalks into 2.5cm/1in pieces. Add the stalks to a pan of boiling water and after 1 minute add the asparagus tips. Simmer for 4–5 minutes until almost tender, then drain and refresh under cold water.

5 Beat together the eggs, ricotta, yogurt, cheese and seasoning. Stir in the asparagus stalks and pour into the pastry case. Arrange the asparagus tips on top, pressing them down slightly.

6 Bake for 35–40 minutes until golden. Serve warm or cold.

ASPARAGUS WITH TARRAGON HOLLANDAISE

THIS IS THE IDEAL APPETIZER FOR AN EARLY SUMMER DINNER PARTY WHEN THE NEW SEASON'S ASPARAGUS IS AT ITS BEST. MAKING HOLLANDAISE SAUCE USING THIS METHOD IS EASY AND VIRTUALLY FOOLPROOF!

SERVES FOUR

INGREDIENTS
500g/1¼lb fresh asparagus
salt
For the Hollandaise sauce
2 eggs yolks
15ml/1 tbsp lemon juice
115g/4oz/½ cup butter
10ml/2 tsp finely chopped
fresh tarragon
salt and freshly ground
black pepper

1 Prepare the asparagus, lay it in a steamer or in an asparagus kettle and place over a pan of rapidly boiling water. Cover and steam for 6–10 minutes until tender (the cooking time will depend on the thickness of the asparagus stems).

2 To make the Hollandaise sauce, place the egg yolks, lemon juice and seasoning in a blender or food processor and process briefly. Melt the butter in a small pan until foaming and then, with the blender running, pour it on to the egg mixture in a slow, steady stream.

3 Stir in the tarragon by hand or process it (for a sauce speckled with green or a pale green sauce, respectively).

4 Arrange the asparagus on small plates and pour over some of the Hollandaise sauce. Serve remaining sauce separately.

Tart: Energy 432kcal/1805kJ; Protein 15g; Carbohydrate 37g, of which sugars 3g; Fat 26g, of which saturates 16g; Cholesterol 78mg; Calcium 329mg; Fibre 3g; Sodium 259mg.
Asparagus: Energy 276kcal/1138kJ; Protein 5g; Carbohydrate 3g, of which sugars 3g; Fat 27g, of which saturates 16g; Cholesterol 162mg; Calcium 53mg; Fibre 2g; Sodium 180mg.

ASPARAGUS SOUP

HOME-MADE ASPARAGUS SOUP HAS A DELICATE FLAVOUR, QUITE UNLIKE THAT FROM A CAN. THIS SOUP IS BEST MADE WITH YOUNG ASPARAGUS, WHICH IS TENDER AND BLENDS WELL. YOU COULD MAKE IT WITH JUST THE STEMS IF YOU WANT TO EAT THE ASPARAGUS TIPS. SERVE IT WITH WAFER-THIN SLICES OF BREAD.

SERVES FOUR

INGREDIENTS
 450g/1lb young asparagus
 40g/1½oz/3 tbsp butter
 6 shallots, sliced
 15g/½oz/⅛ cup plain (all-purpose) flour
 600ml/1 pint/2½ cups vegetable
  stock or water
 15ml/1 tbsp lemon juice
 250ml/8fl oz/1 cup milk
 120ml/4fl oz/½ cup single
  (light) cream
 10ml/2 tsp chopped fresh chervil
 salt and freshly ground black pepper

1 Trim the stalks of the asparagus if necessary. Cut 4cm/1½in off the tops of half the asparagus and set aside for a garnish. Slice the remaining asparagus.

2 Melt 25g/1oz/2 tbsp of the butter in a large pan and gently fry the sliced shallots for 2–3 minutes until soft but not brown, stirring occasionally.

3 Add the sliced asparagus and fry over a gentle heat for about 1 minute. Stir in the flour and cook for 1 minute, then stir in the stock or water and lemon juice and season to taste. Bring to the boil and then simmer, partially covered, for 15–20 minutes until the asparagus is very tender.

4 Cool slightly and then process the soup in a food processor or blender until smooth. Then press the puréed asparagus through a sieve (strainer) placed over a clean pan. Add the milk by pouring and stirring it through the sieve with the asparagus so as to extract the maximum amount of asparagus purée.

5 Melt the remaining butter and fry the reserved asparagus tips gently for about 3–4 minutes to soften.

6 Heat the soup gently for 3–4 minutes. Stir in the cream and the asparagus tips. Continue to heat gently. Serve sprinkled with the chopped fresh chervil.

Energy 241kcal/996kJ; Protein 8g; Carbohydrate 14g, of which sugars 9g; Fat 18g, of which saturates 11g; Cholesterol 47mg; Calcium 154mg; Fibre 3g; Sodium 393mg.

ROAST ASPARAGUS CRÊPES

ROAST ASPARAGUS IS DELICIOUS AND GOOD ENOUGH TO EAT JUST AS IT COMES. HOWEVER, FOR A REALLY SPLENDID APPETIZER, TRY THIS SIMPLE RECIPE. EITHER MAKE SIX LARGE OR TWICE AS MANY COCKTAIL-SIZE PANCAKES TO USE WITH SMALLER STEMS OF ASPARAGUS.

SERVES SIX

INGREDIENTS
    90–120ml/6–8 tbsp olive oil
    450g/1lb fresh asparagus
    175g/6oz/¾ cup mascarpone
    60ml/4 tbsp single (ilght) cream
    25g/1oz/½ cup grated Parmesan cheese
    sea salt
For the pancakes
    175g/6oz/1½ cups plain
        (all-purpose) flour
    2 eggs
    350ml/12fl oz/1½ cups milk
    vegetable oil, for frying
    a pinch of salt

1 To make the pancake batter, mix the flour with the salt in a large bowl, then add the eggs and milk and beat to make a smooth, fairly thin batter.

2 Heat a little oil in a large frying pan and add a small amount of batter, swirling the pan to coat the base evenly. Cook over a moderate heat for about 1 minute, then flip over and cook the other side until golden.

3 Set aside and cook the rest of the pancakes in the same way; the mixture makes six large or 12 smaller pancakes.

4 Preheat the oven to 180°C/350°F/ Gas 4 and lightly grease a large shallow ovenproof dish or roasting pan with some of the olive oil.

5 Trim the asparagus by placing on a board and cutting off the bases. Using a small sharp knife, peel away the woody ends, if necessary.

6 Arrange the asparagus in a single layer in the prepared dish, trickle over the remaining olive oil, rolling the asparagus to coat each one thoroughly. Sprinkle with a little salt and then roast in the oven for about 8–12 minutes, until just tender (the cooking time depends on the stem thickness).

7 Blend the mascarpone with the cream and Parmesan cheese and spread a generous tablespoonful over each of the pancakes, leaving a little extra for the topping. Preheat the grill (broiler).

8 Divide the asparagus spears among the pancakes, roll up and arrange in a single layer in an ovenproof dish. Spoon over the remaining cheese mixture and then place under a moderate grill for 4–5 minutes, until heated through and golden brown. Serve immediately.

Energy 549kcal/2277kJ; Protein 10g; Carbohydrate 27g, of which sugars 5g; Fat 45g, of which saturates 16g; Cholesterol 123mg; Calcium 202mg; Fibre 2g; Sodium 235mg.

ARTICHOKES WITH GARLIC AND HERB BUTTER

IT IS FUN EATING ARTICHOKES AND EVEN MORE FUN TO SHARE ONE BETWEEN TWO PEOPLE. YOU CAN ALWAYS HAVE A SECOND ONE TO FOLLOW SO THAT YOU GET YOUR FAIR SHARE! BE SURE TO PROVIDE AN EMPTY BOWL FOR PUTTING THE DISCARDED LEAVES INTO, AND A FINGERBOWL AND NAPKINS.

SERVES FOUR

INGREDIENTS
    2 large or 4 medium globe artichokes
    salt
For the garlic and herb butter
    75g/3oz/6 tbsp butter
    1 garlic clove, crushed
    15ml/1 tbsp mixed chopped fresh
        tarragon, marjoram and parsley

1 Wash the artichokes well in cold water. Using a sharp knife, cut off the stalks level with the bases. Cut off the top 1cm/½in of leaves. Snip off the pointed ends of the remaining leaves with scissors, if you like.

2 Put the prepared artichokes in a large pan of lightly salted water. Bring to the boil, cover the pan and cook for about 40–45 minutes or until a lower leaf comes away easily when it is pulled.

3 Drain the artichokes upside down for a couple of minutes while making the sauce. Melt the butter over a low heat, add the garlic and cook for 30 seconds. Remove from the heat, stir in the herbs, then pour into one or two serving bowls.

4 Place the artichokes on serving plates and serve with the garlic and herb butter.

COOK'S TIP
To eat an artichoke, pull off each leaf and dip into the garlic and herb butter. Scrape off the soft fleshy base with your teeth. When the centre is reached, pull out the hairy choke and discard it, as it is inedible. The base can be cut up and eaten with the remaining garlic butter.

Energy 160kcal/663kJ; Protein 3g; Carbohydrate 3g, of which sugars 2g; Fat 16g, of which saturates 10g; Cholesterol 40mg; Calcium 50mg; Fibre 0g; Sodium 144mg.

STUFFED ARTICHOKES

THE AMOUNT OF STUFFING NEEDED FOR THIS DISH DEPENDS ON THE SIZE OF THE ARTICHOKES — IF THEY ARE SMALL YOU COULD SERVE ONE PER PERSON. TO INCREASE THE AMOUNT OF STUFFING, ADD EXTRA MOZZARELLA AND LEEK RATHER THAN BACON.

SERVES FOUR

INGREDIENTS
   2 large or 4 medium globe
     artichokes, trimmed
   lemon juice
For the stuffing
   25g/1oz/2 tbsp butter
   2–3 small leeks, sliced
   2–3 bacon rashers (strips),
     chopped (optional)
   75g/3oz mozzarella cheese, cubed
   25g/1oz/½ cup fresh brown or
     white breadcrumbs
   5ml/1 tsp chopped fresh basil
   fresh basil leaves, to garnish
   salt and freshly ground black pepper

1 Place the artichokes in a large pan of salted water. Bring to the boil, cover and cook for 35–40 minutes or until a lower leaf comes away easily.

4 Drain the artichokes, upside down, and when cool enough to handle, cut in half from top to bottom using a sharp knife. Remove the inner leaves, pull out and discard the choke and then sprinkle the inside and base liberally with lemon juice to prevent discoloration.

5 Preheat the grill (broiler). Spoon a little of the stuffing into each artichoke half and place them in a single layer in an ovenproof dish. Set under a moderately hot grill and cook for 5–6 minutes until the stuffing is golden brown. Serve on small plates garnished with basil leaves.

2 To make the stuffing, melt the butter in a pan and gently fry the leeks for 2–3 minutes. Add the bacon, if using, and continue frying until the leeks are soft and the bacon lightly golden brown.

3 Remove the pan from the heat and stir in the mozzarella cubes, breadcrumbs, basil and seasoning to taste.

Energy 155kcal/644kJ; Protein 10g; Carbohydrate 5g, of which sugars 3g; Fat 12g, of which saturates 7g; Cholesterol 32mg; Calcium 128mg; Fibre 1g; Sodium 331mg.

CELERIAC GRATIN

ALTHOUGH CELERIAC HAS A RATHER UNATTRACTIVE APPEARANCE WITH ITS HARD, KNOBBLY SKIN, IT IS A VEGETABLE THAT HAS A VERY DELICIOUS SWEET AND NUTTY FLAVOUR. THIS IS ACCENTUATED IN THIS DISH BY THE ADDITION OF THE SWEET YET NUTTY EMMENTAL CHEESE.

SERVES FOUR

INGREDIENTS
450g/1lb celeriac
juice of ½ lemon
25g/1oz/2 tbsp butter
1 small onion, finely chopped
30ml/2 tbsp plain (all-purpose) flour
300ml/½ pint/1¼ cups milk
25g/1oz/¼ cup grated Emmental cheese
15ml/1 tbsp capers
salt and cayenne pepper

1 Preheat the oven to 190°C/375°F/ Gas 5. Peel the celeriac and cut into 5mm/¼in slices, immediately plunging them into a pan of cold water acidulated with the lemon juice.

3 Melt the butter in a small pan and fry the onion over a gentle heat until soft but not browned. Stir in the flour, cook for 1 minute and then slowly stir in the milk to make a smooth sauce.

VARIATION
For a less strongly flavoured dish, alternate the layers of celeriac with potato. Slice the potato, cook until almost tender, then drain well before assembling the dish.

2 Bring the water to the boil and simmer the celeriac for 10–12 minutes until just tender. Drain and arrange the celeriac in a shallow ovenproof dish.

4 Stir in the cheese, capers and seasoning to taste, then pour over the celeriac. Cook for 15–20 minutes until the top is golden brown.

Energy 122kcal/506kJ; Protein 4g; Carbohydrate 10g, of which sugars 3g; Fat 8g, of which saturates 4g; Cholesterol 19mg; Calcium 122mg; Fibre 6g; Sodium 69mg.

CELERIAC AND BLUE CHEESE ROULADE

CELERIAC ADDS A DELICATE AND SUBTLE FLAVOUR TO THIS ATTRACTIVE DISH. THE SPINACH ROULADE MAKES AN ATTRACTIVE CONTRAST TO THE CREAMY FILLING BUT YOU COULD USE A PLAIN OR CHEESE ROULADE BASE INSTEAD. BE SURE TO ROLL UP THE ROULADE WHILE IT IS STILL WARM AND PLIABLE.

SERVES SIX

INGREDIENTS
  15g/½oz/1 tbsp butter
  225g/8oz cooked spinach, drained
    and chopped
  150ml/¼ pint/⅔ cup single
    (light) cream
  4 large (US extra large) eggs, separated
  15g/½oz/⅙ cup grated Parmesan cheese
  a pinch of nutmeg
  salt and freshly ground black pepper
For the filling
  225g/8oz celeriac
  lemon juice
  75g/3oz St Agur cheese
  115g/4oz/½ cup fromage frais or
    Greek (US strained plain) yogurt
  freshly ground black pepper

1 Preheat the oven to 200°C/400°F/
Gas 6 and line a 34 x 24cm/13 x 9in Swiss
roll tin (jelly roll pan) with non-stick
baking parchment.

2 Melt the butter in a pan and add the
spinach. Cook gently until all the liquid
has evaporated, stirring frequently.
Remove the pan from the heat and stir
in the cream, egg yolks, Parmesan
cheese, nutmeg and seasoning.

3 Whisk the egg whites until stiff, fold
them gently into the spinach mixture and
then spoon into the prepared tin. Spread
the mixture evenly and use a metal spatula
to smooth the surface.

4 Bake in the oven for 10–15 minutes
until the roulade is firm to the touch and
lightly golden on top.

5 Carefully turn out on to a sheet of
greaseproof (waxed) paper or non-stick
baking parchment and peel away the
lining paper. Roll it up with the paper
inside and leave to cool slightly.

6 To make the filling, peel and grate the
celeriac into a bowl and sprinkle well
with lemon juice. Blend the blue cheese
and fromage frais or yogurt and mix with
the celeriac and a little black pepper.

7 Unroll the roulade, spread with
the filling and roll up again. Serve
immediately or wrap loosely and chill.

Energy 222kcal/918kJ; Protein 12g; Carbohydrate 3g, of which sugars 2g; Fat 18g, of which saturates 10g; Cholesterol 202mg; Calcium 232mg; Fibre 3g; Sodium 342mg.

BRAISED CELERY WITH GOAT'S CHEESE

THE SHARP FLAVOUR OF THE CELERY IN THIS DISH IS PERFECTLY COMPLEMENTED BY THE MILD YET TANGY GOAT'S CHEESE. THIS RECIPE IS AN EXAMPLE OF QUICK AND EASY PREPARATION TO MAKE A DELICIOUS ACCOMPANIMENT TO GRILLED (BROILED) MEAT OR STUFFED PANCAKES.

SERVES FOUR

INGREDIENTS
  25g/1oz/2 tbsp butter
  1 head of celery, thinly sliced
  175g/6oz mild medium-fat
    goat's cheese
  45–60ml/3–4 tbsp single
    (light) cream
  salt and freshly ground black pepper

1 Preheat the oven to 180°C/350°F/ Gas 4 and lightly butter a medium, shallow ovenproof dish.

2 Melt the butter in a heavy pan and fry the thinly sliced celery for 2–3 minutes, stirring frequently. Add 45–60ml/3–4 tbsp water to the pan, heat gently and then cover and simmer over a gentle heat for 5–6 minutes, until the celery is nearly tender and the water has almost evaporated completely.

3 Remove the pan from the heat and stir in the goat's cheese and cream. Taste and season with salt and pepper, and then turn into the prepared dish.

4 Cover the dish with buttered baking parchment and cook in the oven for 10–12 minutes. Serve at once.

CELERY, AVOCADO AND WALNUT SALAD

THE CRUNCHINESS OF THE CELERY AND WALNUTS CONTRASTS PERFECTLY WITH THE SMOOTH AVOCADO. SERVE IT WITH A SOUR CREAM DRESSING AS SUGGESTED, OR SIMPLY DRESSED WITH A LITTLE OLIVE OIL AND FRESHLY SQUEEZED LEMON JUICE FOR A LIGHTER TAKE ON THE SALAD.

SERVES FOUR

INGREDIENTS
  3 bacon rashers (strips) (optional)
  8 tender white or green celery sticks,
    very thinly sliced
  3 spring onions (scallions), chopped
  50g/2oz chopped walnuts
  1 ripe avocado
  lemon juice
For the dressing
  120ml/4fl oz/½ cup sour cream
  15ml/1 tbsp olive oil
  a pinch of cayenne pepper

1 Dry-fry the bacon, if using, until golden and then chop into small pieces and place in a salad bowl with the celery, spring onions and walnuts.

2 Halve the avocado and, using a very sharp knife, cut into thin slices. Peel away the skin from each slice and then sprinkle generously with lemon juice and add to the celery mixture.

3 Lightly beat the sour cream, olive oil and cayenne pepper together in a jug (pitcher) or small bowl. Either fold carefully into the salad and serve immediately or serve separately.

Braised: Energy 218kcal/904kJ; Protein 10g; Carbohydrate 1g, of which sugars 1g; Fat 19g, of which saturates 13g; Cholesterol 62mg; Calcium 88mg; Fibre 1g; Sodium 328mg.
Salad: Energy 300kcal/1239kJ; Protein 7g; Carbohydrate 3g, of which sugars 3g; Fat 29g, of which saturates 8g; Cholesterol 29mg; Calcium 80mg; Fibre 2g; Sodium 334mg.

SPRING ROLLS

BAMBOO SHOOTS AND BEANSPROUTS ARE PERFECT COMPANIONS IN THIS POPULAR SNACK, PROVIDING THE CONTRAST IN TEXTURE THAT IS THE PRINCIPAL ELEMENT IN CHINESE COOKING. THE BAMBOO SHOOTS RETAIN THEIR CRISPNESS, WHILE THE BEANSPROUTS BECOME MORE CHEWY WHEN COOKED.

MAKES ABOUT TWENTY

INGREDIENTS
  60ml/4 tbsp vegetable oil
  30ml/2 tbsp dark soy sauce
  30ml/2 tbsp medium dry sherry
  about 1cm/½in fresh root ginger,
    finely grated
  225g/8oz minced Quorn
  50g/2oz rice vermicelli
  4–5 shiitake mushrooms
  4–5 spring onions (scallions)
  200g/7oz can bamboo shoots
  1 garlic clove, crushed
  1 carrot, grated
  75g/3oz beansprouts,
    roughly chopped
  15ml/1 tbsp cornflour (cornstarch),
    blended with 30ml/2 tbsp water
  about 20 15cm/6in spring
    roll wrappers
  vegetable oil, for deep-frying

1 Blend together 30ml/2 tbsp of the oil, the soy sauce, sherry and ginger in a medium bowl. Add the Quorn, stir well and set aside for 10–15 minutes.

2 Place the rice vermicelli in a large bowl, cover with boiling water and leave to stand for 15–20 minutes, until tender. Drain well and then chop roughly.

3 Wipe the mushrooms with kitchen paper, remove the stalks and slice the caps thinly, halving them if the mushrooms are large.

4 Using a sharp knife, cut the spring onions into diagonal slices, including all but the tips of the green parts.

5 Drain the bamboo shoots and rinse them very well under cold running water. Cut in half if they are large.

6 Heat 15ml/1 tbsp of the remaining oil in a wok or large frying pan and cook the garlic for a few seconds. Add the spring onions and stir-fry for 2–3 minutes. Add the mushrooms and stir-fry for a further 3–4 minutes. Transfer the vegetables to a plate, using a slotted spoon.

7 Heat the remaining oil in the wok. Drain the Quorn, reserving the marinade, and then stir-fry for 4–5 minutes.

8 Add the bamboo shoots to the drained Quorn together with the carrot, vermicelli, the mushroom and onion mixture and the reserved marinade, and stir well. Add the beansprouts, stir well and then remove from the heat and cool.

9 Place a level tablespoon of mixture at one corner of a spring roll sheet. Brush the edges of the pastry with the cornflour mixture and roll up, folding the left and right corners inwards as you roll. Continue making spring rolls in this way, until all the mixture is used up.

10 Heat some oil in a large wok or deep-fryer and fry two or three rolls at a time for 3–4 minutes until golden, turning them so that they cook evenly. Drain on kitchen paper and keep warm while you cook the remaining spring rolls. Serve with extra soy sauce.

Energy 38kcal/161kJ; Protein 1.1g; Carbohydrate 6.6g, of which sugars 0.6g; Fat 1g, of which saturates 0.1g; Cholesterol 0mg; Calcium 15mg; Fibre 0.5g; Sodium 88mg.

SAMPHIRE WITH CHILLED FISH CURRY

EVEN IF YOU'RE A BIG CURRY FAN, DON'T BE TEMPTED TO ADD TOO MUCH CURRY PASTE TO THIS DISH OR YOU MAY SPOIL IT. YOU NEED ONLY THE MEREST HINT OF MILD CURRY PASTE SO THAT THE FLAVOUR OF THE SAMPHIRE AND FISH CAN STILL BE APPRECIATED.

SERVES FOUR

INGREDIENTS
175g/6oz samphire
350g/12oz fresh salmon steak or fillet
350g/12oz lemon sole fillets
fish stock or water
115g/4oz large peeled prawns (shrimp)
25g/1oz/2 tbsp butter
1 small onion, very finely chopped
10ml/2 tsp mild curry paste
5–10ml/1–2 tsp apricot jam
150ml/¼ pint/⅔ cup sour cream
a sprig of mint, to garnish (optional)

1 Trim the samphire and blanch in boiling water for about 5 minutes until tender. Drain and set aside.

2 Place the salmon and lemon sole in a large frying pan, cover with fish stock or water and bring to the boil. Reduce the heat, cover and cook for 6–8 minutes until the fish is tender.

COOK'S TIP
As the samphire has a fresh salty tang of the sea, there is not really any need to add extra salt to this recipe.

3 Transfer the fish to a plate and when cool enough to handle, break the salmon and sole into bitesize pieces, removing any skin and bones. Place in a mixing bowl with the prawns.

4 Melt the butter in a pan and gently fry the onion for 3–4 minutes until soft but not brown. Add the curry paste, cook for 30 seconds, then remove from the heat. Stir in the jam. Allow to cool and then stir in the sour cream.

5 Pour the curry cream over the fish. Arrange the samphire around the edge of a serving plate and spoon the fish into the centre. Garnish with a sprig of mint.

Energy 255kcal/1483kJ; Protein 40g; Carbohydrate 6g, of which sugars 5g; Fat 19g, of which saturates 7g; Cholesterol 175mg; Calcium 120mg; Fibre 1g; Sodium 242mg.

FENNEL <u>AND</u> MUSSEL PROVENÇAL

THE ANISEED FLAVOUR OF FENNEL IS THE PERFECT PARTNER TO SWEET MUSSELS IN THIS DISH.

SERVES FOUR

INGREDIENTS
2 large fennel bulbs
1.75kg/4–4½lb fresh mussels in
  their shells, well scrubbed under
  cold water and beards removed
175ml/6fl oz/¾ cup water
a sprig of thyme
25g/1oz/2 tbsp butter
4 shallots, finely chopped
1 garlic clove, crushed
250ml/8fl oz/1 cup white wine
10ml/2 tsp plain (all-purpose) flour
175ml/6fl oz/¾ cup single
  (light) cream
15ml/1 tbsp chopped fresh parsley
salt and freshly ground black pepper
a sprig of dill, to garnish

1 Trim the fennel, cut into slices
5mm/¼in thick and then cut into
1cm/½in sticks. Cook in a little salted
water until just tender and drain.

2 Discard any mussels that are
damaged or do not close. Put in a large
pan, add the water and thyme, cover
tightly, bring to the boil and cook for
about 5 minutes until the mussels open,
shaking occasionally.

3 Transfer the mussels to a plate and
discard any that are unopened. When
the mussels are cool enough to handle,
remove them from their shells and place
in a large bowl, reserving a few in their
shells for a garnish.

4 Melt the butter in a pan and fry the
shallots and garlic for 3–4 minutes until
softened but not browned. Add the fennel,
fry for 30–60 seconds, then stir in the
wine and simmer until reduced by half.

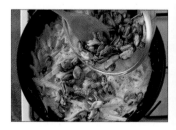

5 Blend the flour with a little extra wine
or water. Add the cream, parsley and
seasoning and heat gently. Stir in the
flour and the mussels. Cook over a low
heat until the sauce thickens. Season and
pour into a serving dish. Garnish with dill
and the reserved mussels in their shells.

BRAISED FENNEL <u>WITH</u> TOMATOES

THIS IS AN IDEAL MAKE-AHEAD DISH AND IS LOVELY SERVED WITH ROAST CHICKEN.

SERVES FOUR

INGREDIENTS
3 small fennel bulbs
30–45ml/2–3 tbsp olive oil
5–6 shallots, sliced
2 garlic cloves, crushed
4 tomatoes, peeled and chopped
about 175ml/6fl oz/¾ cup dry
  white wine
15ml/1 tbsp chopped fresh basil or
  2.5ml/½ tsp dried
50g/2oz/1 cup fresh white
  breadcrumbs
salt and freshly ground black pepper

1 Preheat the oven to 150°C/300°F/
Gas 2. Trim the fennel bulbs and cut into
slices about 1cm/½ in thick.

2 Heat the olive oil in a large pan and
fry the shallots and garlic for about
4–5 minutes over a moderate heat until
the shallots are slightly softened. Add the
tomatoes, stir-fry briefly and then stir in
150ml/¼ pint/⅔ cup of the wine, the basil
and seasoning. Bring to the boil, add the
fennel, then cover and cook for 5 minutes.

3 Arrange the fennel in layers in an
ovenproof dish. Pour over the tomato
mixture and sprinkle the top with half
the breadcrumbs. Bake for about 1 hour,
occasionally pressing down on the crust
with the back of a spoon and sprinkling
over another layer of breadcrumbs and a
little more wine.

Fennel: Energy 175kcal/738kJ; Protein 18g; Carbohydrate 9g, of which sugars 3g; Fat 3g, of which saturates 0g; Cholesterol 60mg; Calcium 89mg; Fibre 2g; Sodium 372mg.
Braised: Energy 206kcal/860kJ; Protein 3g; Carbohydrate 15g, of which sugars 7g; Fat 12g, of which saturates 2g; Cholesterol 0mg; Calcium 61mg; Fibre 2g; Sodium 103mg.

ROOTS RECIPES

PATATAS BRAVAS

THIS IS A CLASSIC SPANISH TAPAS DISH OF DEEP-FRIED CUBES OF POTATO WITH A SPICY TOMATO SAUCE.

SERVES FOUR

INGREDIENTS
675g/1½lb potatoes, such as Maris
  Piper or Estima
oil, for deep-frying
For the sauce
  15ml/1 tbsp olive oil
  1 small onion, chopped
  1 garlic clove, crushed
  400g/14oz can tomatoes
  10ml/2 tsp Worcestershire sauce
  5ml/1 tsp wine vinegar
  about 5ml/1 tsp Tabasco sauce

1 Peel and cut the potatoes into small cubes and place in a large bowl of cold water to remove the excess starch.

2 Heat the oil in a medium frying pan and fry the onion and garlic for 3–4 minutes until the onion is soft and just beginning to brown.

3 Pour the tomatoes into a blender or processor, process until smooth and then pour into the pan with the onion. Simmer, uncovered, over a moderate heat for 8–10 minutes until the mixture is thick and reduced, stirring occasionally.

4 Heat the oil in a deep-fryer. Drain the potatoes and pat dry with kitchen paper. Fry the potatoes in the hot oil, in batches if necessary, until golden brown. Drain on kitchen paper.

5 Stir the Worcestershire sauce, wine vinegar and Tabasco sauce into the tomato mixture. Add the potatoes, stirring well so that all the potatoes are coated with the sauce.

6 Spoon into individual serving dishes and serve immediately.

POTATOES DAUPHINOIS

RICH, WARMING AND DELICIOUS, THIS MAKES A LOVELY ACCOMPANIMENT OR CAN BE SERVED ON ITS OWN.

SERVES FOUR

INGREDIENTS
675g/1½lb potatoes, peeled and
  thinly sliced
½ garlic clove
25g/1oz/2 tbsp butter
300ml/½ pint/1¼ cups single
  (light) cream
50ml/2fl oz/¼ cup milk
salt and white pepper

1 Preheat the oven to 150°C/300°F/Gas 2. Place the potato slices in a bowl of cold water. Drain and pat dry.

2 Rub the garlic around the inside of a wide shallow ovenproof dish. Butter the dish generously.

3 Blend the cream and milk in a jug (pitcher). Cover the base of the dish with a layer of potatoes. Dot a little butter over the potato layer, season with salt and pepper and then pour over a little of the cream and milk mixture.

4 Continue making layers, until all the ingredients have been used up, ending with a layer of cream.

5 Bake in the oven for about 1¼ hours. If the dish browns too quickly and seems to be drying out, cover with a lid or with a piece of foil. The potatoes are ready when they are very soft and the top is golden brown.

COOK'S TIP
For a slightly speedier version of this recipe, par-boil the potato slices for 3–4 minutes. Drain well, leave to steam to remove excess moisture and assemble as above. Cook at 160°C/325°F/Gas 3 for 45–50 minutes until the potatoes are completely tender.

Patatas: Energy 256kcal/1070kJ; Protein 3.3g; Carbohydrate 30g, of which sugars 4.9g; Fat 14.4g, of which saturates 2.2g; Cholesterol 0mg; Calcium 14mg; Fibre 2.4g; Sodium 20mg.
Dauphinois: Energy 319kcal/1329kJ; Protein 6g; Carbohydrate 31g, of which sugars 3g; Fat 20g, of which saturates 12g; Cholesterol 55mg; Calcium 76mg; Fibre 3g; Sodium 71mg.

HASSELBACK POTATOES

A VERY UNUSUAL WAY WITH POTATOES. EACH POTATO HALF IS SLICED ALMOST TO THE BASE AND THEN ROASTED WITH OIL AND BUTTER. THE CRISPY POTATOES ARE THEN COATED IN AN ORANGE GLAZE AND RETURNED TO THE OVEN UNTIL DEEP GOLDEN BROWN AND CRUNCHY.

SERVES FOUR TO SIX

INGREDIENTS
    4 large potatoes
    25g/1oz/2 tbsp butter, melted
    45ml/3 tbsp olive oil
For the glaze
    juice of 1 orange
    grated rind of ½ orange
    15ml/1 tbsp demerara (raw) sugar
    freshly ground black pepper

1 Preheat the oven to 190°C/375°F/ Gas 5. Cut each potato in half lengthways, place flat-side down and then cut down as if making very thin slices, but leaving the bottom 1cm/½in intact.

2 Place the potatoes in a large roasting dish. Using a pastry brush, coat the potatoes generously with the melted butter and pour the olive oil over the base and around the potatoes.

3 Bake the potatoes in the oven for 40–50 minutes until they begin to brown. Baste occasionally during cooking.

4 Meanwhile, place the orange juice, orange rind and sugar in a small pan and heat gently, stirring until the sugar has dissolved. Simmer for 3–4 minutes until the glaze is fairly thick and then remove from the heat.

5 When the potatoes begin to brown, brush them all over with the orange glaze and return to the oven to roast for a further 15 minutes or until the potatoes are a deep golden brown. Serve immediately.

Energy 188kcal/784kJ; Protein 2g; Carbohydrate 21g, of which sugars 4g; Fat 11g, of which saturates 3g; Cholesterol 9mg; Calcium 8mg; Fibre 2g; Sodium 34mg.

PUFFY CREAMED POTATOES

THIS ACCOMPANIMENT CONSISTS OF CREAMED POTATOES INCORPORATED INTO MINI YORKSHIRE PUDDINGS. SERVE THEM WITH ROAST DUCK OR BEEF, OR WITH A VEGETARIAN CASSEROLE. FOR A MEAL ON ITS OWN, SERVE TWO OR THREE PER PERSON AND ACCOMPANY WITH A SALAD.

MAKES SIX

INGREDIENTS
275g/10oz potatoes
creamy milk and butter for mashing
5ml/1 tsp chopped fresh parsley
5ml/1 tsp chopped fresh tarragon
75g/3oz/⅔ cup plain (all-purpose) flour
1 egg
about 120ml/4fl oz/½ cup milk
oil or sunflower fat, for baking
salt and freshly ground black pepper

1 Boil the potatoes until tender and mash with a little milk and butter. Stir in the chopped parsley and tarragon and season well to taste. Preheat the oven to 200°C/400°F/Gas 6.

2 Process the flour, egg, milk and a little salt in a food processor or blender to make a smooth batter.

3 Place about 2.5ml/½ tsp oil or a small knob (pat) of sunflower fat in each of six ramekin dishes and place in the oven on a baking tray for 2–3 minutes until the oil or fat is very hot.

4 Working quickly, pour a small amount of batter (about 20ml/4 tsp) into each ramekin dish. Add a heaped tablespoon of mashed potatoes and then pour an equal amount of the remaining batter in each dish. Place in the oven and bake for 15–20 minutes until the puddings are puffy and golden brown.

5 Using a palette knife or metal spatula, carefully ease the puddings out of the ramekin dishes and arrange on a large warm serving dish. Serve immediately.

Energy 144kcal/602kJ; Protein 4g; Carbohydrate 19g, of which sugars 2g; Fat 6g, of which saturates 2g; Cholesterol 47mg; Calcium 56mg; Fibre 1g; Sodium 44mg.

PARSNIP AND CHESTNUT CROQUETTES

THE SWEET NUTTY TASTE OF CHESTNUTS BLENDS PERFECTLY WITH THE SIMILARLY SWEET BUT EARTHY FLAVOUR OF PARSNIPS. FRESH CHESTNUTS NEED TO BE PEELED BUT FROZEN CHESTNUTS ARE EASY TO USE AND ARE NEARLY AS GOOD AS FRESH FOR THIS RECIPE.

MAKES TEN TO TWELVE

INGREDIENTS
450g/1lb parsnips, cut roughly into
   small pieces
115g/4oz frozen chestnuts
25g/1oz/2 tbsp butter
1 garlic clove, crushed
15ml/1 tbsp chopped fresh
   coriander (cilantro)
1 egg, beaten
50g/2oz/1 cup fresh white or
   brown breadcrumbs
vegetable oil, for frying
salt and freshly ground
   black pepper
a sprig of coriander (cilantro),
   to garnish

1 Place the parsnips in a pan with enough water to cover. Bring to the boil, cover and simmer for 15–20 minutes until completely tender.

2 Place the frozen chestnuts in a pan of water, bring to the boil and simmer for 8–10 minutes until very tender. Drain, place in a bowl and mash roughly.

3 Melt the butter in a small pan and cook the garlic for 30 seconds. Drain the parsnips and mash with the garlic butter. Stir in the chestnuts and chopped coriander, then season well with salt and ground black pepper.

4 Take about 15ml/1tbsp of the mixture at a time and form into small croquettes, about 7.5cm/3in long. Dip each croquette into the beaten egg and then roll in the breadcrumbs.

5 Heat a little oil in a frying pan and fry the croquettes for 3–4 minutes until golden, turning frequently so they brown evenly. Drain on kitchen paper and then serve, garnished with coriander.

Energy 107kcal/445kJ; Protein 1.8g; Carbohydrate 10.8g, of which sugars 2.9g; Fat 6.6g, of which saturates 1.8g; Cholesterol 21mg; Calcium 27mg; Fibre 2.2g; Sodium 52mg.

PARSNIP, AUBERGINE AND CASHEW BIRYANI

THIS COLOURFUL INDIAN DISH IS A MEAL IN ITSELF AS IT CONTAINS CARBOHYDRATES, VEGETABLES AND PROTEIN IN THE FORM OF CASHEW NUTS AND HARD-BOILED EGGS. IT IS QUITE SWEET, AS IT CONTAINS PARSNIPS AND DRIED FRUIT, BUT THIS IS OFFSET BY THE FRESH HERBS.

SERVES FOUR TO SIX

INGREDIENTS

1 small aubergine (eggplant), sliced
275g/10oz basmati rice
3 parsnips, peeled
3 onions
2 garlic cloves
2.5cm/1in piece fresh root
   ginger, peeled
about 60ml/4 tbsp vegetable oil
175g/6oz/1½ cups unsalted cashew nuts
40g/1½oz/⅓ cup sultanas
   (golden raisins)
1 red (bell) pepper, seeded and sliced
5ml/1 tsp ground cumin
5ml/1 tsp ground coriander
2.5ml/½ tsp chilli powder
120ml/4fl oz/½ cup natural
   (plain) yogurt
300ml/½ pint/1¼ cups stock
25g/1oz/2 tbsp butter
salt and freshly ground black pepper
sprigs of coriander (cilantro),
   to garnish
2 hard-boiled eggs, quartered

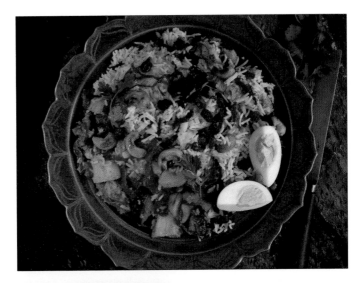

1 Sprinkle the aubergine with salt and leave for 30 minutes. Rinse, pat dry and cut into bitesize pieces. Soak the rice in a bowl of cold water for 40 minutes. Cut into 1cm/½in pieces. Roughly chop 1 onion and put in a food processor with the garlic and ginger. Add 30–45ml/ 2–3 tbsp water and process to a paste.

2 Finely slice the remaining onions. Heat 45ml/3 tbsp of the oil in a large flameproof casserole.

3 Fry the onions gently for 10–15 minutes until deep golden brown. Remove and drain. Add 40g/1½oz of the cashew nuts to the pan and stir-fry for 2 minutes. Add the sultanas and fry until they swell. Remove and drain. Add the aubergine and pepper to the pan and stir-fry for 4–5 minutes.

4 Drain on kitchen paper. Fry the parsnips for 4–5 minutes. Stir in the remaining cashew nuts and fry for 1 minute. Transfer to the plate with the aubergines.

5 Add the remaining oil to the pan. Add the onion paste. Cook, stirring over a moderate heat for 4–5 minutes until golden. Stir in the cumin, coriander and chilli powder. Cook, stirring, for 1 minute, then reduce the heat and add the yogurt.

6 Bring the mixture to the boil and stir in the stock, parsnips, aubergines and peppers. Season, cover and simmer for 30–40 minutes until the parsnips are tender. Rransfer to an ovenproof casserole.

7 Preheat the oven to 150°C/300°F/ Gas 2. Drain the rice and add to 300ml/ ½ pint/1¼ cups of salted boiling water. Cook gently for 5–6 minutes.

8 Drain the rice and pile it in a mound on top of the parsnips. Make a hole from the top to the base. Scatter the fried onions, cashew nuts and sultanas over the rice and dot with butter. Cover with a double layer of foil and secure in place with a lid. Cook for 35–40 minutes.

9 Spoon on to a serving dish and garnish with coriander sprigs and eggs.

Energy 562kcal/2360kJ; Protein 16g; Carbohydrate 81g, of which sugars 10g; Fat 22g, of which saturates 6g; Cholesterol 88mg; Calcium 92mg; Fibre 4g; Sodium 181mg.

MEDITERRANEAN CHICKEN WITH TURNIPS

TURNIPS ARE POPULAR IN ALL PARTS OF THE MEDITERREAN, COOKED WITH TOMATOES AND SPINACH IN SIMPLE VEGETARIAN DISHES, OR TEAMED WITH FISH OR POULTRY FOR A MORE SUBSTANTIAL MEAL. THIS RECIPE COMES FROM THE EASTERN MEDITERRANEAN.

SERVES FOUR

INGREDIENTS

30ml/2 tbsp sunflower oil
8 chicken thighs or 4 chicken pieces
4 small turnips
2 onions, chopped
2 garlic cloves, crushed
6 tomatoes, peeled and chopped
250ml/8fl oz/1 cup tomato juice
250ml/8fl oz/1 cup chicken stock
120ml/4fl oz/½ cup white wine
5ml/1 tsp paprika
a good pinch of cayenne pepper
20 black olives, pitted
½ lemon, cut into wedges
salt and freshly ground black pepper
fresh parsley, to garnish
couscous, to serve

1 Preheat the oven to 160°C/325°F/ Gas 3. Heat 15ml/1 tbsp of the oil in a large frying pan and fry the chicken pieces until lightly browned. Peel the turnips and cut into julienne strips.

2 Transfer the chicken to a large casserole. Add the remaining oil to the pan and fry the onions and garlic for 4–5 minutes until lightly golden brown, stirring occasionally.

3 Add the turnip and stir-fry for about 2–3 minutes. Add the tomatoes, tomato juice, stock, wine, paprika, cayenne and seasoning. Bring to the boil. Pour over the chicken. Stir in the olives and lemon.

4 Cover tightly and cook in the oven for 1–1¼ hours until the chicken is tender.

5 Garnish with fresh parsley and serve on a bed of couscous.

SWEDE CRISPS

TENDER SLICES OF SWEDE WITH A CRUNCHY BREADCRUMB COATING PROVIDE A FEAST FOR THE SENSES. THE SLIGHTLY PEPPERY FLAVOUR OF SWEDE IS COMPLEMENTED BY THE SPICY BREADCRUMB MIXTURE.

SERVES FOUR

INGREDIENTS

1 small swede (rutabaga)
50g/2oz/1 cup fresh brown or
    white breadcrumbs
15ml/1 tbsp plain (all-purpose) flour
2.5ml/½ tsp paprika
2.5ml/½ tsp ground coriander
2.5ml/½ tsp ground cumin
a pinch of cayenne pepper
1 egg, beaten
salt and freshly ground black pepper
oil, for deep frying
mango chutney, to serve

1 Peel the swede, cut in half and slice thinly. Cook in a pan of boiling water for 3–5 minutes until just tender. Drain well.

2 Mix together the breadcrumbs, flour, paprika, coriander, cumin, cayenne pepper and seasoning. Dip the swede slices first in the egg and then in the breadcrumb mixture.

3 Heat the oil in a deep-fryer or wok and fry the swede discs, in batches if necessary, for 4–5 minutes until golden on the outside and soft inside. Drain on kitchen paper and serve with mango chutney.

COOK'S TIP
Fry the discs until the swede (rutabaga) is tender, so that the crunchiness of the breadcrumb coating contrasts with the soft vegetable.

Chicken: Energy 415kcal/1739kJ; Protein 41g; Carbohydrate 12g, of which sugars 10g; Fat 23g, of which saturates 5g; Cholesterol 186mg; Calcium 69mg; Fibre 4g; Sodium 658mg.
Swede: Energy 169kcal/706kJ; Protein 4g; Carbohydrate 12g, of which sugars 3g; Fat 12g, of which saturates 2g; Cholesterol 58mg; Calcium61mg; Fibre 2g; Sodium 96mg.

GLAZED CARROTS WITH CIDER

THIS RECIPE IS EXTREMELY SIMPLE TO MAKE. THE CARROTS ARE COOKED IN THE MINIMUM OF LIQUID TO BRING OUT THE BEST OF THEIR FLAVOUR, AND THE CIDER ADDS A PLEASANT SHARPNESS.

SERVES FOUR

INGREDIENTS
    450g/1lb young carrots
    25g/1oz/2 tbsp butter
    15ml/1 tbsp soft light brown sugar
    120ml/4fl oz/½ cup cider
    60ml/4 tbsp vegetable stock or water
    5ml/1 tsp Dijon mustard
    15ml/1 tbsp chopped fresh parsley

1 Trim the tops and bottoms of the carrots. Peel or scrape them. Using a sharp knife, cut them into julienne strips.

2 Melt the butter in a frying pan, add the carrots and sauté for 4–5 minutes, stirring frequently. Sprinkle over the sugar and cook, stirring for 1 minute or until the sugar has dissolved.

3 Add the cider and stock or water, bring to the boil and stir in the Dijon mustard. Partially cover the pan and simmer for about 10–12 minutes until the carrots are just tender.

4 Remove the lid and continue cooking until the liquid has reduced to a sauce.

5 Remove the pan from the heat, stir in the parsley and then spoon into a warmed serving dish. Serve as an accompaniment to grilled (broiled) meat or fish or with a vegetarian dish.

COOK'S TIP
If the carrots are cooked before the liquid in the pan has reduced, transfer the carrots to a serving dish and rapidly boil the liquid until thick. Pour over the carrots and sprinkle with parsley.

CARROT, APPLE AND ORANGE COLESLAW

THIS DISH IS AS DELICIOUS AS IT IS EASY TO MAKE. THE GARLIC AND HERB DRESSING ADDS THE NECESSARY CONTRAST TO THE SWEETNESS OF THE SALAD.

SERVES FOUR

INGREDIENTS
    350g/12oz/3 cups finely grated
        young carrots
    2 eating apples
    15ml/1 tbsp lemon juice
    1 large orange
For the dressing
    45ml/3 tbsp olive oil
    60ml/4 tbsp sunflower oil
    45ml/3 tbsp lemon juice
    1 garlic clove, crushed
    60ml/4 tbsp natural (plain) yogurt
    15ml/1 tbsp chopped mixed fresh
        herbs: tarragon, parsley, chives
    salt and freshly ground black pepper

1 Place the carrots in a large serving bowl. Quarter the apples, remove the core and then slice thinly. Sprinkle with lemon juice to prevent them discolouring and then add to the carrots.

2 Using a sharp knife, remove the peel and pith from the orange and then separate into segments.

3 To make the dressing, place all the ingredients in a jar with a tight-fitting lid and shake vigorously to blend.

4 Just before serving, pour the dressing over the salad and toss well together.

Glazed: Energy 122kcal/507kJ; Protein 1g; Carbohydrate 11.1g, of which sugars 10.4g; Fat 8.6g, of which saturates 2.8g; Cholesterol 1mg; Calcium 32mg; Fibre 2.7g; Sodium 85mg.
Coleslaw: Energy 339kcal/1404kJ; Protein 4g; Carbohydrate 19g, of which sugars 19g; Fat 28g, of which saturates 4g; Cholesterol 4mg; Calcium 139mg; Fibre 4g; Sodium 72mg.

CARROT AND CORIANDER SOUP

NEARLY ALL ROOT VEGETABLES MAKE EXCELLENT SOUPS AS THEY PURÉE WELL AND HAVE AN EARTHY FLAVOUR THAT COMPLEMENTS THE SHARPER FLAVOURS OF HERBS AND SPICES. CARROTS ARE PARTICULARLY VERSATILE AND THIS SIMPLE SOUP IS ELEGANT IN BOTH FLAVOUR AND APPEARANCE.

SERVES FOUR TO SIX

INGREDIENTS

450g/1lb carrots, preferably young
  and tender
15ml/1 tbsp sunflower oil
40g/1½oz/3 tbsp butter
1 onion, chopped
1 celery stick, sliced plus 2–3 pale
  leafy celery tops
2 small potatoes, chopped
1 litre/1¾ pints/4 cups chicken stock
10–15ml/2–3 tsp ground coriander
15ml/1 tbsp chopped fresh
  coriander (cilantro)
200ml/7fl oz/⅞ cup milk
salt and freshly ground black pepper

1 Trim the carrots, peel if necessary and cut into chunks. Heat the oil and 25g/1oz/2 tbsp of the butter in a large flameproof casserole or heavy pan and fry the onion over for 3–4 minutes until slightly softened but not browned.

2 Cut the celery stick into slices. Add the celery and potatoes to the onion in the pan, cook for a few minutes and then add the carrots. Fry over a gentle heat for 3–4 minutes, stirring frequently, and then cover. Reduce the heat even further and sweat for about 10 minutes. Shake the pan or stir occasionally so the vegetables do not stick to the base.

3 Add the stock, bring to the boil and then partially cover and simmer for a further 8–10 minutes until the carrots and potatoes are tender.

4 Remove 6–8 tiny celery leaves for garnish and finely chop the remaining celery tops (about 15ml/1 tbsp once chopped). Melt the remaining butter in a small pan and fry the ground coriander for about 1 minute, stirring constantly.

5 Reduce the heat and add the chopped celery and fresh coriander and fry for about 1 minute. Set aside.

6 Process the soup in a food processor or blender and pour into a clean pan. Stir in the milk, coriander mixture and seasoning. Heat gently, taste and adjust the seasoning. Serve garnished with the reserved celery.

COOK'S TIP
For a more piquant flavour, add a little lemon juice just before serving.

Energy 161kcal/667kJ; Protein 3g; Carbohydrate 15g, of which sugars 9g; Fat 10g, of which saturates 5g; Cholesterol 19mg; Calcium 70mg; Fibre 3g; Sodium 472mg.

BORSCHT

THIS CLASSIC SOUP WAS THE STAPLE DIET OF PRE-REVOLUTION RUSSIAN PEASANTS FOR HUNDREDS OF YEARS. THERE ARE MANY VARIATIONS AND IT IS RARE TO FIND TWO RECIPES THE SAME. THIS ONE IS SIMPLE TO MAKE AND TASTES AS DELICIOUS AS IT LOOKS.

SERVES SIX

INGREDIENTS

- 350g/12oz whole, uncooked beetroot (beets)
- 15ml/1 tbsp sunflower oil
- 115g/4oz/⅔ cup chopped streaky (fatty) bacon
- 1 large onion
- 1 large carrot, cut into julienne strips
- 3 celery sticks, thinly sliced
- 1.5 litres/2½ pints/6¼ cups chicken stock
- about 225g/8oz tomatoes, peeled, seeded and sliced
- about 30ml/2 tbsp lemon juice or wine vinegar
- 30ml/2 tbsp chopped dill
- 115g/4oz white cabbage, thinly sliced
- 150ml/¼ pint/⅔ cup sour cream
- salt and freshly ground black pepper

1 Peel the beetroot, slice and then cut into very thin strips.

2 Heat the oil in a large, heavy pan and fry the bacon over a gentle heat for 3–4 minutes. Add the onion, fry for 2–3 minutes and then add the carrot, celery and beetroot.

3 Cook for 4–5 minutes, stirring frequently, until the oil has been completely absorbed.

4 Add the stock, tomatoes, lemon juice or wine vinegar, half of the dill and seasoning. Bring to the boil and simmer for about 30–40 minutes until the vegetables are completely tender.

5 Add the cabbage and simmer for 5 minutes until tender. Adjust the seasoning and serve sprinkled with remaining dill and the sour cream.

Energy 84kcal/348kJ; Protein 0.5g; Carbohydrate 0.5g, of which sugars 0.1g; Fat 9g, of which saturates 3.4g; Cholesterol 8mg; Calcium 2mg; Fibre 0g; Sodium 672mg.

ARTICHOKE RÖSTI

THIS FLAVOURSOME 'CAKE' MAKES AN UNUSUAL ACCOMPANIMENT TO SAUSAGES OR LAMB CHOPS.

SERVES FOUR TO SIX

INGREDIENTS
450g/1lb Jerusalem artichokes, peeled
juice of 1 lemon
450g/1lb potatoes, peeled
about 50g/2oz/4 tbsp butter
salt

1 Place the Jerusalem artichokes in a pan of water with the lemon juice and a pinch of salt. Bring to the boil and cook for about 5 minutes until barely tender.

2 Place the potatoes in a separate pan of salted water. Bring to the boil and cook until barely tender – they will take slightly longer than the artichokes.

3 Drain and cool both the artichokes and potatoes, and then coarsely grate them into a large mixing bowl. Mix them to combine with your fingers, without breaking them up too much. Pat dry with kitchen paper to remove excess liquid.

4 Melt the butter in a large, heavy frying pan. Add the artichoke mixture, spreading it out. Cook gently for about 10 minutes. Invert the 'cake' on to a plate and slide back into the pan. Cook for 10 minutes until golden. Serve immediately.

ARTICHOKE TIMBALES WITH SPINACH SAUCE

THESE TIMBALES CAN BE SERVED AS A VERY HEALTHY APPETIZER OR LIGHT LUNCH.

SERVES SIX

INGREDIENTS
900g/2lb Jerusalem artichokes, peeled
juice of 1 lemon
25g/1oz/2 tbsp butter
15ml/1 tbsp oil
1 onion, finely chopped
1 garlic clove, crushed
50g/2oz/1 cup fresh white breadcrumbs
1 egg
60–75ml/4–5 tbsp vegetable stock
  or milk
15ml/1 tbsp chopped fresh parsley
5ml/1 tsp finely chopped sage
salt and freshly ground black pepper
For the sauce
225g/8oz fresh spinach, prepared
15g/½oz/1 tbsp butter
2 shallots, finely chopped
150ml/¼ pint/⅔ cup single (light) cream
175ml/6fl oz/¾ cup vegetable stock
salt and freshly ground black pepper

1 Preheat the oven to 180°C/350°F/ Gas 4. Grease six 150ml/¼ pint/⅔ cup ramekin dishes, and then place a circle of non-stick baking parchment in each base.

2 Place the artichokes in a pan with the lemon juice and water to cover. Simmer for about 10 minutes until tender. Drain and mash with the butter.

3 Heat the oil in a frying pan and fry the onion and garlic until soft. Purée in a food processor with the breadcrumbs, egg, stock or milk, parsley, sage and seasoning. Add the artichokes and process briefly. Do not over-process.

4 Put the mixture in the prepared dishes and smooth the tops. Cover with non-stick baking parchment, place in a roasting pan half-filled with boiling water and bake for 35–40 minutes until firm.

5 To make the sauce, cook the spinach without water, in a large covered pan, for 2–3 minutes. Shake the pan occasionally. Strain and press out the excess liquid.

6 Melt the butter in a small pan and fry the shallots gently until slightly softened but not browned. Place in a food processor or blender with the spinach and blitz to make a smooth purée.

7 Pour back into the pan, add the cream and seasoning, and keep warm over a very low heat. Do not allow the mixture to boil.

8 Allow the timbales to stand for a few minutes after cooking and then turn out on to warmed serving plates. Spoon the warm sauce over them and serve.

COOK'S TIP
When puréeing the artichokes in a food processor or blender, use the pulse button and process for a very short time. The mixture will become cloying if it is over-processed.

Rösti: Energy 119kcal/500kJ; Protein 1.7g; Carbohydrate 12.8g, of which sugars 1.7g; Fat 7.2g, of which saturates 4.6g; Cholesterol 19mg; Calcium 37mg; Fibre 1.6g; Sodium 116mg.
Timbales: Energy 122kcal/977kJ; Protein 5g; Carbohydrate 24g, of which sugars 5g; Fat 14g, of which saturates 7g; Cholesterol 28mg; Calcium 152mg; Fibre 2g; Sodium 205mg.

YAM FRITTERS

YAMS HAVE A SLIGHTLY DRIER FLAVOUR THAN POTATOES AND ARE PARTICULARLY GOOD WHEN MIXED WITH SPICES AND THEN FRIED. THE FRITTERS CAN ALSO BE MOULDED INTO SMALL BALLS AND DEEP-FRIED. THIS IS A FAVOURITE AFRICAN WAY OF SERVING YAMS.

MAKES ABOUT TWENTY

INGREDIENTS
675g/1½lb yams
milk, for mashing
2 small (US medium) eggs, beaten
45ml/3 tbsp chopped tomato flesh
45ml/3 tbsp finely chopped spring
   onions (scallions)
1 green chilli, seeded and
   finely sliced
flour, for shaping
40g/1½oz/¾ cup white breadcrumbs
vegetable oil, for shallow-frying
salt and freshly ground black pepper

1 Peel the yams and cut into chunks. Place in a pan of salted water and boil for 20–30 minutes until tender. Drain and mash with a little milk and about 45ml/3 tbsp of the beaten eggs.

2 Add the chopped tomato, spring onions, chilli and seasoning and stir well to mix thoroughly.

3 Using floured hands, shape the yam and vegetable mixture into round fritters, about 7.5cm/3in in diameter.

4 Dip each in the remaining beaten egg and then coat with the breadcrumbs. Heat a little oil in a large frying pan and fry the yam fritters for about 4–5 minutes until golden brown. Turn the fritters over once during cooking. Drain well on kitchen paper and serve.

EDDO, CARROT AND PARSNIP MEDLEY

EDDO (TARO), LIKE YAMS, IS WIDELY EATEN IN AFRICA AND THE CARIBBEAN, OFTEN AS A PURÉE. HERE, IT IS ROASTED AND COMBINED WITH MORE COMMON ROOT VEGETABLES TO MAKE A COLOURFUL DISPLAY.

SERVES FOUR TO SIX

INGREDIENTS
450g/1lb eddoes (taros)
350g/12oz parsnips
450g/1lb carrots
25g/1oz/2 tbsp butter
45ml/3 tbsp sunflower oil
For the dressing
30ml/2 tbsp fresh orange juice
30ml/2 tbsp demerara (raw) sugar
10ml/2 tsp soft green peppercorns
salt
fresh parsley, to garnish

1 Preheat the oven to 200°C/400°F/ Gas 6. Thickly peel the eddoes, making sure to remove all the skin as this can be an irritant. Cut the peeled flesh into pieces about 5 x 2cm/2 x ¾in by 2cm/¾in, and place them in a large mixing bowl.

2 Peel the parsnips, halve lengthways and remove the inner core if necessary. Cut into the same size pieces as the eddo and add to the bowl. Blanch in boiling water for 2 minutes and then drain. Peel or scrub the carrots, and halve or quarter them according to their size.

3 Place the butter and sunflower oil in a roasting pan and heat in the oven for 3–4 minutes. Add the vegetables, turning them in the oil to coat evenly. Roast in the oven for 30 minutes.

4 Meanwhile, blend the orange juice, sugar and soft green peppercorns in a small bowl. Remove the roasting pan from the oven and allow to cool for a minute or so and then carefully pour the mixture over the vegetables, stirring to coat them all. (If the liquid is poured on immediately, the hot oil will spit.)

5 Return the roasting pan to the oven and cook for a further 20 minutes until the vegetables are crisp and golden.

6 Transfer to a warmed serving plate and sprinkle with salt. Garnish with parsley to serve.

Yam: Energy 100kcal/419kJ; Protein 2g; Carbohydrate 12g, of which sugars 1g; Fat 5g, of which saturates 1g; Cholesterol 23mg; Calcium 17mg; Fibre 1g; Sodium 21mg.
Medley: Energy 263kcal/1102kJ; Protein 3g; Carbohydrate 39g, of which sugars 39g; Fat 15g, of which saturates 12g; Cholesterol 3mg; Calcium 9mg; Fibre 7g; Sodium 54mg.

CASSAVA AND VEGETABLE KEBABS

THIS IS AN ATTRACTIVE AND DELICIOUS ASSORTMENT OF AFRICAN VEGETABLES, MARINATED IN A SPICY GARLIC SAUCE. IF CASSAVA IS UNAVAILABLE, USE SWEET POTATO OR YAM INSTEAD.

SERVES FOUR

INGREDIENTS
175g/6oz cassava, peeled
1 onion, cut into wedges
1 aubergine (eggplant), cut into
  bitesize pieces
1 courgette (zucchini), sliced
1 ripe plantain, sliced
1 red (bell) pepper or ½ red pepper,
  ½ green pepper, sliced
16 cherry tomatoes
For the marinade
60ml/4 tbsp lemon juice
60ml/4 tbsp olive oil
45–60/3–4 tbsp soy sauce
15ml/1 tbsp tomato purée (paste)
1 fresh green chilli, seeded and
  finely chopped
½ onion, grated
2 garlic cloves, crushed
5ml/1 tsp mixed (apple pie) spice
a pinch of dried thyme
rice or couscous, to serve

1 Cut the cassava into bitesize pieces. Place in a bowl, cover with boiling water and leave for 5 minutes. Drain well.

2 Place all the vegetables, including the cassava, in a large bowl.

3 Blend together all the marinade ingredients and pour over the prepared vegetables. Set aside for 1–2 hours.

4 Preheat the grill (broiler) and thread all the vegetables and cherry tomatoes on to eight skewers.

5 Grill (broil) the vegetables under a low heat for about 15 minutes until tender and browned, turning frequently and basting occasionally with the marinade.

6 Meanwhile, pour the remaining marinade into a small pan and simmer for 10 minutes until slightly reduced.

7 Arrange the vegetable kebabs on a serving plate and strain the sauce into a small jug (pitcher). Serve with rice or couscous.

Energy 317kcal/1328kJ; Protein 5g; Carbohydrate 40g, of which sugars 14g; Fat 16g, of which saturates 2g; Cholesterol 0mg; Calcium 65mg; Fibre 6g; Sodium 670mg.

POUSSINS WITH SWEET POTATO CHIPS

GAME CHIPS, OFTEN MADE WITH PARSNIPS, SWEET POTATOES OR OTHER SWEET ROOT VEGETABLES, MAKE A LOVELY ACCOMPANIMENT TO ROASTED GAME BIRDS, SUCH AS POUSSINS, AS HERE.

SERVES FOUR

INGREDIENTS
  4 poussins, 275–350g/10–12oz each
  175–250ml/6–8fl oz/¾–1 cup stock
  175ml/6fl oz/¾ cup white wine
  30ml/2 tbsp lemon juice
  15ml/1 tbsp chopped fresh tarragon or
    10ml/2 tsp dried
  25g/1oz butter
  10ml/2 tsp plain (all-purpose) flour
  salt and freshly ground black pepper
For the stuffing
  1 sweet potato, about 225g/8oz
  15ml/1 tbsp lemon juice
  25g/1oz butter or margarine
  2 shallots, finely chopped
  25g/1oz flaked (sliced) almonds
  50g/2oz ready-to-eat dried
    apricots, chopped
  25g/1oz fresh breadcrumbs
  5ml/1 tsp chopped fresh thyme
  salt and freshly ground black pepper
For the sweet potato chips
  450g/1lb sweet potatoes
  juice of ½ lemon
  flour, for coating
  a good pinch of cayenne pepper
  a good pinch of ground coriander
  a good pinch of ground cumin
  oil, for deep-frying

1 Preheat the oven to 180°C/350°F/
Gas 4 and prepare the stuffing. Peel the
sweet potato and cook in boiling water
with the lemon juice until tender. Drain
and mash with half of the butter.

2 Melt the remaining butter in a small
frying pan and fry the shallots for
2–3 minutes until softened. Add the
almonds and continue frying until both
the almonds and shallots are flecked
with brown. Stir into the mashed potato
together with the apricots, breadcrumbs,
thyme and seasoning to taste.

3 Loosely stuff the poussins with the
mixture and place them in a roasting
pan. Mix together the stock, white wine
and lemon juice in a small pan and bring
to the boil. Pour over the poussins.

4 Sprinkle each with tarragon and
seasoning and use half the butter to dot
over each bird. Cover loosely with foil
and roast in the oven for 35–45 minutes,
basting often with the juices.

5 To prepare the sweet potato chips,
peel and thinly slice the potatoes and
place in a bowl of water with the lemon
juice. Mix the flour, cayenne pepper,
coriander, cumin and salt on a plate.

6 Ten minutes before the poussins are
ready, heat the oil in a deep-fryer or wok.
Drain, then dry the potato slices with
kitchen paper and dip into the seasoned
flour. Fry the slices, in batches, for
2–3 minutes until golden. Drain well on
kitchen paper and keep warm.

7 When the poussins are cooked and
the juices run clear, increase the oven
temperature to 220°C/425°F/Gas 7. Cook
uncovered for 5 minutes or until well
browned. Transfer to a serving plate and
arrange the chips around the edge.

8 Pour the cooking juices into a pan
and heat gently. Mix the remaining butter
and flour to a paste and add small pieces
to the stock, whisking well between each
addition. Pour the sauce into a jug
(pitcher) and serve with the poussins
and potato chips.

Energy 749kcal/3134kJ; Protein 36g; Carbohydrate 50g, of which sugars 16g; Fat 47g, of which saturates 14g; Cholesterol 86mg; Calcium 98mg; Fibre 8g; Sodium 371mg.

PAN-FRIED SWEET POTATOES WITH BACON

THIS IS A COMFORTING DISH TO EAT ON A COLD WINTER'S EVENING. BACON AND ONION COUNTERACT THE SWEETNESS OF THE SWEET POTATO, AND THE CAYENNE PEPPER GIVES THE NECESSARY EXTRA 'BITE'. IT WOULD BE LOVELY SERVED WITH SOME FRESH STEAMED GREENS.

SERVES FOUR

INGREDIENTS

675–900g/1½–2lb sweet potatoes
juice of 1 lemon
15ml/1 tbsp plain (all-purpose) flour
a good pinch of cayenne pepper
about 45ml/3 tbsp sunflower oil
1 large onion, chopped
115g/4oz/⅔ cup chopped streaky
   (fatty) bacon
50g/2oz/1 cup fresh breadcrumbs
salt

1 Peel the sweet potatoes and cut into chunks about 4cm/1½in square. Place in a pan of boiling water with the lemon juice and a little salt and simmer for 8–10 minutes until cooked but not soft.

3 Heat 15ml/1tbsp of the oil in a large frying pan and fry the onion for about 2 minutes. Add the bacon and fry over a gentle heat for 6–8 minutes until the onion and bacon are golden. Transfer to a plate using a slotted spoon.

4 Add the breadcrumbs and fry, stirring, for about 1–2 minutes until golden. Add to the plate with the bacon.

2 Mix together the flour, cayenne pepper and a pinch of salt. Drain the potatoes and then dust with the seasoned flour, coating the pieces well.

5 Heat the remaining oil. Fry the potatoes for 5–6 minutes, turning often. Stir in the breadcrumb mixture; cook for 1 minute.

Energy 419kcal/1763kJ; Protein 11g; Carbohydrate 56g, of which sugars15g; Fat 19g, of which saturates 4g; Cholesterol 21mg; Calcium 87mg; Fibre 6g; Sodium 537mg.

SALSIFY GRATIN

THE SPINACH IN THIS RECIPE ADDS COLOUR AND MAKES IT GO FURTHER. HOWEVER, IF YOU CAN OBTAIN SALSIFY EASILY AND HAVE THE PATIENCE TO PEEL A LOT OF IT, INCREASE THE QUANTITY AND LEAVE OUT THE SPINACH. FOR VEGETARIANS USE VEGETABLE INSTEAD OF CHICKEN STOCK.

SERVES FOUR

INGREDIENTS
450g/1lb salsify, cut into
  5cm/2in lengths
juice of 1½ lemons
450g/1lb spinach, prepared
150ml/¼ pint/⅔ cup chicken stock
300ml/½ pint/1¼ cups single
  (light) cream
salt and freshly ground black pepper

3 Cook the spinach in a large pan over a moderate heat for 2–3 minutes until the leaves have wilted, shaking the pan occasionally. Place the stock, cream and seasoning in a small pan and heat through very gently, stirring.

4 Arrange the salsify and spinach in layers in the prepared ovenproof dish. Carefully pour over the stock and cream mixture and bake in the oven for about 1 hour until the top is golden brown and bubbling.

1 Trim away the tops and bottoms of the salsify and peel or scrape away the outer skin. Place each peeled root immediately in water with lemon juice added, to prevent discoloration.

2 Preheat the oven to 160°C/325°F/ Gas 3 and butter an ovenproof dish. Place the salsify in a pan of boiling water with the lemon juice. Simmer for about 10 minutes until the salsify is just tender, then drain.

Energy 206kcal/853kJ; Protein 7g; Carbohydrate 15g, of which sugars 6g; Fat 16g, of which saturates 9g; Cholesterol 41mg; Calcium 309mg; Fibre 4.4g; Sodium 324mg.

GREENS RECIPES

BROCCOLI AND CHICKEN LASAGNE

THIS MAKE-AHEAD DISH IS USUALLY POPULAR WITH CHILDREN AND IS A COMPLETE MEAL IN ONE.

SERVES SIX

INGREDIENTS
  450g/1lb broccoli, broken into florets
  450g/1lb skinless chicken breast fillets
  15ml/1 tbsp sunflower oil
  25g/1oz/2 tbsp butter
  1 onion, finely chopped
  1 garlic clove, chopped
  600ml/1 pint/2½ cups passata
    (bottled strained tomatoes)
  2.5ml/½ tsp thyme
  2.5ml/½ tsp oregano
  about 12 sheets precooked lasagne
  275g/10oz/1¼ cups fromage frais
    or cream
  75g/3oz/1 cup grated Parmesan cheese
  225g/8oz mozzarella cheese,
    thinly sliced
  salt and freshly ground black pepper

1 Preheat the oven to 180°C/350°F/
Gas 4. Butter a large, shallow ovenproof
dish. Steam the broccoli until just tender.

2 Cut the chicken into thin strips. Heat
the oil and butter in a frying pan and
fry the chicken for a few minutes until
lightly browned. Transfer to a plate using
a slotted spoon and set aside.

3 Add the onion and garlic to the pan
and fry for 3–4 minutes until the onion
has softened and is lightly golden brown.
Stir in the passata, thyme, oregano and
seasoning, and cook for 3–4 minutes
over a moderate heat until the sauce is
slightly thickened, stirring regularly.

4 Spoon half the tomato sauce into the
prepared dish. Add a layer of lasagne
and then half the chicken and half the
broccoli. Dot with half the fromage frais
or cream and sprinkle with half the
Parmesan. Put another layer of lasagne on
top and spoon over the remaining tomato
sauce, chicken, broccoli and fromage frais
or cream. End with a layer of lasagne.

5 Arrange the mozzarella slices on top
and sprinkle with the remaining Parmesan.
Bake for 30–35 minutes until golden.

BROCCOLI CRUMBLE

THIS SAVOURY CRUMBLE MAKES A GREAT MAIN COURSE FOR A VEGETARIAN IF YOU USE VEGETARIAN CHEESE.

SERVES FOUR

INGREDIENTS
  25g/1oz/2 tbsp butter or margarine
  2 leeks, thinly sliced
  25g/1oz/¼ cup plain (all-purpose) flour
  150ml/¼ pint/⅔ cup milk
  120ml/4fl oz/½ cup water
  225g/8oz broccoli, broken into florets
  25g/1oz/⅓ cup grated Parmesan cheese
  salt and freshly ground black pepper
For the topping
  115g/4oz/1 cup plain (all-purpose) flour
  5ml/1 tsp dried basil
  75g/3oz/6 tbsp butter or margarine
  50g/2oz/1 cup fresh breadcrumbs
  a pinch of salt

1 Preheat the oven to 190°C/375°F/Gas 5.
Melt the butter in a flameproof casserole
and fry the leeks for 2–3 minutes until
softened. Stir in the flour, then add the
milk and water. Bring to the boil, add the
broccoli, season and simmer for 5 minutes.

2 Stir in the Parmesan cheese, season
and pour into an ovenproof dish. To make
the topping, mix the flour with the basil
and salt. Rub in the fat, then stir in the
breadcrumbs. Sprinkle over the broccoli.
Bake for 20–25 minutes until golden.

Lasagne: Energy 527kcal/2214kJ; Protein 42g; Carbohydrate 40g, of which sugars 9g; Fat 23g, of which saturates 13g; Cholesterol 99mg; Calcium 389mg; Fibre 3g; Sodium 379mg.
Crumble: Energy 404kcal/1686kJ; Protein 11g; Carbohydrate 35g, of which sugars 5g; Fat 25g, of which saturates 15g; Cholesterol 64mg; Calcium 215mg; Fibre 3g; Sodium 282mg.

SPINACH AND CANNELLINI BEANS

THIS HEARTY DISH CAN BE MADE WITH ALMOST ANY DRIED BEAN, SUCH AS BLACK-EYED BEANS, HARICOT BEANS OR CHICKPEAS. IT IS A GOOD DISH TO SERVE ON A COLD EVENING. IF USING CANNED BEANS, DRAIN THEM, THEN RINSE UNDER COLD WATER.

SERVES FOUR

INGREDIENTS

225g/8oz cannellini beans,
    soaked overnight
60ml/4 tbsp olive oil
1 slice white bread
1 onion, chopped
3–4 tomatoes, peeled and chopped
a good pinch of paprika
450g/1lb spinach
1 garlic clove, halved
salt and freshly ground black pepper

1 Drain the beans, place in a pan and cover with water. Bring to the boil and boil rapidly for 10 minutes. Cover and simmer for about 1 hour until the beans are tender. Drain.

2 Heat 30ml/2 tbsp of the oil in a frying pan and fry the bread until golden brown. Transfer to a plate.

3 Fry the onion in 15ml/1 tbsp of the oil over a gentle heat until soft but not brown, then add the tomatoes and continue cooking over a gentle heat.

4 Heat the remaining oil in a large pan, stir in the paprika and then add the spinach. Cover and cook for a few minutes until the spinach has wilted.

5 Add the onion and tomato mixture to the spinach, mix well and stir in the cannellini beans.

6 Place the garlic and fried bread in a food processor and process until smooth. Stir into the spinach and bean mixture.

7 Add 150ml/¼ pint/⅔ cup cold water and then cover and simmer gently for 20–30 minutes, adding more water if necessary.

Energy 376kcal/1576kJ; Protein 16g; Carbohydrate 42g, of which sugars 9g; Fat 17g, of which saturates 3g; Cholesterol 0mg; Calcium 264mg; Fibre 17g; Sodium 236mg.

SPINACH IN FILO WITH THREE CHEESES

A GOOD CHOICE TO SERVE WHEN VEGETARIANS AND MEAT EATERS ARE GATHERED FOR A MEAL AS, WHATEVER THEIR PREFERENCE, EVERYONE SEEMS PARTIAL TO THIS TASTY DISH. JUST CHECK THAT THE CHEESE IS SUITABLE FOR VEGETARIANS IF THEY ARE STRICT ABOUT ANIMAL PRODUCTS.

SERVES FOUR

INGREDIENTS
 450g/1lb spinach
 15ml/1 tbsp sunflower oil
 15g/½oz/1 tbsp butter
 1 small onion, finely chopped
 175g/6oz/¾ cup ricotta cheese
 115g/4oz feta cheese, cut into
  small cubes
 75g/3oz/¾ cup grated Gruyère or
  Emmenthal cheese
 15ml/1 tbsp fresh chopped chervil
 5ml/1 tsp fresh chopped marjoram
 salt and freshly ground black pepper
 5 large or 10 small sheets filo pastry
 50g/2oz/4 tbsp butter, melted

1 Preheat the oven to 190°C/375°F/ Gas 5. Cook the spinach in a pan for 3–4 minutes until the leaves have wilted, shaking the pan occasionally. Strain and press out the excess liquid.

2 Heat the oil and butter in a pan and fry the onion for 3–4 minutes until softened. Remove from the heat and add half of the spinach. Combine, using a metal spoon to break up the spinach.

3 Add the ricotta cheese and stir until evenly combined. Stir in the remaining spinach, again chopping it into the mixture with a metal spoon.

4 Fold in the feta and Gruyère or Emmenthal cheese, chervil, marjoram and seasoning to taste and stir to combine well.

5 Lay a sheet of filo pastry measuring about 30cm/12in square on a work surface. (If you have small filo sheets, lay them side by side, overlapping in the middle.) Brush with butter and cover with a second sheet; brush this with butter and build up five layers of pastry in this way.

6 Spread the filling over the pastry, leaving a 2.5cm/1in border. Fold the sides inwards and then roll up.

7 Place the roll, seam side down, on a greased baking sheet and brush with the remaining butter. Bake for 30 minutes.

Energy 430kcal/1785kJ; Protein 18g; Carbohydrate 19g, of which sugars 4g; Fat 32g, of which saturates 17g; Cholesterol 83mg; Calcium 548mg; Fibre 5g; Sodium 681mg.

SPINACH RAVIOLI

HOME-MADE RAVIOLI IS TIME-CONSUMING, YET IT IS WORTH THE EFFORT AS EVEN THE BEST STORE-BOUGHT PASTA NEVER TASTES QUITE AS FRESH. TO COMPLEMENT THIS EFFORT, MAKE THE FILLING EXACTLY TO YOUR LIKING, TASTING IT FOR THE RIGHT BALANCE OF SPINACH AND CHEESE.

3 Melt half the butter in a small pan and fry the onion over a gentle heat for about 5–6 minutes until soft. Place in a bowl with the chopped spinach, the Parmesan and Dolcelatte cheeses, and seasoning. Mix well.

4 Grease a ravioli tin (pan). Roll out half or a quarter of the pasta dough to a thickness of about 3mm/⅛in. Lay the dough over the ravioli tin, pressing it well into each of the squares.

5 Spoon a little spinach mixture into each cavity, then roll out a second piece of dough and lay it on top. Press a rolling pin evenly over the top of the tin to seal the edges and then cut the ravioli into squares using a pastry cutter.

6 Place the ravioli in a large pan of boiling water and simmer for about 4–5 minutes until cooked through but al dente. Drain well and then toss with the remaining butter and the parsley.

7 Divide between four serving plates and serve scattered with shavings of Parmesan cheese.

COOK'S TIP
For a small ravioli tin (pan) of 32 holes, divide the dough into quarters. Roll the dough out until it covers the tin comfortably – it takes some time but the pasta needs to be thin otherwise the ravioli will be too stodgy. For a large ravioli tin of 64 holes, divide the dough in half.

SERVES FOUR

INGREDIENTS
225g/8oz fresh spinach
40g/1½oz/3 tbsp butter
1 small onion, finely chopped
25g/1oz/⅓ cup grated Parmesan cheese
40g/1½oz Dolcelatte cheese, crumbled
15ml/1 tbsp chopped fresh parsley
salt and freshly ground black pepper
shavings of Parmesan cheese, to serve
For the pasta dough
350g/12oz/3 cups strong white flour
4ml/¾ tsp salt
2 eggs
15ml/1 tbsp olive oil

1 To make the pasta dough, mix together the flour and salt in a large bowl or food processor. Add the eggs, olive oil and about 45ml/3 tbsp of cold water or enough to make a pliable dough. If working by hand, mix the ingredients together and then knead the dough for about 15 minutes until very smooth. Or, process for about 1½ minutes in a food processor. Place the dough in a plastic bag and chill for at least 1 hour (or overnight if more convenient).

2 Cook the spinach in a large, covered pan for 3–4 minutes, until the leaves have wilted. Strain and press out the excess liquid. Set aside to cool a little and then chop finely.

Energy 547kcal/2283kJ; Protein 15.9g; Carbohydrate 43.4g, of which sugars 3.6g; Fat 35.6g, of which saturates 21.5g; Cholesterol 114mg; Calcium 222mg; Fibre 2.1g; Sodium 252mg.

CAULIFLOWER, PRAWN AND BROCCOLI TEMPURA

ALL SORTS OF VEGETABLES ARE DELICIOUS DEEP-FRIED JAPANESE-STYLE (TEMPURA). FIRM VEGETABLES,
SUCH AS CAULIFLOWER AND BROCCOLI, ARE BEST BLANCHED BEFORE FRYING BUT MANGETOUTS, RED AND
GREEN PEPPER SLICES, AND MUSHROOMS CAN SIMPLY BE DIPPED IN THE BATTER AND FRIED.

SERVES FOUR

INGREDIENTS
½ cauliflower
275g/10oz broccoli
8 raw prawns (shrimp)
8 button (white) mushrooms (optional)
sunflower or vegetable oil, for
    deep-frying
lemon wedges and sprigs of coriander
    (cilantro), to garnish (optional)
soy sauce, to serve
For the batter
115g/4oz/1 cup plain
    (all-purpose) flour
a pinch of salt
2 eggs, separated
175ml/6fl oz/¾ cup iced water
30ml/2 tbsp sunflower or
    vegetable oil

1 Cut the cauliflower and broccoli into medium florets. Blanch all the florets for 1–2 minutes. Drain. Refresh under cold running water. Put to one side. Peel the prawns but leave their tails intact. Put to one side.

2 To make the batter, place the flour and salt in a bowl, blend together the egg yolks and water and stir into the flour, beating well to make a smooth batter.

3 Beat in the oil and then whisk the egg whites until stiff and fold into the batter. Heat the oil for deep-frying to 190°C/ 375°F. Coat a few of the vegetables and prawns in the batter. Fry for 2–3 minutes until lightly golden and puffy. Transfer to a plate lined with kitchen paper and keep warm while frying the remaining tempura.

4 Arrange on individual plates, garnish with lemon and coriander, if liked, and serve with little bowls of soy sauce.

VARIATION
Try cooking other vegetables in this way, such as aubergines (eggplants) and courgettes (zucchini).

Energy 584kcal/2435kJ; Protein 19.7g; Carbohydrate 82.9g, of which sugars 7.5g; Fat 18.2g, of which saturates 2.6g; Cholesterol 0mg; Calcium 242mg; Fibre 5.8g; Sodium 984mg.

CAULIFLOWER AND MUSHROOM GOUGÈRE

THIS IS AN ALL-ROUND FAVOURITE VEGETARIAN DISH. WHEN COOKING THIS DISH FOR MEAT LOVERS, CHOPPED ROAST HAM OR FRIED BACON CAN BE ADDED.

SERVES FOUR TO SIX

INGREDIENTS
300ml/½ pint/1¼ cups water
115g/4oz/½ cup butter or margarine
150g/5oz/1¼ cups plain
   (all-purpose) flour
4 eggs
115g/4oz Gruyère or Cheddar cheese,
   finely diced
5ml/1 tsp Dijon mustard
salt and freshly ground black pepper
For the filling
½ x 400g/14oz can tomatoes
15ml/1 tbsp sunflower oil
15g/½oz/1 tbsp butter or margarine
1 onion, chopped
115g/4oz button (white) mushrooms,
   halved if large
1 small cauliflower, broken into florets
a sprig of thyme
salt and freshly ground black pepper

1 Preheat the oven to 200°C/400°F/
Gas 6 and butter a large ovenproof dish.
Place the water and butter together in a
large pan and heat until the butter has
melted. Remove from the heat and add
all the flour at once. Beat well with a
wooden spoon for about 30 seconds,
until smooth. Allow to cool slightly.

2 Beat in the eggs, one at a time, and
continue beating until the mixture is
thick and glossy. Stir in the cheese
and mustard and season with salt and
pepper to taste. Spread the mixture
evenly around the sides of the ovenproof
dish, leaving a hollow in the centre for
the filling.

3 To make the filling, purée the
tomatoes in a blender or food processor
and then pour into a measuring jug
(cup). Add enough water to make up to
300ml/½ pint/1¼ cups of liquid.

4 Heat the oil and butter in a flameproof
casserole and fry the onion for about
3–4 minutes until softened but not
browned. Add the mushrooms and cook
for 2–3 minutes until they begin to be
flecked with brown. Add the cauliflower
florets and stir-fry for 1 minute.

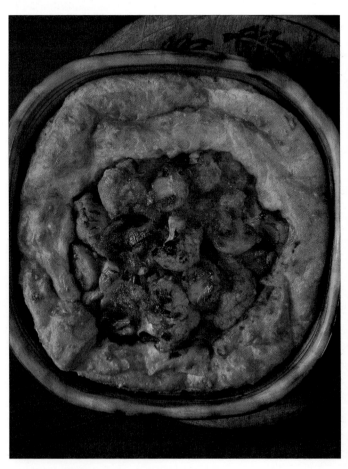

5 Add the tomato liquid, thyme and
seasoning. Cook, uncovered, over a
gentle heat for about 5 minutes until the
cauliflower is only just tender.

6 Spoon the mixture into the hollow in
the ovenproof dish, adding all the liquid.
Bake for 35–40 minutes, until the outer
pastry is well risen and golden brown.

VARIATION
Add about 115–150g/4–5oz sliced roast
ham to the sauce at the end of step 5.

BALTI-STYLE CAULIFLOWER ᵂᴵᵀᴴ TOMATOES

BALTI IS A TYPE OF MEAT AND VEGETABLE COOKING FROM PAKISTAN AND NORTHERN INDIA. IT CAN REFER BOTH TO THE PAN USED FOR COOKING, WHICH IS LIKE A LITTLE WOK, AND THE SPICES USED.

SERVES FOUR

INGREDIENTS
30ml/2 tbsp vegetable oil
1 onion, chopped
2 garlic cloves, crushed
1 cauliflower, broken into florets
5ml/1 tsp ground coriander
5ml/1 tsp ground cumin
5ml/1 tsp ground fennel seeds
2.5ml/½ tsp garam masala
a pinch of ground ginger
2.5ml/½ tsp chilli powder
4 plum tomatoes, peeled, seeded
  and quartered
175ml/6fl oz/¾ cup water
175g/6oz fresh spinach,
  roughly chopped
15–30ml/1–2 tbsp lemon juice
salt and freshly ground
  black pepper

1 Heat the oil in a balti pan, wok, or large frying pan. Add the onion and garlic and stir-fry for 2–3 minutes over a high heat until the onion begins to brown. Add the cauliflower florets and stir-fry for a further 2–3 minutes until the cauliflower is flecked with brown.

2 Add the coriander, cumin, fennel seeds, garam masala, ginger and chilli powder and cook over a high heat for 1 minute, stirring all the time; then add the tomatoes, water and salt and pepper. Bring to the boil and then reduce the heat, cover and simmer for 5–6 minutes until the cauliflower is just tender.

3 Stir in the chopped spinach, cover and cook for 1 minute until the spinach is tender. Add enough lemon juice to sharpen the flavour and adjust the seasoning to taste.

4 Serve straight from the pan, with an Indian meal or with chicken or meat.

Energy 149kcal/621kJ; Protein 6g; Carbohydrate 11g, of which sugars 8g; Fat 9g, of which saturates 1g; Cholesterol 0mg; Calcium 126mg; Fibre 5g; Sodium 81mg.

HOT BROCCOLI TARTLETS

*IN FRANCE, HOME OF THE CLASSIC QUICHE LORRAINE, YOU CAN ALSO FIND A WHOLE VARIETY OF
SAVOURY TARTLETS, FILLED WITH ONIONS, LEEKS, MUSHROOMS AND BROCCOLI. THIS VERSION IS SIMPLE
TO PREPARE AND WOULD MAKE AN ELEGANT START TO A MEAL.*

MAKES EIGHT TO TEN

INGREDIENTS
    15ml/1 tbsp oil
    1 leek, finely sliced
    175g/6oz broccoli, broken into florets
    15g/½oz/1 tbsp butter
    15g/½oz/⅛ cup plain (all-purpose) flour
    150ml/¼ pint/⅔ cup milk
    50g/2oz/½ cup grated goat's Cheddar
      or farmhouse Cheddar
    fresh chervil, to garnish
For the pastry
    175g/6oz/1½ cups plain
      (all-purpose) flour
    75g/3oz/6 tbsp butter
    1 egg
    a pinch of salt

1 To make the pastry, place the flour
and salt in a large bowl and rub in the
butter and egg to make a dough. Add
a little cold water if necessary, knead
lightly, then wrap and chill for 1 hour.

2 Preheat the oven to 190°C/375°F/
Gas 5. Let the dough return to room
temperature for 10 minutes and then roll
out on a lightly floured surface and line
8–10 deep patty tins (muffin pans).

3 Prick the bases with a fork and bake
in the oven for about 10–15 minutes
until the pastry is firm and lightly golden.
Increase the oven temperature to
200°C/400°F/Gas 6.

4 Heat the oil in a frying pan and sauté
the leek for 4–5 minutes until soft. Add the
broccoli, stir-fry for about 1 minute and
then add a little water. Cover and steam
for 3–4 minutes until the broccoli is
just tender.

5 Melt the butter in a separate large
pan, stir in the flour and cook for a
minute, stirring all the time. Slowly add
the milk and stir to make a smooth
sauce. Add half of the cheese and
season with salt and pepper.

6 Spoon a little broccoli and leek into
each tartlet case and then spoon over
the sauce. Sprinkle each tartlet with
the remaining cheese and then bake
in the oven for about 10 minutes, until
golden brown.

7 Leave to cool slightly. Serve the
tartlets warm or cold as part of a buffet
or as an appetizer or nibble with drinks,
garnished with chervil.

Energy 193kcal/806kJ; Protein 5g; Carbohydrate16 g, of which sugars 2g; Fat 12g, of which saturates 7g; Cholesterol 49mg; Calcium 99mg; Fibre 1g; Sodium 108mg.

CHARD PASTIES

CHARD, LIKE SPINACH, GOES PARTICULARLY WELL IN PASTIES. UNLIKE SOME GREEN VEGETABLES, IT CAN SURVIVE A LITTLE EXTRA COOKING AND IS SUBSTANTIAL ENOUGH TO BE THE PRINCIPAL INGREDIENT. FOR A MORE SAVOURY PASTRY, REPLACE A LITTLE OF THE BUTTER WITH GRATED CHEESE.

SERVES FOUR

INGREDIENTS
    675g/1½lb Swiss chard
    25g/1oz/2 tbsp butter or margarine
    1 onion, finely chopped
    75g/3oz/½ cup chopped streaky
        (fatty) bacon
    50g/2oz/½ cup grated Gruyère cheese
    25g/1oz/½ cup fresh breadcrumbs
    90ml/6 tbsp single (light) cream
    salt and freshly ground black pepper
For the pastry
    275g/10oz/2½ cups plain
        (all-purpose) flour
    150g/5oz/10 tbsp butter or margarine
    a pinch of salt
    beaten egg for glazing

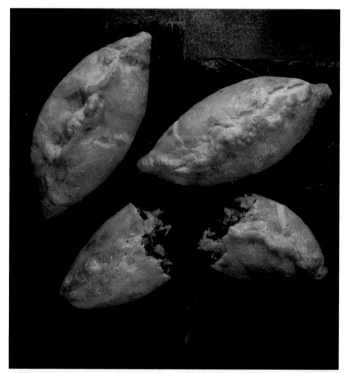

1 To make the pastry, place the flour and salt in a mixing bowl and rub in the fat. Add a little cold water and mix to a soft dough. Knead on a floured surface. Wrap and chill for 30 minutes.

2 Trim the stalks of the chard and then chop both the leaves and stalk. Place in a heavy pan, cover and cook over a low heat for 6–8 minutes until the stalks are tender and the leaves wilted. Shake the pan occasionally. Strain and press out the excess liquid using the back of a spoon, then place in a mixing bowl and leave to cool.

3 Melt the butter in a small frying pan and fry the onion and bacon for about 4–5 minutes, until the onion is lightly golden and the bacon is browned.

4 Add the onion and bacon to the chard and stir in the cheese, breadcrumbs, cream and seasoning to taste. Preheat the oven to 200°C/400°F/Gas 6.

5 Divide the pastry into four and roll out into rounds.

6 Spoon the filling on to the centre of each and dampen the edges with water. Bring the sides together over the filling and press together to seal. Brush with beaten egg and then put on an oiled baking sheet. Bake for 15–20 minutes, until the pastry is golden.

Energy 752kcal/3136kJ; Protein 18g; Carbohydrate 62g, of which sugars 3g; Fat 50g, of which saturates 30g; Cholesterol 132mg; Calcium 337mg; Fibre 3g; Sodium 996mg.

PASTA WITH SAVOY CABBAGE AND GRUYÈRE

THIS IS AN INEXPENSIVE AND SIMPLE DISH WITH A SURPRISING TEXTURE AND FLAVOUR. THE CABBAGE IS COOKED SO THAT IT HAS PLENTY OF 'BITE' TO IT, CONTRASTING WITH THE SOFTNESS OF THE PASTA.

SERVES FOUR

INGREDIENTS

1 small Savoy or green cabbage,
    thinly sliced
25g/1oz/2 tbsp butter
1 small onion, chopped
350g/12oz pasta, e.g. tagliatelle,
    fettucine or penne
15ml/1 tbsp chopped fresh parsley
150ml/¼ pint/⅔ cup single (light) cream
50g/2oz/½ cup grated Gruyère or
    Cheddar cheese
about 300ml/½ pint/1¼ cups hot
    vegetable or chicken stock
salt and freshly ground
    black pepper

1 Preheat the oven to 180°C/350°F/
Gas 4 and butter a large casserole.
Place the cabbage in a mixing bowl.

2 Melt the butter in a small frying pan
and fry the onion until softened. Stir into
the cabbage in the bowl.

3 Cook the pasta according to the
instructions, until al dente.

4 Drain well and stir into the bowl with
the cabbage and onion. Add the parsley
and mix well and then pour into the
prepared casserole.

5 Beat together the cream and Gruyère
or Cheddar cheese and then stir in the
hot stock. Season well and pour over the
cabbage and pasta, so that it comes
about halfway up the casserole. If
necessary, add a little more stock.

6 Cover tightly with foil or a lid and cook
in the oven for 30–35 minutes, until the
cabbage is tender and the stock is
bubbling. Remove the lid for the last
5 minutes of the cooking time to brown
the top.

Energy 428kcal/1808kJ; Protein 16g; Carbohydrate 70g, of which sugars 7g; Fat 12g, of which saturates 6g; Cholesterol 26mg; Calcium 185mg; Fibre 7g; Sodium 257mg.

CABBAGE SALAD <u>WITH</u> PESTO MAYONNAISE

BOTH THE PESTO AND THE MAYONNAISE CAN BE MADE FOR THIS DISH. HOWEVER, IF TIME IS SHORT, YOU CAN BUY THEM BOTH READY-PREPARED AND IT WILL TASTE JUST AS GOOD.

SERVES FOUR TO SIX

INGREDIENTS
    1 small or ½ medium white cabbage
    3–4 carrots, grated
    4 spring onions (scallions),
        finely sliced
    25–40g/1–1½oz pine nuts
    15ml/1 tbsp chopped fresh mixed
        herbs; parsley, basil and chervil
For the pesto mayonnaise
    1 egg yolk
    about 10ml/2 tsp lemon juice
    200ml/7fl oz/⅞ cup sunflower oil
    10ml/2 tsp pesto
    60ml/4 tbsp natural (plain) yogurt
    salt and freshly ground black pepper

1 To make the mayonnaise, place the egg yolk in a blender or food processor and process with the lemon juice. With the machine running, very slowly add the oil, pouring it a little more quickly as the mayonnaise emulsifies.

2 Season to taste with salt and pepper and a little more lemon juice if necessary. Alternatively, make the mayonnaise by hand using a balloon whisk.

3 Spoon 75ml/5 tbsp of mayonnaise into a bowl and stir in the pesto and yogurt, beating well to make a fairly thin dressing. (The remaining mayonnaise will keep for about 3–4 weeks in a screw-top jar in the refrigerator.)

4 Using a food processor or a sharp knife, thinly slice the cabbage and place in a large salad bowl.

5 Add the carrots and spring onions, together with the pine nuts and herbs, mixing thoroughly with your hands. Stir the pesto dressing into the salad or serve separately in a small dish if preferred.

Energy 443kcal/1704kJ; Protein 4g; Carbohydrate 10g, of which sugars 9g; Fat 40g, of which saturates 5g; Cholesterol 37mg; Calcium 112mg; Fibre 3g; Sodium 47mg.

KOHLRABI STUFFED WITH PEPPERS

IF YOU HAVEN'T SAMPLED KOHLRABI, OR HAVE ONLY EATEN IT IN STEWS WHERE ITS FLAVOUR IS LOST, THIS DISH IS RECOMMENDED. THE SLIGHTLY SHARP, FRESH FLAVOUR OF THE PEPPERS IS AN EXCELLENT FOIL TO THE MORE EARTHY FLAVOUR OF THE KOHLRABI.

SERVES FOUR

INGREDIENTS
    4 small kohlrabi, about 175–225g/
        6–8oz each
    about 400ml/14fl oz/1¾ cups hot
        vegetable stock
    15ml/1 tbsp olive or sunflower oil
    1 onion, chopped
    1 small red and 1 small green (bell)
        pepper, seeded and sliced
    salt and freshly ground
        black pepper
    flat leaf parsley, to garnish (optional)

1 Preheat the oven to 180°C/350°F/ Gas 4. Trim and top and tail the kohlrabi and arrange in the base of a lightly greased medium ovenproof dish.

2 Pour over the stock to come about halfway up the vegetables. Cover and braise in the oven for about 30 minutes until tender. Transfer to a plate and allow to cool, reserving the stock.

3 Heat the oil in a frying pan and fry the onion for 3–4 minutes over a gentle heat, stirring occasionally. Add the peppers and cook for a further 2–3 minutes, until the onion is lightly browned.

4 Add the reserved vegetable stock and a little seasoning, then simmer, uncovered, over a moderate heat until the stock has almost evaporated.

5 Scoop out the flesh from the kohlrabi and roughly chop it into bitesize pieces. Stir the flesh into the onion and pepper mixture, taste and adjust the seasoning as necessary. Arrange the shells in a shallow ovenproof dish.

6 Spoon the filling into the kohlrabi shells. Place in the oven for 5–10 minutes to heat through and then serve immediately, garnished with flat leaf parsley, if you like.

Energy 68kcal/281kJ; Protein 2g; Carbohydrate 6g, of which sugars 5g; Fat 4g, of which saturates 1g; Cholesterol 0mg; Calcium 23mg; Fibre 2g; Sodium 133mg.

TURNIP TOPS WITH PARMESAN AND GARLIC

TURNIP TOPS HAVE A PRONOUNCED FLAVOUR AND ARE GOOD WHEN COOKED WITH OTHER STRONG-FLAVOURED INGREDIENTS SUCH AS ONIONS, GARLIC AND PARMESAN CHEESE. THEY DO NOT REQUIRE LONG COOKING AS THE LEAVES ARE QUITE TENDER.

SERVES FOUR

INGREDIENTS
    45ml/3 tbsp olive oil
    2 garlic cloves, crushed
    4 spring onions (scallions), sliced
    350g/12oz turnip tops, thinly sliced,
      tough stalk removed
    50g/2oz/½ cup grated Parmesan cheese
    salt and freshly ground black pepper
    shavings of Parmesan cheese,
      to garnish

1 Heat the olive oil in a large pan and fry the garlic for a few seconds. Add the spring onions, stir-fry for 2 minutes and then add the turnip tops.

2 Stir-fry for a few minutes so that the greens are coated in oil, then add about 50ml/2fl oz/¼ cup water. Bring to the boil, cover and simmer until the greens are tender. Stir occasionally and do not allow the pan to boil dry.

3 Bring the liquid to the boil and allow the excess to evaporate and then stir in the Parmesan cheese.

4 Serve immediately with extra shavings of cheese, if liked.

Energy 169kcal/700kJ; Protein 6g; Carbohydrate 2g, of which sugars 2g; Fat 15g, of which saturates 4g; Cholesterol 12mg; Calcium 158mg; Fibre 1.1g; Sodium 196mg.

STIR-FRIED BRUSSELS SPROUTS

STIR-FRYING IS ONE OF THE BEST WAYS OF COOKING BRUSSELS SPROUTS.

SERVES FOUR

INGREDIENTS
    450g/1lb Brussels sprouts
    15ml/1 tbsp sunflower oil
    6–8 spring onions (scallions), cut into
        2.5cm/1in lengths
    2 slices fresh root ginger
    50g/2oz/½ cup slivered almonds
    150–175ml/5–6fl oz/⅔–¾ cup
        vegetable or chicken stock
    salt

1 Remove any large outer leaves and trim the bases of the Brussels sprouts. Cut into slices about 7mm/⅓in thick.

2 Heat the oil in a wok or frying pan and fry the spring onions and the ginger for 2–3 minutes, stirring. Add the almonds and stir-fry over a moderate heat until the onions and almonds begin to brown.

3 Remove and discard the ginger, reduce the heat and stir in the Brussels sprouts. Stir-fry for a few minutes and then pour in the stock and cook over a gentle heat for 5–6 minutes or until the sprouts are nearly tender.

4 Add a little salt, if necessary, and then increase the heat to boil off the excess liquid. Spoon into a warmed serving dish and serve immediately.

BRUSSELS SPROUTS GRATIN

THIS LOVELY GRATIN CAN BE SERVED AS A MAIN COURSE OR A SIDE DISH.

SERVES FOUR

INGREDIENTS
    15g/½oz/1 tbsp butter
    150ml/¼ pint/⅔ cup whipping cream
    150ml/¼ pint/⅔ cup milk
    25g/1oz/⅓ cup grated
        Parmesan cheese
    675g/1½lb Brussels sprouts,
        thinly sliced
    1 garlic clove, finely chopped
    salt and freshly ground black pepper

1 Preheat the oven to 150°C/300°F/ Gas 2 and butter a shallow ovenproof dish. Blend together the cream, milk, Parmesan cheese and seasoning.

2 Place a layer of Brussels sprouts in the base of the prepared dish, sprinkle with a little garlic and pour over about a quarter of the cream mixture. Add another layer of sprouts and continue building layers in this way, ending with the remaining cream and milk.

3 Cover and bake for 1–1¼ hours. Halfway through cooking, remove the cover and press the sprouts under the liquid. Return to the oven to brown.

Stir-fried: Energy 150kcal/625kJ; Protein 6g; Carbohydrate 7g, of which sugars 5g; Fat 11g, of which saturates 1g; Cholesterol 0mg; Calcium 79mg; Fibre 6g; Sodium 92mg.

Gratin: Energy 68kcal/281kJ; Protein 2g; Carbohydrate 6g, of which sugars 5g; Fat 4g, of which saturates 1g; Cholesterol 0mg; Calcium 23mg; Fibre 2g; Sodium 133mg.

PAK CHOI <u>WITH</u> LIME DRESSING

FOR THIS THAI RECIPE, THE COCONUT DRESSING IS TRADITIONALLY MADE USING FISH SAUCE, BUT VEGETARIANS COULD USE MUSHROOM SAUCE INSTEAD. BEWARE, THIS IS A FIERY DISH, BUT YOU CAN ALWAYS REDUCE THE AMOUNT OF CHILLI USED OR OMIT IT ALTOGETHER IF PREFERRED.

SERVES FOUR

INGREDIENTS
   6 spring onions (scallions)
   2 pak choi (bok choy)
   30ml/2 tbsp oil
   3 fresh red chillies, cut into
     thin strips
   4 garlic cloves, thinly sliced
   15ml/1 tbsp crushed peanuts
For the dressing
   15–30ml/1–2 tbsp Thai fish sauce
   30ml/2 tbsp lime juice
   250ml/8fl oz/1 cup coconut milk

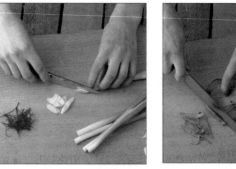

1 To make the dressing, blend together the Thai fish sauce and lime juice, and then stir in the coconut milk.

2 Cut the spring onions diagonally into slices, including all but the very tips of the green parts.

3 Using a large sharp knife, cut the pak choi into very fine shreds.

4 Heat the oil in a wok and stir-fry the chillies for 2–3 minutes until crisp. Transfer to a plate using a slotted spoon.

5 Stir-fry the garlic for 30–60 seconds until golden brown and transfer to the plate with the chillies.

6 Stir-fry the white parts of the spring onions for about 2–3 minutes and then add the green parts and stir-fry for a further 1 minute. Add to the plate with the chillies and garlic.

7 Bring a large pan of salted water to the boil and add the pak choi; stir twice and then drain immediately.

8 Place the warmed pak choi in a large bowl, add the coconut dressing and stir well. Spoon into a large serving bowl and sprinkle with the peanuts and the stir-fried chilli mixture. Serve either warm or cold.

COOK'S TIP
Coconut milk is available in cans from large supermarkets and Chinese stores. Alternatively, creamed coconut is available in packets. To use creamed coconut, place about 115g/4oz in a jug (pitcher) and pour over 250ml/8fl oz/ 1 cup boiling water. Stir until dissolved.

Energy 93kcal/384kJ; Protein 2.9g; Carbohydrate 6.2g, of which sugars 5.7g; Fat 6.4g, of which saturates 0.9g; Cholesterol 0mg; Calcium 157mg; Fibre 2.1g; Sodium 354mg.

DOLMADES

DOLMADES ARE STUFFED VINE LEAVES, A TRADITIONAL GREEK DISH. IF YOU CAN'T OBTAIN FRESH VINE LEAVES, USE A PACKET OF BRINED VINE LEAVES. SOAK THE LEAVES IN HOT WATER FOR 10 MINUTES THEN RINSE AND DRY WELL ON KITCHEN PAPER BEFORE USE.

4 Stir in 30ml/2 tbsp of the pine nuts, the almonds, sultanas, chives, mint, lemon juice and seasoning and mix well.

5 Lay a vine leaf on a clean work surface, veined side uppermost. Place a spoonful of filling near the stem, fold the lower part of the leaf over it and roll up, folding in the sides as you go. Continue stuffing the vine leaves in the same way.

6 Line the base of a deep frying pan with four large vine leaves. Place the stuffed vine leaves close together in the pan, seam side down, in a single layer.

7 Add the wine and enough stock to just cover the vine leaves. Place a plate directly over the leaves, then cover and simmer gently for 30 minutes, checking to make sure the pan does not boil dry.

8 Leave the vine leaves to cool, then chill. Serve garnished with the remaining pine nuts, a sprig of mint and a little Greek yogurt.

MAKES TWENTY TO TWENTY FOUR

INGREDIENTS
20–30 fresh young vine leaves
30ml/2 tbsp olive oil
1 large onion, finely chopped
1 garlic clove, crushed
225g/8oz/generous 1 cup cooked long
  grain rice
about 45ml/3 tbsp pine nuts
15ml/1 tbsp flaked (sliced) almonds
40g/1½oz/¼ cup sultanas (golden
  raisins)
15ml/1 tbsp snipped chives
15ml/1 tbsp finely chopped mint
juice of ½ lemon
150ml/¼ pint/⅔ cup white wine
hot vegetable stock
salt and freshly ground black pepper
a sprig of mint, to garnish
Greek (US strained plain) yogurt

1 Bring a large pan of water to the boil and cook the vine leaves for about 2–3 minutes. They will darken and go limp after about 1 minute and simmering for a further minute or so ensures they are pliable. If using leaves from a packet, place them in a large bowl, cover with boiling water and leave for a few minutes until the leaves can be easily separated. Rinse them under cold water and drain on kitchen paper.

2 Heat the oil in a small frying pan and fry the onion and garlic for 3–4 minutes over a gentle heat until soft.

3 Spoon the onion and garlic mixture into a bowl and add the cooked rice.

Energy 43kcal/181kJ; Protein 0.7g; Carbohydrate 6.7g, of which sugars 1.7g; Fat 1.1g, of which saturates 0.1g; Cholesterol 0mg; Calcium 12mg; Fibre 0.3g; Sodium 2mg.

BEAN, PEA AND SEED RECIPES

LAMB AND BROAD BEAN COUSCOUS

THIS FLAVOURSOME DISH IS SERVED WITH A SPICY TABASCO SAUCE, BUT IT COULD BE SERVED ON ITS OWN.

SERVES FOUR

INGREDIENTS
30–45ml/2–3 tbsp vegetable oil
350g/12oz lean lamb, cut into cubes
3 skinless chicken pieces, cut into
  large chunks
1 large onion, chopped
2 garlic cloves, crushed
3 carrots, cut into 4cm/1½in lengths
1 small parsnip, cut into chunks
4 tomatoes, skinned and chopped
400ml/14fl oz/1⅔ cups chicken stock
1 cinnamon stick
2.5ml/½ tsp ground ginger
a sprig of thyme
1 small red or green (bell) pepper,
  seeded and sliced
225g/8oz shelled broad (fava) beans
5–10ml/1–2 tsp Tabasco or chilli sauce
salt and freshly ground black pepper
For the couscous
400g/14oz couscous
15ml/1 tbsp olive oil
a pinch of salt

1 Heat 30ml/2 tbsp oil in a flameproof
casserole and fry the cubes of lamb until
browned. Drain and transfer to a plate.

2 Add the chicken pieces and cook until
brown. Drain and put on the plate.

3 Heat a further 15ml/1 tbsp oil and fry
the onion and garlic for 4–5 minutes
until softened. Add the carrots and
parsnip, stir-fry for a few minutes, then
add the tomatoes, stock, cinnamon stick,
ginger, thyme, seasoning and meat.

4 Bring to the boil, stirring occasionally,
then reduce the heat, cover and simmer
for 45–60 minutes until the meat is tender.

5 Meanwhile, rub the olive oil and salt
into the couscous. Mix in 120ml/4fl oz/
½ cup warm water. Leave for 10 minutes.

6 Place the soaked couscous in a
colander. Set over the stew, cover and
steam for 15 minutes.

7 Add the pepper and broad beans to
the stew and simmer for 10 minutes,
until the vegetables are cooked.

8 Just before serving, ladle about
150ml/¼ pint/⅔ cup of the cooking liquid
into a pan. Add a little Tabasco or chilli
sauce and heat gently. Taste and add
more Tabasco or chilli sauce, if liked, then
pour into a warmed serving jug (pitcher).

9 Spoon the couscous on to a large
warmed serving plate and pour the stew
over. Serve with the hot sauce.

BROAD BEANS À LA PAYSANNE

A COLOURFUL COMBINATION OF VEGETABLES AND HAM, THIS IS LOVELY SERVED WITH AN OMELETTE.

SERVES FOUR

INGREDIENTS
15ml/1 tbsp olive oil
1 onion, finely chopped
1 thick slice lean ham, finely diced
350g/12oz shelled broad (fava) beans
2 Little Gem (Bibb) lettuces, chopped
75ml/3fl oz/⅓ cup chicken or
  vegetable stock
50ml/2fl oz/¼ cup single (light) cream
salt and freshly ground black pepper
sprigs of mint or chervil, to garnish

1 Heat the oil in a pan. Fry the onion
and ham until soft. Add the beans and
lettuce. Cover and cook for 6–8 minutes.

2 Stir in the stock, cream and seasoning
and cook over a very low heat for
20–30 minutes. Stir occasionally, taking
care not to break up the beans.

3 Turn into a warmed serving dish and
garnish with a sprig of mint or chervil.

COOK'S TIP
Larger broad (fava) beans sometimes
have a tough outer skin. It is a good idea
to cook them briefly, peel off the outer
skin and use the tender green centres.

Lamb: Energy 674kcal/2819kJ; Protein 48g; Carbohydrate 75g, of which sugars 16g; Fat 22g, of which saturates 5g; Cholesterol 117mg; Calcium 106mg; Fibre 6g; Sodium 340mg.
Paysanne: Energy 164kcal/984kJ; Protein 10g; Carbohydrate 10g, of which sugars 4g; Fat 10g, of which saturates 3g; Cholesterol 22mg; Calcium 48mg; Fibre 1g; Sodium 259mg.

PEAS WITH BABY ONIONS AND CREAM

IDEALLY, USE FRESH PEAS AND FRESH BABY ONIONS. FROZEN PEAS ARE AN ACCEPTABLE SUBSTITUTE IF FRESH ONES AREN'T AVAILABLE, BUT FROZEN ONIONS TEND TO BE INSIPID AND ARE NOT WORTH USING. ALTERNATIVELY, USE THE WHITE PARTS OF SPRING ONIONS (SCALLIONS).

SERVES FOUR

INGREDIENTS

175g/6oz baby (pearl) onions
15g/½oz/1 tbsp butter
900g/2lb fresh peas (about
   350g/12oz shelled or frozen)
150ml/¼ pint/⅔ cup double
   (heavy) cream
15g/½oz/⅛ cup plain (all-purpose) flour
10ml/2 tsp chopped fresh parsley
15–30ml/1–2 tbsp lemon juice
   (optional)
salt and freshly ground black pepper

1 Peel the onions and halve them if necessary. Melt the butter in a flame-proof casserole and fry the onions for 5–6 minutes over a moderate heat, until they begin to be flecked with brown.

3 Using a small whisk, blend the cream with the flour. Remove the pan from the heat and stir in the combined cream and flour, parsley and seasoning to taste.

4 Cook over a gentle heat for about 3–4 minutes, until the sauce is thick. Taste and adjust the seasoning; add a little lemon juice to sharpen, if liked.

2 Add the peas and stir-fry for a few minutes. Add 120ml/4fl oz/¼ cup water and bring to the boil. Partially cover and simmer for about 10 minutes until both the peas and onions are tender. There should be a thin layer of water on the base of the pan – add a little more water if necessary or, if there is too much liquid, remove the lid and increase the heat until the liquid is reduced.

Energy 161kcal/670kJ; Protein 9.1g; Carbohydrate 15.9g, of which sugars 6.8g; Fat 7.4g, of which saturates 3.7g; Cholesterol 13mg; Calcium 73mg; Fibre 6.5g; Sodium 47mg.

MANGETOUTS WITH CHICKEN

MANGETOUTS ARE SO DELICATE AND FRESH-TASTING THAT IT SEEMS A CRIME TO DO ANYTHING AT ALL WITH THEM, BARRING FLASH COOKING AND SERVING THEM HOT OR COLD WITH A LITTLE BUTTER OR A VINAIGRETTE DRESSING. THEY ARE EXCELLENT IN STIR-FRIES, ADDING COLOUR AND TEXTURE.

SERVES FOUR

INGREDIENTS

    4 skinless chicken breast fillets
    225g/8oz mangetouts (snow peas)
    45ml/3 tbsp vegetable oil, plus
        oil for deep-frying
    3 garlic cloves, finely chopped
    2.5cm/1in piece fresh root ginger,
        freshly grated
    5–6 spring onions (scallions),
        cut into 4cm/1½in lengths
    10ml/2 tsp sesame oil
For the marinade
    5ml/1 tsp cornflour (cornstarch)
    15ml/1 tbsp light soy sauce
    15ml/1 tbsp medium dry sherry
    15ml/1 tbsp vegetable oil
For the sauce
    5ml/1 tsp cornflour (cornstarch)
    10–15ml/2–3 tsp dark soy sauce
    120ml/4fl oz/½ cup chicken stock
    30ml/2 tbsp oyster sauce
    boiled rice, to serve

1 Cut the chicken into strips about 1 x 4cm/½ x 1½in. To make the marinade, blend together the cornflour and soy sauce. Stir in the sherry and oil. Pour over the chicken, turning the pieces over to coat evenly, and leave for 30 minutes.

2 Trim the mangetouts and plunge them into a pan of boiling salted water. Bring back to the boil and then drain the mangetouts and refresh them under cold running water.

3 To make the sauce, mix together the cornflour, soy sauce, stock and oyster sauce and set aside.

4 Heat the oil in a deep fryer. Drain the chicken strips and fry, in batches if necessary, for about 30 seconds to brown. Drain and transfer to a plate using a slotted spoon.

5 Heat 15ml/1 tbsp of the vegetable oil in a wok and add the garlic and ginger. Stir-fry for 30 seconds. Add the mangetouts and stir-fry for 1–2 minutes. Transfer to a plate and keep warm.

6 Heat the remaining vegetable oil in the wok, add the spring onions and stir-fry for 1–2 minutes. Add the chicken and stir-fry for 2 minutes. Pour in the sauce, reduce the heat and cook until it thickens and the chicken is cooked through.

7 Stir in the sesame oil, and pour over the mangetouts. Serve with boiled rice.

Energy 208kcal/1246kJ; Protein 33g; Carbohydrate 7g, of which sugars 3g; Fat 15g, of which saturates 2g; Cholesterol 88mg; Calcium 57mg; Fibre 3g; Sodium 619mg.

FRENCH BEANS WITH BACON AND CREAM

THIS COMFORTING, TASTY DISH IS IDEAL FOR A LUNCH OR LIGHT SUPPER, SERVED WITH SOME WARM CRUSTY BREAD TO MOP UP THE CREAMY JUICES. YOU COULD USE HAM IN PLACE OF THE BACON.

SERVES FOUR

INGREDIENTS
  350g/12oz French (green) beans
  75g/3oz/½ cup chopped bacon
  25g/1oz/2 tbsp butter or margarine
  15ml/1 tbsp plain (all-purpose) flour
  350ml/12fl oz/1½ cups milk
    and single (light) cream, mixed
  salt and freshly ground black pepper

1 Preheat the oven to 190°C/375°F/ Gas 5. Trim the beans and cook in salted boiling water for 5 minutes until just tender. Drain and place in an ovenproof dish.

2 Dry-fry the bacon until it is crisp, then crumble into very small pieces and stir into the beans.

3 Melt the butter or margarine in a medium pan, stir in the flour and then add the milk and cream to make a smooth sauce. Season well with salt and pepper to taste.

4 Pour the sauce over the beans and carefully mix it in. Cover lightly with a piece of foil and bake in the oven for 15–20 minutes until hot.

Energy 312kcal/1292kJ; Protein 9.1g; Carbohydrate 11.8g, of which sugars 5.2g; Fat 25.7g, of which saturates 12.3g; Cholesterol 56mg; Calcium 118mg; Fibre 3.9g; Sodium 206mg.

FRENCH BEAN SALAD

ALTHOUGH BEAN SALADS ARE DELICIOUS SERVED WITH A SIMPLE VINAIGRETTE DRESSING, THIS DISH IS A LITTLE MORE ELABORATE. IT DOES, HOWEVER, ENHANCE THE FRESH FLAVOUR OF THE BEANS.

SERVES FOUR

INGREDIENTS
- 450g/1lb French (green) beans
- 15ml/1 tbsp olive oil
- 25g/1oz/2 tbsp butter
- ½ garlic clove, crushed
- 50g/2oz/1 cup fresh breadcrumbs
- 15ml/1 tbsp chopped fresh flat leaf parsley
- 1 egg, hard-boiled and finely chopped

For the dressing
- 30ml/2 tbsp olive oil
- 30ml/2 tbsp sunflower oil
- 10ml/2 tsp white wine vinegar
- ½ garlic clove, crushed
- 1.5ml/¼ tsp French mustard
- a pinch of sugar
- a pinch of salt

1 Trim the French beans and cook in boiling salted water for 5–6 minutes until tender. Drain the beans and refresh them under cold running water and place in a serving bowl.

2 Make the salad dressing by blending the oils, vinegar, garlic, mustard, sugar and salt thoroughly together. Pour over the beans and toss to mix.

COOK'S TIP
For a more substantial salad, boil about 450g/1lb scrubbed new potatoes until tender, cool and then cut them into bitesize chunks. Stir into the French (green) beans and then add the dressing.

3 Heat the oil and butter in a frying pan and fry the garlic for 1 minute. Stir in the breadcrumbs and fry over a moderate heat for about 3–4 minutes until golden brown, stirring frequently.

4 Remove the pan from the heat and stir in the parsley and then the egg. Sprinkle the breadcrumb mixture over the French beans. Serve warm or at room temperature.

Energy 237kcal/976kJ; Protein 6g; Carbohydrate 5g, of which sugars 4g; Fat 21g, of which saturates 6g; Cholesterol 20mg; Calcium 137mg; Fibre 2.6g; Sodium 60mg.

RUNNER BEANS WITH GARLIC

DELICATE AND FRESH-TASTING FLAGEOLET BEANS AND GARLIC ADD A DISTINCT FRENCH FLAVOUR TO THIS SIMPLE SIDE DISH. SERVE TO ACCOMPANY ROAST LAMB OR VEAL.

SERVES FOUR

INGREDIENTS
225g/8oz flageolet (small
   cannellini) beans
15ml/1 tbsp olive oil
25g/1oz/2 tbsp butter
1 onion, finely chopped
1–2 garlic cloves, crushed
3–4 tomatoes, peeled and chopped
350g/12oz runner (green) beans,
   prepared and sliced
150ml/¼ pint/⅔ cup white wine
150ml/¼ pint/⅔ cup vegetable stock
30ml/2 tbsp chopped fresh parsley
salt and freshly ground black pepper

1 Place the flageolet beans in a large pan of water, bring to the boil and simmer for ¾–1 hour until tender. Drain well in a colander or sieve (strainer).

2 Heat the oil and butter in a large frying pan and sauté the onion and garlic for 3–4 minutes until soft. Add the chopped tomatoes and continue cooking over a gentle heat until they are soft.

3 Stir the flageolet beans into the onion and tomato mixture, then add the runner beans, wine, stock, and a little salt. Stir well. Cover and simmer for 5–10 minutes until the runner beans are tender.

4 Increase the heat to reduce the liquid, then stir in the parsley and season with a little more salt, if necessary, and pepper.

Energy 248kcal/1040kJ; Protein 13g; Carbohydrate 23g, of which sugars 23g; Fat 17g, of which saturates 5g; Cholesterol 13mg; Calcium 236mg; Fibre 20g; Sodium 88mg.

INDIAN–STYLE OKRA

WHEN OKRA IS SERVED IN RESTAURANTS IT IS OFTEN FLAT AND SOGGY BECAUSE IT HAS BEEN OVERCOOKED OR LEFT STANDING. HOWEVER, WHEN YOU MAKE THIS DISH, YOU WILL DISCOVER HOW DELICIOUS IT CAN BE.

SERVES FOUR

INGREDIENTS
350g/12oz okra
2 small onions
2 garlic cloves, crushed
1cm/½in piece fresh
  root ginger
1 green chilli, seeded
10ml/2 tsp ground cumin
10ml/2 tsp ground coriander
30ml/2 tbsp vegetable oil
juice of 1 lemon

3 Reduce the heat and add the garlic and ginger mixture. Cook for about 2–3 minutes, stirring frequently, and then add the okra, lemon juice and 105ml/7 tbsp water.

4 Stir well, cover tightly and simmer over a low heat for about 10 minutes until the okra are just tender.

5 Transfer the mixture to a serving dish, sprinkle with the fried onion rings and serve immediately.

1 Trim the okra and cut into 1cm/½in lengths. Roughly chop one of the onions and place in a food processor or blender with the garlic, ginger, chilli and 90ml/ 6 tbsp water. Process to a paste. Add the cumin and coriander and blend again to combine thoroughly.

2 Thinly slice the remaining onion into half rings and fry in the oil for 6–8 minutes until golden brown. Transfer to a plate using a slotted spoon.

Energy 113kcal/470kJ; Protein 3g; Carbohydrate 7g, of which sugars 5g; Fat 9g, of which saturates 1g; Cholesterol 0mg; Calcium 164mg; Fibre 5g; Sodium 11mg.

CORN AND CHEESE PASTRIES

THESE TASTY PASTRIES ARE REALLY SIMPLE TO MAKE AND EXTREMELY MOREISH — WHY NOT MAKE DOUBLE THE AMOUNT — THEY'LL GO LIKE HOT CAKES.

<u>MAKES EIGHTEEN TO TWENTY</u>

INGREDIENTS
250g/9oz corn
115g/4oz feta cheese
1 egg, beaten
30ml/2 tbsp whipping cream
15g/½oz/⅓ cup grated Parmesan cheese
3 spring onions (scallions), chopped
8–10 small sheets filo pastry
115g/4oz/½ cup butter, melted
freshly ground black pepper

1 Preheat the oven to 190°C/375°F/ Gas 5 and lightly butter two patty tins (muffin pans).

2 If using fresh corn, strip the kernels from the cob using a sharp knife and simmer in a little salted water for 3–5 minutes, until tender. For canned corn, drain and rinse well under cold running water.

3 Crumble the feta cheese into a bowl and stir in the corn. Add the egg, cream, Parmesan cheese, spring onions and ground black pepper, and stir well.

4 Take a sheet of pastry and cut it in half to make a square. (Keep the remaining pastry covered with a damp cloth to prevent it drying out.) Brush with melted butter and then fold into four, to make a smaller square (about 7.5cm/3in).

5 Place a heaped teaspoon of the corn and feta mixture in the centre of each pastry square and then squeeze the pastry securely around the filling to make a 'money bag' casing.

6 Continue making pastries until all the mixture is used up. Brush the outside of each 'bag' with any remaining butter and then bake in the oven for about 15 minutes until golden. Serve hot.

CORN AND SCALLOP CHOWDER

FRESH HOME-GROWN CORN IS IDEAL FOR THIS CHOWDER, ALTHOUGH CANNED OR FROZEN CORN ALSO WORKS WELL. THIS SOUP IS ALMOST A MEAL IN ITSELF AND MAKES A PERFECT LUNCH DISH.

SERVES FOUR TO SIX

INGREDIENTS

2 ears of corn or 200g/7oz frozen
    or canned corn
600ml/1 pint/2½ cups milk
15g/½oz/1 tbsp butter or margarine
1 small leek or onion, chopped
40g/1½oz/¼ cup chopped smoked
    streaky (fatty) bacon
1 small garlic clove, crushed
1 small green (bell) pepper, seeded
    and diced
1 celery stick, chopped
1 medium potato, diced
15ml/1 tbsp plain (all-purpose) flour
300ml/½ pint/1¼ cups chicken
    or vegetable stock
4 scallops
115g/4oz cooked fresh mussels
a pinch of paprika
150ml/¼ pint/⅔ cup single (light)
    cream (optional)
salt and freshly ground
    black pepper

1 Using a sharp knife, slice down the ears of the corn to remove the kernels. Place half of the kernels in a food processor or blender and process with a little of the milk.

2 Melt the butter or margarine in a large pan and gently fry the leek or onion, bacon and garlic for 4–5 minutes until the leek is soft but not browned. Add the green pepper, celery and potato and sweat over a gentle heat for a further 3–4 minutes, stirring frequently.

3 Stir in the flour and cook for about 1–2 minutes until the mixture is golden and frothy. Gradually stir in the milk and corn mixture, stock, the remaining milk and corn kernels and seasoning.

4 Bring to the boil and then reduce the heat to a gentle simmer, and cook, partially covered, for 15–20 minutes, until the vegetables are tender.

5 Pull the corals away from the scallops and slice the white flesh into 5mm/¼in slices. Stir the scallops into the soup, cook for 4 minutes and then stir in the corals, mussels and paprika.

6 Allow to heat through for a few minutes and then stir in the cream, if using. Adjust the seasoning to taste and serve.

Energy 200kcal/845kJ; Protein 13g; Carbohydrate 23.6g, of which sugars 10.5g; Fat 6.7g, of which saturates 3.2g; Cholesterol 31mg; Calcium 150mg; Fibre 1.9g; Sodium 326mg.

SQUASH RECIPES

ONION SQUASH RISOTTO

A CREAMY RISOTTO IS ONE OF THE BEST WAYS IN WHICH TO SHOWCASE SQUASH OR PUMPKIN. SAVOURY BACON AND FRESH-TASTING PARSLEY LEND AN EXTRA DIMENSION TO THIS TASTY RECIPE.

SERVES FOUR

INGREDIENTS
  1 onion squash or pumpkin, about
    900g–1kg/2–2¼lb
  30ml/2 tbsp olive oil
  1 onion, chopped
  1–2 garlic cloves, crushed
  115g/4oz/⅔ cup chopped streaky
    (fatty) bacon
  115g/4oz/generous ½ cup arborio rice
  600–750ml/1–1¼ pints/2½–3 cups
    chicken stock
  40g/1½oz/½ cup grated
    Parmesan cheese
  15ml/1 tbsp chopped fresh parsley
  salt and freshly ground black pepper

1 Quarter the squash or pumpkin, remove the seeds and skin, then cut into chunks about 1–2cm/ ½–¾in in size.

2 Heat the oil in a flameproof casserole and fry the onion and garlic for about 3–4 minutes, stirring frequently. Add the bacon and continue frying until both the onion and bacon are lightly golden.

3 Add the squash or pumpkin, stir-fry for a few minutes. Add the rice and cook for about 2 minutes, stirring all the time.

4 Pour in about half of the stock and season. Stir, then half cover and simmer for about 20 minutes, stirring occasionally. As the liquid is absorbed, add more stock and stir to prevent the mixture sticking.

5 When the squash and rice are nearly tender, add a little more stock. Cook, uncovered for 5–10 minutes. Stir in the Parmesan cheese and parsley and serve.

PUMPKIN SOUP

THE SWEET FLAVOUR OF PUMPKIN IS GOOD IN SOUPS, TEAMING WELL WITH OTHER MORE SAVOURY INGREDIENTS SUCH AS ONIONS AND POTATOES TO MAKE A WARM AND COMFORTING DISH.

SERVES FOUR TO SIX

INGREDIENTS
  15ml/1 tbsp sunflower oil
  25g/1oz/2 tbsp butter
  1 large onion, sliced
  675g/1½lb pumpkin, cut into chunks
  450g/1lb potatoes, sliced
  600ml/1 pint/2½ cups vegetable stock
  a good pinch of nutmeg
  5ml/1 tsp chopped fresh tarragon
  600ml/1 pint/2½ cups milk
  about 5–10ml/1–2 tsp lemon juice
  salt and freshly ground black pepper

1 Heat the oil and butter in a heavy pan and fry the onion for 4–5 minutes over a gentle heat until soft but not browned, stirring frequently.

2 Add the pumpkin and potato, stir well and then cover and sweat over a low heat for about 10 minutes, until the vegetables are almost tender, stirring occasionally to prevent them from sticking to the pan.

3 Stir in the stock, nutmeg, tarragon and seasoning. Bring to the boil and then simmer for about 10 minutes until the vegetables are completely tender.

4 Allow to cool slightly, then pour into a food processor or blender and process until smooth.

5 Pour back into a clean pan and add the milk. Heat gently and then taste, adding the lemon juice and extra seasoning if necessary. Serve piping hot with crusty brown bread.

Risotto: Energy 333kcal/1385kJ; Protein 13g; Carbohydrate 30g, of which sugars 6g; Fat 17g, of which saturates 5g; Cholesterol 28mg; Calcium 186mg; Fibre 2g; Sodium 729mg.
Pumpkin: Energy 301kcal/1252kJ; Protein 12g; Carbohydrate 19g, of which sugars 10g; Fat 20g, of which saturates 12g; Cholesterol 57mg; Calcium 341mg; Fibre 2g; Sodium 536mg.

BAKED COURGETTES

WHEN SMALL AND VERY FRESH COURGETTES ARE USED FOR THIS RECIPE IT IS WONDERFUL, BOTH SIMPLE AND DELICIOUS, ALTHOUGH IT ALSO GOOD WITH STORE-BOUGHT VEGETABLES. THE CREAMY YET TANGY GOAT'S CHEESE CONTRASTS WELL WITH THE DELICATE FLAVOUR OF THE YOUNG COURGETTES.

SERVES FOUR

INGREDIENTS

8 small courgettes (zucchini), about
450g/1lb total weight
15ml/1 tbsp olive oil, plus extra
for greasing
75–115g/3–4oz goat's cheese,
cut into thin strips
a small bunch fresh mint,
finely chopped
freshly ground black pepper

1 Preheat the oven to 180°C/350°F/
Gas 4. Cut out eight rectangles of foil
large enough to encase each courgette
and brush each with a little oil.

2 Trim the courgettes and cut a thin slit
along the length of each.

3 Insert pieces of goat's cheese in the
slits. Add a little mint and sprinkle with
the olive oil and black pepper.

4 Wrap each courgette in the foil
rectangles, place on a baking sheet and
bake for about 25 minutes until tender.

COOK'S TIP
Almost any cheese could be used in this
recipe. Mild cheeses, however, such as
a mild cheddar or mozzarella, will best
allow the flavour of the courgettes to
be appreciated.

Energy 314kcal/1302kJ; Protein 23.3g; Carbohydrate 7.2g, of which sugars 5.4g; Fat 21.6g, of which saturates 10.2g; Cholesterol 169mg; Calcium 562mg; Fibre 1.8g; Sodium 504mg.

COURGETTES ITALIAN-STYLE

USING A GOOD QUALITY OLIVE OIL TOGETHER WITH SOME SUNFLOWER OIL ENABLES THE OLIVE OIL TO GIVE THIS CLASSIC ITALIAN ACCOMPANIMENT A DELICIOUS FRAGRANCE WITHOUT IT OVERPOWERING THE SUBTLE FLAVOUR OF THE FRESH, TENDER COURGETTES.

SERVES FOUR

INGREDIENTS
    15ml/1 tbsp olive oil
    15ml/1 tbsp sunflower oil
    1 large onion, chopped
    1 garlic clove, crushed
    4–5 medium courgettes, cut into
      1cm/½in slices
    150ml/¼ pint/⅔ cup chicken
      or vegetable stock
    2.5ml/½ tsp fresh chopped oregano
    salt and freshly ground black pepper
    chopped fresh parsley, to garnish

3 Stir in the stock, oregano and seasoning and simmer gently for 8–10 minutes, until the liquid has almost evaporated.

4 Spoon the courgettes into a warmed serving dish, sprinkle with chopped parsley and serve immediately.

1 Heat the oils in a large frying pan and fry the onion and garlic over a moderate heat for 5–6 minutes until the onion has softened and is beginning to brown.

2 Add the courgettes and fry for about 4 minutes until they just begin to be flecked with brown. Stir frequently.

Energy 118kcal/487kJ; Protein 4g; Carbohydrate 8g, of which sugars 6g; Fat 8g, of which saturates 1g; Cholesterol 0mg; Calcium 54mg; Fibre 1g; Sodium 64mg.

MARROWS WITH GNOCCHI

A SIMPLE WAY WITH MARROW, THIS DISH MAKES AN EXCELLENT ACCOMPANIMENT TO MEAT BUT IT IS ALSO GOOD WITH A VEGETARIAN DISH, OR SIMPLY SERVED WITH COOKED TOMATOES. GNOCCHI ARE AVAILABLE FROM MOST SUPERMARKETS; ITALIAN DELICATESSENS MAY ALSO SELL FRESH GNOCCHI.

SERVES FOUR

INGREDIENTS

   1 small marrow (large zucchini),
      cut into bitesize chunks
   50g/2oz/4 tbsp butter
   400g/14oz packet gnocchi
   ½ garlic clove, crushed
   salt and freshly ground black pepper
   chopped fresh basil, to garnish

1 Preheat the oven to 180°C/350°F/ Gas 4 and butter a large ovenproof dish. Place the marrow, more or less in a single layer, in the dish. Dot all over with the remaining butter.

2 Place a double piece of buttered baking parchment over the top. Cover with an ovenproof plate or lid so that it presses the marrow down, and then place a heavy, ovenproof weight on top of that. (Use a couple of old-fashioned scale weights.)

3 Put in the oven to bake for about 15 minutes, by which time the marrow should just be tender.

4 Cook the gnocchi in a large pan of boiling salted water for 2–3 minutes, or according to the instructions on the packet. Drain well.

5 Stir the garlic and gnocchi into the marrow. Season and then place the baking parchment over the marrow and return to the oven for 5 minutes (the weights are not necessary).

6 Just before serving, sprinkle the top with a little chopped fresh basil.

Energy 244kcal/1016kJ; Protein 3g; Carbohydrate 33g, of which sugars 3g; Fat 10g, of which saturates 7g; Cholesterol 27mg; Calcium 29mg; Fibre 1g; Sodium 576mg.

BAKED MARROW IN CREAM AND PARSLEY

THIS IS A REALLY GLORIOUS WAY WITH A SIMPLE AND MODEST VEGETABLE. TRY TO FIND A SMALL, FIRM AND UNBLEMISHED MARROW FOR THIS RECIPE, AS THE FLAVOUR WILL BE SWEET, FRESH AND DELICATE. YOUNG MARROWS DO NOT NEED PEELING; MORE MATURE ONES DO.

SERVES FOUR

INGREDIENTS
1 small young marrow (large zucchini),
  about 900g/2lb
30ml/2 tbsp olive oil
15g/½oz/1 tbsp butter
1 onion, chopped
15ml/1 tbsp plain (all-purpose) flour
300ml/½ pint/1¼ cups milk
  and single (light) cream mixed
30ml/2 tbsp chopped fresh parsley
salt and freshly ground black pepper

1 Preheat the oven to 180°C/350°F/
Gas 4 and cut the marrow into pieces
measuring about 5 x 2.5cm/2 x 1in.

2 Heat the oil and butter in a flameproof
casserole and fry the onion over a gentle
heat until very soft.

3 Add the marrow and sauté for
1–2 minutes and then stir in the flour.
Cook for a few minutes, then stir in the
milk and cream mixture.

4 Add the parsley and seasoning, stir
well and then cover and cook in the oven
for 30–35 minutes. If liked, remove the
lid for the final 5 minutes of cooking to
brown the top. Alternatively, serve the
marrow in its rich pale sauce.

VARIATION
Chopped fresh basil or a mixture of
basil and chervil also tastes good in
this dish.

Energy 203kcal/543kJ; Protein 5g; Carbohydrate 15g, of which sugars 10g; Fat 14g, of which saturates 5g; Cholesterol 18mg; Calcium 149mg; Fibre 3g; Sodium 59mg.

CUCUMBER AND TROUT MOUSSE

THIS IS A VERY LIGHT, REFRESHING MOUSSE, MAKING THE MOST OF THE CLEAN TASTE OF CUCUMBER.
SERVE IT AS AN APPETIZER OR FOR A LIGHT LUNCH WITH A GREEN SALAD. YOU COULD ALSO ARRANGE
A CHERVIL LEAF OR A VERY THIN LEMON SLICE ON THE TOPPING.

4 Sprinkle the gelatine over 30ml/2 tbsp of water in a bowl and leave to soak for a few minutes. Place the bowl over a pan of simmering water and stir until completely dissolved.

5 Heat the stock. Stir in the dissolved gelatine and leave until cool but not set. Pour the gelatine over the trout mixture and stir in the olives, lemon juice, tarragon and seasoning.

6 Lightly whip the cream and whisk the egg whites until stiff. Carefully fold the cream into the trout mixture, followed by the egg whites.

7 Spoon the mousse into the ramekin dishes, levelling the surface. Cover with clear film (plastic wrap) and chill in the refrigerator for 1–2 hours and then unmould on to serving plates

8 Garnish the mousses with a few peeled prawns and serve immediately with lettuce leaves and any remaining tarragon leaves.

SERVES SIX

INGREDIENTS
1 small cucumber
2–3 smoked trout fillets, about
   175g/6oz total weight
115g/4oz/½ cup fromage frais or
   sour cream
15ml/1 tbsp powdered gelatine
150ml/¼ pint/⅔ cup vegetable stock
12–14 pimiento stuffed olives, sliced
30ml/2 tbsp lemon juice
5ml/1 tsp finely chopped fresh tarragon
150ml/¼ pint/⅔ cup whipping cream
2 egg whites
salt and freshly ground black pepper
peeled prawns (shrimp) and lettuce
   leaves, to garnish
For the topping
15ml/1 tbsp powdered gelatine
90ml/6 tbsp vegetable stock

1 Lightly oil six ramekin dishes. To prepare the topping, take one quarter of the cucumber and slice thinly. Sprinkle the gelatine over the stock, leave to soak for a few minutes and then place over a pan of simmering water and stir until completely dissolved.

2 Spoon a little of the gelatine mixture into each dish and arrange two or three cucumber slices on top. Put in the refrigerator to set. Pour over the remaining gelatine mixture and return to the refrigerator to set.

3 To make the mousse, peel and very finely dice the remaining cucumber and put in a bowl. Flake the fish, discarding the skin and any bones and add to the cucumber. Beat in the fromage frais or sour cream.

Energy 170kcal/702kJ; Protein 10g; Carbohydrate 2g, of which sugars 2; Fat 14g, of which saturates 7g; Cholesterol 28mg; Calcium 55mg; Fibre 1g; Sodium 271mg.

LOOFAH RATATOUILLE

LOOFAHS HAVE A SIMILAR FLAVOUR TO COURGETTES AND CONSEQUENTLY TASTE EXCELLENT WITH OTHER RATATOUILLE INGREDIENTS, SUCH AS AUBERGINES AND TOMATOES. UNLESS USING VERY YOUNG LOOFAHS, WHICH ARE BEST, ENSURE THAT YOU PEEL AWAY THE ROUGH SKIN, AS IT CAN BE SHARP.

SERVES FOUR

INGREDIENTS

 1 large or 2 medium
   aubergines (eggplants)
 450g/1lb young loofahs or
   sponge gourds
 1 large red (bell) pepper, cut
   into large chunks
 225g/8oz cherry tomatoes
 225g/8oz shallots, peeled
 10ml/2 tsp ground coriander
 60ml/4 tbsp olive oil
 2 garlic cloves, finely chopped
 a few coriander (cilantro) leaves
 salt and freshly ground
   black pepper

1 Cut the aubergine into thick chunks and sprinkle the pieces with salt. Set aside in a colander for about 45 minutes and then rinse well under cold running water and pat dry.

2 Preheat the oven to 220°C/425°F/ Gas 7. Slice the loofahs into 2cm/¾in pieces. Place the aubergine, loofah and pepper pieces, together with the tomatoes and shallots in a roasting pan which is large enough to take all the vegetables in a single layer.

3 Sprinkle with the ground coriander and olive oil and then scatter the chopped garlic and coriander leaves on top. Season to taste.

4 Roast for about 25 minutes, stirring the vegetables occasionally, until the loofah is golden brown and the peppers are beginning to char at the edges.

Energy 215kcal/892kJ; Protein 4g; Carbohydrate 15g, of which sugars 13g; Fat 16g, of which saturates 2g; Cholesterol 0mg; Calcium 48mg; Fibre 7g; Sodium 15mg.

PUMPKIN AND HAM FRITTATA

A FRITTATA IS AN ITALIAN VERSION OF THE SPANISH TORTILLA, A SUBSTANTIAL OMELETTE MADE OF EGGS AND VEGETABLES, AND SOMETIMES HAM, AS HERE. SERVE WARM OR HOT WITH CRUSTY BREAD.

SERVES FOUR

INGREDIENTS
30ml/2 tbsp sunflower oil
1 large onion, chopped
450g/1lb pumpkin, chopped into
   bitesize pieces
200ml/7fl oz/scant 1 cup chicken
   stock
115g/4oz/⅔ cup smoked ham, chopped
6 eggs
10ml/2 tsp chopped fresh marjoram
salt and freshly ground black pepper

1 Preheat the oven to 190°C/375°F/Gas 5 and oil a large, shallow ovenproof dish. Heat the oil in a large frying pan and fry the onion for 3–4 minutes until softened.

2 Add the pumpkin and fry over a brisk heat for 3–4 minutes, stirring frequently. Stir in the stock, cover and simmer over a gentle heat for 5–6 minutes until the pumpkin is slightly tender. Add the ham.

3 Pour the mixture into the prepared dish. Beat the eggs with the marjoram and a little seasoning. Pour into the dish, then bake for 20–25 minutes until the frittata is firm and lightly golden.

Energy 304kcal/1265kJ; Protein 21g; Carbohydrate 7g, of which sugars 5g; Fat 21g, of which saturates 5g; Cholesterol 348mg; Calcium 107mg; Fibre 1; Sodium 787mg.

CHOCOLATE ZUCCHINI CAKE

THE RECIPE FOR THIS MOIST CHOCOLATE CAKE FLAVOURED WITH ZUCCHINI, OR COURGETTES, COMES FROM AMERICA. ALTHOUGH AN UNLIKELY COMBINATION, IT IS A VARIATION WELL WORTH TRYING.

SERVES FOUR TO SIX

INGREDIENTS
    115g/4oz/½ cup margarine
    130ml/4½fl oz/½ cup sunflower oil
    115g/4oz/generous ½ cup caster
       (superfine) sugar
    225g/8oz/1 cup soft light brown sugar
    3 eggs, beaten
    130ml/4½fl oz/½ cup milk
    350g/12oz/3 cups plain
       (all-purpose) flour
    10ml/2 tsp baking powder
    60ml/4 tbsp unsweetened
       cocoa powder
    2.5ml/½ tsp ground allspice
    450g/1lb courgettes (zucchini),
       peeled and grated
    5ml/1 tsp vanilla extract
    225g/8oz plain (semisweet)
       chocolate drops

1 Preheat the oven to 190°C/375°F/ Gas 5, then grease and line a 23 x 33cm/ 9 x13in baking tin (pan) with non-stick baking parchment.

2 Cream the margarine, oil and sugars together until light and fluffy, then gradually beat in the eggs and milk.

3 Sift the flour, baking powder, cocoa powder and ground allspice together and fold gently into the mixture.

4 Stir in the grated courgettes and vanilla extract and spoon the mixture into the prepared tin. Smooth the top using a palette knife and sprinkle the chocolate dots over the top.

5 Bake in the oven for 35–45 minutes until the cake is firm and a knife comes out clean. Cut into squares while still warm and then leave to cool completely on a wire rack.

Energy 1022kcal/4283kJ; Protein 14g; Carbohydrate 130g, of which sugars 85g; Fat 54g, of which saturates 14g; Cholesterol 122mg; Calcium 129mg; Fibre 2g; Sodium 382mg.

FRUIT RECIPES

AUBERGINE AND COURGETTE BAKE

THIS IS A GREAT MAKE-AHEAD VEGETARIAN MAIN DISH.

INGREDIENTS
  1 large aubergine (eggplant)
  salt and freshly ground black pepper
  30ml/2 tbsp olive oil
  1 large onion, chopped
  1–2 garlic cloves, crushed
  900g/2lb tomatoes, peeled and chopped
  a handful of basil leaves, shredded
    or 5ml/1tsp dried basil
  15ml/1 tbsp chopped fresh parsley
  2 courgettes (zucchini),
    sliced lengthways
  plain (all-purpose) flour, for coating
  75–90ml/5–6 tbsp sunflower oil
  350g/12oz mozzarella cheese, sliced
  25g/1oz/⅓ cup grated Parmesan cheese

1 Slice the aubergine, sprinkle with salt and set aside for 1 hour. Heat the oil in a frying pan. Fry the onion and garlic for 4 minutes until softened. Stir in the tomatoes, half the basil, the parsley and seasoning. Bring to the boil. Reduce the heat and cook for 25–35 minutes until pulped.

2 Rinse and dry the aubergines. Dust the aubergines and courgettes with flour. Heat the sunflower oil in another frying pan and fry the aubergine and courgettes until golden brown. Set aside.

3 Preheat the oven to 180°C/350°F/ Gas 4. Butter an ovenproof dish. Put a layer of aubergines and then courgettes in the dish, pour over half the sauce and arrange with half the mozzarella. Sprinkle over most of the remaining basil and some parsley. Repeat, ending with mozzarella. Sprinkle the Parmesan and remaining herbs on top and bake for 30–35 minutes.

AUBERGINES WITH TZATZIKI

THESE DELECTABLE DEEP-FRIED AUBERGINES MAKE A LOVELY APPETIZER.

INGREDIENTS
  2 medium aubergines (eggplants)
  oil, for deep-frying
  salt
For the batter
  75g/3oz/⅔ cup plain (all-purpose) flour
  1 egg
  120–150ml/4–5fl oz/½–⅔ cup milk
  a pinch of salt
For the tzatziki
  ½ cucumber, peeled and diced
  150ml/¼ pint/⅔ cup natural
    (plain) yogurt
  1 garlic clove, crushed
  15ml/1 tbsp chopped fresh mint

1 To make the tzatziki, place the cucumber in a colander, sprinkle with salt and leave for 30 minutes. Rinse, drain and pat dry. Mix the yogurt, garlic, mint and cucumber in a bowl. Cover and chill. Slice the aubergine lengthways. Sprinkle with salt. Leave for 1 hour.

2 To make the batter, sift the flour and salt into a large bowl, add the egg and milk and beat until smooth.

3 Rinse the aubergine slices and pat dry. Heat 1cm/½in of oil in a large frying pan. Dip the aubergine slices in the batter and fry them for 3–4 minutes until golden, turning once. Drain on kitchen paper.

Bake: Energy 395kcal/1639kJ; Protein 15g; Carbohydrate 10g, of which sugars 9g; Fat 33g, of which saturates 11g; Cholesterol 38mg; Calcium 298mg; Fibre 4g; Sodium 279mg.

Tzatziki: Energy 268kcal/1120kJ; Protein 8g; Carbohydrate 22g, of which sugars 7g; Fat 17g, of which saturates 4g; Cholesterol 67mg; Calcium 165mg; Fibre 3g; Sodium 69mg.

GAZPACHO

GAZPACHO IS A CLASSIC SPANISH SOUP. IT IS POPULAR ALL OVER SPAIN BUT NOWHERE MORE SO THAN IN ANDALUCIA, WHERE THERE ARE HUNDREDS OF VARIATIONS. IT IS A COLD SOUP OF TOMATOES, TOMATO JUICE, GREEN PEPPER AND GARLIC, WHICH IS SERVED WITH A SELECTION OF GARNISHES.

SERVES FOUR

INGREDIENTS
  1.5kg/3½lb ripe tomatoes
  1 green (bell) pepper, seeded and
    roughly chopped
  2 garlic cloves, crushed
  2 slices white bread, crusts removed
  60ml/4 tbsp olive oil
  60ml/4 tbsp tarragon wine vinegar
  150ml/¼ pint/⅔ cup tomato juice
  a good pinch of sugar
  salt and freshly ground
    black pepper
  ice cubes, to serve
For the garnishes
  30ml/2 tbsp sunflower oil
  2–3 slices white bread, diced
  1 small cucumber, peeled and
    finely diced
  1 small onion, finely chopped
  1 red and 1 green (bell) pepper,
    seeded and finely diced
  2 hard-boiled eggs, chopped

1 Skin the tomatoes, then quarter them and remove the cores.

2 Place the pepper in a food processor and process for a few seconds. Add the tomatoes, garlic, bread, olive oil and vinegar and process again.

3 Add the tomato juice, sugar, seasoning to taste and a little extra tomato juice or cold water and process. The consistency should be thick but not too stodgy; add a little more tomato juice or water if required.

4 Pour into a bowl and chill for at least 2 hours but no more than 12 hours, otherwise the textures deteriorate.

5 To prepare the bread cubes to use as a garnish, heat the oil in a frying pan and fry them over a moderate heat for 4–5 minutes until golden brown. Drain well on kitchen paper.

6 Place each garnish in a separate small dish, or alternatively arrange them in rows on a large plate.

7 Just before serving, stir a few ice cubes into the soup and then spoon into serving bowls. Serve with the garnishes.

Energy 356kcal/1494kJ; Protein 7.6g; Carbohydrate 41.9g, of which sugars 21.5g; Fat 18.8g, of which saturates 2.9g; Cholesterol 0mg; Calcium 90mg; Fibre 6.7g; Sodium 346mg.

TOMATO AND BASIL TART

IN FRANCE, PÂTISSERIES DISPLAY MOUTHWATERING SAVOURY TARTS IN THEIR WINDOWS. THIS IS A VERY SIMPLE YET EXTREMELY TASTY TART MADE WITH RICH SHORTCRUST PASTRY, TOPPED WITH SLICES OF MOZZARELLA CHEESE AND TOMATOES AND ENRICHED WITH OLIVE OIL AND BASIL LEAVES.

SERVES FOUR

INGREDIENTS

   150g/5oz mozzarella cheese,
    thinly sliced
   4 large tomatoes, thickly sliced
   about 10 basil leaves
   30ml/2 tbsp olive oil
   2 garlic cloves, thinly sliced
   sea salt and freshly ground
    black pepper
For the pastry
   115g/4oz/1 cup plain (all-purpose) flour
   50g/2oz/4 tbsp butter or margarine
   1 egg yolk
   a pinch of salt

1 To prepare the pastry, mix together the flour and salt, then rub in the butter and egg yolk. Add enough cold water to make a smooth dough and knead lightly on a floured surface. Place in a plastic bag and chill for about 1 hour.

2 Preheat the oven to 190°C/375°F/ Gas 5. Remove the pastry from the refrigerator and allow about 10 minutes for it to return to room temperature. Roll the pastry out into a 20cm/8in round. Press into the base of a 20cm/8in flan dish or tin (pan).

3 Prick the base all over with a fork, then bake in the oven for about 10 minutes until firm but not brown. Allow to cool slightly. Reduce the oven temperature to 180°C/350°F/Gas 4.

4 Arrange the mozzarella slices over the pastry base. On top, arrange a single layer of the sliced tomatoes, overlapping them slightly. Dip the basil leaves in olive oil and arrange them on the tomatoes.

5 Sprinkle the garlic on top, drizzle with the remaining olive oil and season with a little salt and a good sprinkling of black pepper. Bake for 40–45 minutes, until the tomatoes are well cooked. Serve hot.

Energy 330kcal/1380kJ; Protein 12g; Carbohydrate 27g, of which sugars 5g; Fat 20g, of which saturates 12g; Cholesterol 99mg; Calcium 198mg; Fibre 3g; Sodium 241mg.

ITALIAN ROAST PEPPERS

SIMPLE AND EFFECTIVE, THIS DISH WILL DELIGHT ANYONE WHO LIKES PEPPERS. IT CAN BE EATEN EITHER AS AN APPETIZER SERVED WITH FRENCH BREAD, OR AS A LIGHT LUNCH WITH COUSCOUS OR RICE.

SERVES FOUR

INGREDIENTS
4 small red (bell) peppers, halved,
    cored and seeded
30–45ml/2–3 tbsp capers, chopped
10–12 black olives, pitted
    and chopped
2 garlic cloves, finely chopped
50–75g/2–3oz mozzarella
    cheese, grated
40g/1½oz/¾ cup fresh white
    breadcrumbs
120ml/4fl oz/½ cup white wine
45ml/3 tbsp olive oil
5ml/1 tsp finely chopped
    fresh mint
5ml/1 tsp chopped fresh parsley
freshly ground black pepper

1 Preheat the oven to 180°C/350°F/ Gas 4 and butter a shallow ovenproof dish. Place the peppers tightly together in the dish and sprinkle over the chopped capers, black olives, garlic, mozzarella and breadcrumbs.

2 Pour over the wine and olive oil and then sprinkle with the mint, parsley and freshly ground black pepper.

3 Bake for 30–40 minutes until the topping is crisp and golden brown.

Energy 214kcal/897kJ; Protein 6g; Carbohydrate 14g, of which sugars 8g; Fat 15g, of which saturates 4g; Cholesterol 9mg; Calcium 85mg; Fibre 4g; Sodium 206mg.

SWEET PEPPER CHOUX WITH ANCHOVIES

THE RATATOUILLE VEGETABLES IN THIS DISH ARE ROASTED INSTEAD OF STEWED, AND HAVE A WONDERFUL AROMATIC FLAVOUR. ANY COMBINATION OF RED, GREEN OR YELLOW PEPPERS CAN BE USED.

SERVES SIX

INGREDIENTS
- 300ml/½ pint/1¼ cups water
- 115g/4oz/½ cup butter or margarine
- 150g/5oz/1¼ cups plain
  (all-purpose) flour
- 4 eggs
- 115g/4oz Gruyère or Cheddar cheese,
  finely diced
- 5ml/1 tsp Dijon mustard
- salt

For the filling
- 3 (bell) peppers; red, yellow and green
- 1 large onion, cut into eighths
  or sixteenths
- 3 tomatoes, peeled and quartered
- 1 courgette (zucchini), sliced
- 6 basil leaves, torn in strips
- 1 garlic clove, crushed
- 30ml/2 tbsp olive oil
- about 18 black olives, pitted
- 45ml/3 tbsp red wine
- 175ml/6fl oz/¾ cup passata (bottled
  strained tomatoes) or puréed
  canned tomatoes
- 50g/2oz can anchovy fillets, drained
- salt and freshly ground black pepper

1 Preheat the oven to 240°C/475°F/Gas 9. Grease six individual ovenproof dishes. Halve the peppers, seed and core and cut into 2.5cm/1in chunks.

2 Place the peppers, onion, tomatoes and courgette in a roasting pan. Add the basil, garlic and olive oil, stirring so the vegetables are well coated. Sprinkle with salt and pepper and then roast for about 25–30 minutes until the vegetables are just beginning to blacken at the edges.

3 Reduce the oven temperature to 200°C/400°F/Gas 6. To make the choux pastry, put the water and butter together in a large pan and heat until the butter melts. Remove from the heat and add all the flour in one go. Beat well with a wooden spoon for about 30 seconds until smooth. Allow to cool slightly.

4 Beat in the eggs, one at a time, and then continue beating until the mixture is thick and glossy. Stir in the cheese and mustard, then season with salt and pepper. Spoon the mixture around the sides of the prepared dishes.

5 Spoon the vegetables into a large mixing bowl, together with any juices or scrapings from the base of the pan. Add the olives and stir in the wine and passata or puréed tomatoes. (Or you can stir these into the roasting tin but allow the pan to cool slightly otherwise the liquid will boil and evaporate.)

6 Divide the pepper mixture between the six dishes and arrange the drained anchovy fillets on top.

7 Bake in the oven for about 25–35 minutes until the choux pastry is puffy and golden. Serve hot from the oven with a fresh green salad.

Energy 484kcal/2015kJ; Protein 17g; Carbohydrate 30g, of which sugars 9g; Fat 34g, of which saturates 16g; Cholesterol 222mg; Calcium 294mg; Fibre 4g; Sodium 739mg.

EGGS FLAMENCO

A VARIATION OF THE POPULAR BASQUE DISH PIPERADE, THE EGGS ARE COOKED WHOLE INSTEAD OF BEATING THEM BEFORE ADDING TO THE PEPPERS. THE RECIPE MAKES A GOOD LUNCH OR SUPPER DISH.

SERVES FOUR

INGREDIENTS
2 red (bell) peppers
1 green (bell) pepper
30ml/2 tbsp olive oil
1 large onion, finely sliced
2 garlic cloves, crushed
5–6 tomatoes, peeled and chopped
120ml/4fl oz/½ cup puréed canned
  tomatoes or tomato juice
a good pinch of dried basil
4 eggs
40ml/8 tsp single (light) cream
a pinch of cayenne
  pepper (optional)
salt and freshly ground
  black pepper

1 Preheat the oven to 180°C/350°F/ Gas 4. Seed and thinly slice the peppers. Heat the olive oil in a large frying pan. Fry the onion and garlic gently for about 5 minutes, stirring, until softened.

2 Add the peppers to the onion in the frying pan and fry for 10 minutes. Stir in the tomatoes and tomato purée or juice, the basil and seasoning. Cook gently for a further 10 minutes until the peppers are soft.

3 Spoon the mixture into four ovenproof dishes, preferably earthenware. Make a hole in the centre and break an egg into each. Spoon 10ml/2 tsp cream over the yolk of each egg and sprinkle with a little black pepper or cayenne, as preferred.

4 Bake in the oven for 12–15 minutes until the white of the egg is lightly set. Serve immediately with chunks of crusty warm French or Spanish bread.

Energy 257kcal/1072kJ; Protein 11g; Carbohydrate 16g, of which sugars 14g; Fat 17g, of which saturates 4g; Cholesterol 237mg; Calcium 82mg; Fibre 5g; Sodium 118mg.

SPINACH AND PEPPER PIZZA

THIS PIZZA IS PACKED WITH FLAVOUR AS WELL AS BENEFICIAL NUTRIENTS, MAKING IT A HEALTHY AND DELICIOUS CHOICE FOR DINNER — UNLIKE MANY FAT- AND SALT-LADEN STORE-BOUGHT PIZZAS.

MAKES TWO 30cm/12in PIZZAS

INGREDIENTS
450g/1lb fresh spinach
60ml/4 tbsp single (light) cream
25g/1oz/⅓ cup grated Parmesan cheese
15ml/1 tbsp olive oil
1 large onion, chopped
1 garlic clove, crushed
½ green and ½ red (bell) pepper,
    seeded and thinly sliced
175–250ml/6–8fl oz/¾–1 cup passata
    (bottled strained tomatoes)
50g/2oz black olives, pitted
    and chopped
15ml/1 tbsp chopped fresh basil
175g/6oz/1½ cups grated
    mozzarella cheese
175g/6oz/1½ cups grated
    Cheddar cheese
salt
For the dough
25g/1oz fresh yeast or 15ml/1 tbsp
    dried yeast and 5ml/1 tsp sugar
about 225ml/7fl oz/⅞ cup warm water
350g/12oz/3 cups strong white
    bread flour
30ml/2 tbsp olive oil
5ml/1 tsp salt

1 To make the dough, cream together the fresh yeast and 150ml/¼ pint/⅔ cup of the water and set aside until frothy. If using dried yeast, stir the sugar into 150ml/¼ pint/⅔ cup water, sprinkle over the yeast and leave until frothy.

2 Place the flour and salt in a large bowl, make a well in the centre and pour in the olive oil and yeast mixture. Add the remaining water. Mix to make a dough. Knead for 10 minutes until smooth.

3 Shape the dough into a ball and place in an oiled bowl, cover and leave for about 1 hour until it has doubled in size.

4 To prepare the topping, cook the spinach for 4–5 minutes until the leaves have wilted. Strain and press out the excess liquid. Place in a bowl and mix with the cream, Parmesan and salt.

5 Heat the oil in a frying pan and fry the onion and garlic over a moderate heat for 3–4 minutes until the onion has slightly softened. Add the peppers and continue cooking until the onion is lightly golden, stirring regularly.

6 Preheat the oven to 220°C/425°F/Gas 7. Knead the dough briefly on a lightly floured surface. Divide the dough and roll out into two 30cm/12in rounds.

7 Spread each base with the passata. Add the onions and peppers and then spread over the spinach mixture. Sprinkle over the olives, basil leaves, mozzarella cheese and Cheddar cheese.

8 Bake in the preheated oven for 15–20 minutes, or until the crust is lightly browned and the top is beginning to turn golden. Allow to cool slightly before serving.

Energy 1661kcal/6590kJ; Protein 74g; Carbohydrate 152g, of which sugars 19g; Fat 88g, of which saturates 41g; Cholesterol 164mg; Calcium 1814mg; Fibre 20g; Sodium 3114mg.

ENCHILADAS WITH HOT CHILLI SAUCE

IN MEXICO, CHILLIES APPEAR IN ALMOST EVERY SAVOURY DISH, EITHER IN THE FORM OF CHILLI POWDER OR CHOPPED, SLICED OR WHOLE. BY MEXICAN STANDARDS, THIS IS A LOW-HEAT VERSION OF THE POPULAR CHICKEN ENCHILADAS. IF YOU LIKE YOUR FOOD HOT, ADD EXTRA CHILLIES TO THE SAUCE.

SERVES FOUR

INGREDIENTS

8 wheat tortillas
175g/6oz/1½ cups grated
  Cheddar cheese
1 onion, finely chopped
350g/12oz cooked chicken,
  cut into small chunks
300ml/½ pint/1¼ cups sour cream
1 avocado, sliced and tossed in
  lemon juice, to garnish

For the *salsa picante*
1–2 green chillies
15ml/1 tbsp vegetable oil
1 onion, chopped
1 garlic clove, crushed
400g/14oz can chopped tomatoes
30ml/2 tbsp tomato purée (paste)
salt and freshly ground
  black pepper

3 Preheat the oven to 180°C/350°F/ Gas 4 and butter a shallow ovenproof dish. Sprinkle each tortilla with cheese and onion, about 40g/1½oz of chicken and 15ml/1 tbsp *salsa picante*. Pour over 15ml/1 tbsp sour cream, roll up and place, seam side down, in the dish.

4 Pour the remaining *salsa* over the top and sprinkle with the remaining cheese and onion. Bake for about 25–30 minutes until the top is golden. Serve with the remaining sour cream either poured over, or separately, and garnish with the sliced avocado.

1 To make the *salsa picante*, cut the chillies in half lengthways and carefully remove the cores and seeds. Slice the chillies very finely. Heat the oil in a frying pan and fry the onion and garlic for about 3–4 minutes until softened. Add the tomatoes, tomato purée and chillies. Simmer gently, uncovered, for about 12–15 minutes, stirring frequently.

2 Pour the sauce into a food processor or blender, and process until smooth. Return the sauce to the heat and cook very gently, uncovered, for a further 15 minutes, until thickened. Season to taste then set aside.

Energy 932kcal/3899kJ; Protein 48g; Carbohydrate 79g, of which sugars 12g; Fat 49g, of which saturates 23g; Cholesterol 179mg; Calcium 563mg; Fibre 5g; Sodium 787mg.

HOT SOUR CHICKPEAS

THIS DISH, KHATTE CHOLE, IS EATEN AS A SNACK ALL OVER INDIA, SOLD BY ITINERANT STREET VENDORS. THE HEAT OF THE CHILLIES IS TEMPERED PARTLY BY THE CORIANDER AND CUMIN, WHILE THE LEMON JUICE ADDS A WONDERFUL SOURNESS.

SERVES FOUR

INGREDIENTS

  350g/12oz chickpeas, soaked in cold
    water overnight
  60ml/4 tbsp vegetable oil
  2 medium onions, very finely chopped
  225g/8oz tomatoes, peeled and
    finely chopped
  15ml/1 tbsp ground coriander
  15ml/1 tbsp ground cumin
  5ml/1 tsp ground fenugreek
  5ml/1 tsp ground cinnamon
  1–2 hot green chillies, seeded
    and finely sliced
  about 2.5cm/1in fresh root
    ginger, grated
  60ml/4 tbsp lemon juice
  15ml/1 tbsp chopped fresh
    coriander (cilantro)
  salt

1 Drain the chickpeas, place in a large pan, cover with water and bring to the boil. Cover and simmer for 1–1¼ hours until tender, making sure they do not boil dry. Drain, reserving the cooking liquid.

2 Heat the oil in a large flameproof casserole. Reserve about 30ml/2 tbsp of the chopped onions and fry the remainder in the casserole over a moderate heat for 4–5 minutes, stirring frequently, until tinged with brown.

3 Add the tomatoes and continue cooking over a moderately low heat for 5–6 minutes until soft. Stir frequently, mashing the tomatoes to a pulp.

4 Stir in the coriander, cumin, fenugreek and cinnamon. Cook for 30 seconds and then add the chickpeas and 350ml/12fl oz/1½ cups of the reserved cooking liquid. Season with salt, cover and simmer very gently for about 15–20 minutes, stirring occasionally and adding more cooking liquid if the mixture becomes too dry.

5 Meanwhile, mix the reserved finely chopped onion with the chilli, ginger and lemon juice in a small bowl. Stir to combine well.

6 Just before serving, stir the onion and chilli mixture and the chopped fresh coriander into the chickpeas, and adjust the seasoning as required.

Energy 454kcal/1905kJ; Protein 20g; Carbohydrate 52g, of which sugars 8g; Fat 20g, of which saturates 2g; Cholesterol 0mg; Calcium 168mg; Fibre 13g; Sodium59mg.

GUACAMOLE

THIS IS QUITE A FIERY VERSION OF A POPULAR MEXICAN DISH, ALTHOUGH PROBABLY NOWHERE NEAR AS HOT AS YOU WOULD BE SERVED IN MEXICO, WHERE IT SEEMS HEAT KNOWS NO BOUNDS! IF YOU ARE SERVING THIS TO CHILDREN OR DON'T LIKE HEAT, YOU CAN OMIT THE CHILLI ALTOGETHER.

SERVES FOUR

INGREDIENTS
2 ripe avocados, peeled and
  stoned (pitted)
2 tomatoes, peeled, seeded
  and finely chopped
6 spring onions (scallions),
  finely chopped
1–2 chillies, seeded and
  finely chopped
30ml/2 tbsp fresh lime or
  lemon juice
15ml/1 tbsp chopped fresh
  coriander (cilantro)
salt and freshly ground black pepper
coriander (cilantro) sprigs, to garnish

1 Put the avocado halves into a large bowl and mash them roughly with a large fork.

2 Add the remaining ingredients. Mix well and season according to taste. Serve garnished with fresh coriander.

Energy 156kcal/645kJ; Protein 2.1g; Carbohydrate 3.7g, of which sugars 2.5g; Fat 14.7g, of which saturates 3.1g; Cholesterol 0mg; Calcium 26mg; Fibre 3.5g; Sodium 11mg.

PLANTAIN APPETIZER

PLANTAINS ARE A TYPE OF COOKING BANANA WITH A LOWER SUGAR CONTENT THAN DESSERT BANANAS.
THEY ARE UNSUITABLE FOR EATING RAW BUT CAN BE USED IN A WIDE RANGE OF COOKED DISHES. THIS
DELICIOUS ASSORTMENT OF SWEET AND SAVOURY PLANTAINS IS A POPULAR DISH IN AFRICA.

SERVES FOUR

INGREDIENTS
   2 green plantains
   45ml/3 tbsp vegetable oil
   1 small onion, very thinly sliced
   1 yellow plantain
   ½ garlic clove, crushed
   salt and cayenne pepper
   vegetable oil, for frying

1 Peel one of the green plantains and cut into wafer-thin rounds, preferably using a potato peeler.

2 Heat about 15ml/1 tbsp of the oil in a large frying pan and fry the plantain slices for 2–3 minutes until golden, turning occasionally. Transfer to a plate lined with kitchen paper and keep warm.

3 Coarsely grate the other green plantain and mix with the onion.

4 Heat 15ml/1 tbsp of the remaining oil in the pan and fry the plantain and onion mixture for 2–3 minutes until golden, turning occasionally. Transfer to the plate with the plantain slices.

5 Peel the yellow plantain, cut into small chunks. Sprinkle with cayenne pepper. Heat the remaining oil and fry the yellow plantain and garlic for 4–5 minutes until brown. Drain and sprinkle with salt.

Energy 294kcal/1234kJ; Protein 2g; Carbohydrate 57g, of which sugars 12g; Fat 8g, of which saturates 1g; Cholesterol 0mg; Calcium 22mg; Fibre 5g; Sodium 8mg.

SALAD VEGETABLE RECIPES

CHICKEN LIVERS AND GREEN SALAD

THIS SIMPLE SALAD IS VERY NUTRITIOUS, QUICK TO MAKE AND PACKED WITH FLAVOUR.

SERVES FOUR

INGREDIENTS
a selection of fresh salad leaves
4 spring onions (scallions), sliced
15ml/1 tbsp roughly chopped
    flat leaf parsley
115g/4oz/⅔ cup chopped unsmoked
    streaky bacon
450g/1lb chicken livers
seasoned flour, for dusting
15ml/1 tbsp sunflower oil
25g/1oz/2 tbsp butter or margarine
salt and freshly ground black pepper
For the dressing
100ml/3½fl oz/⅓ cup sunflower oil
30–45ml/2–3 tbsp lemon juice
5ml/1 tsp French mustard
1 small garlic clove, crushed
salt and freshly ground black pepper

1 To make the dressing, place the oil, lemon juice, mustard, garlic and seasoning in a screw-top jar and shake vigorously to mix.

2 Place the salad leaves in a large serving bowl with the spring onions and parsley. Pour over the dressing, toss briefly and then arrange on four individual serving plates.

3 Dry-fry the bacon in a frying pan until golden brown. Transfer to a plate lined with kitchen paper using a slotted spoon and keep warm.

4 Trim the chicken livers of all fat, gristle and any green bits, pat dry on kitchen paper and then dust them thoroughly with the seasoned flour.

5 Heat the oil and butter in a frying pan and fry the livers over a fairly high heat for about 8 minutes, turning occasionally until cooked to your preference, either cooked through or slightly pink inside.

6 Arrange the chicken livers on the salad leaves and scatter the crisp bacon pieces over the top.

CAESAR SALAD

A CLASSIC SALAD WITH AN EGG YOLK DRESSING, THIS SHOULD BE MADE USING COS LETTUCE. YOU COULD ADD SOME SHREDDED COOKED CHICKEN IF YOU HAVE SOME TO HAND.

SERVES FOUR

INGREDIENTS
1 garlic clove, crushed
60–75ml/4–5 tbsp olive oil
75g/3oz stale white bread,
    cut into cubes
1 cos or romaine lettuce
8 anchovies, chopped
40g/1½oz shavings of
    Parmesan cheese
For the dressing
2 egg yolks
2.5ml/½ tsp French mustard
50ml/2fl oz/¼ cup olive oil
50ml/2fl oz/¼ cup sunflower oil
15ml/1 tbsp white wine vinegar
a pinch of salt

1 Place the garlic in the oil and set aside for about 30 minutes for the garlic flavour to infuse into the oil.

2 To make the dressing, place the egg yolks, French mustard, olive oil, sunflower oil, vinegar and salt in a screw-top jar and shake well.

3 To make the croûtons, strain the garlic oil into a frying pan and discard the garlic. When hot, fry the bread until golden and then drain on kitchen paper.

4 Arrange the lettuce leaves in a salad bowl. Pour over the dressing and gently fold in the anchovies and croûtons. Sprinkle with Parmesan shavings.

Chicken: Energy 313kcal/1299kJ; Protein 17g; Carbohydrate 8.3g, of which sugars 8g; Fat 23.7g, of which saturates 4.1g; Cholesterol 333mg; Calcium 42mg; Fibre 2.4g; Sodium 72mg.
Caesar: Energy 198kcal/824kJ; Protein 5.6g; Carbohydrate 13.8g, of which sugars 1.7g; Fat 13.8g, of which saturates 2.1g; Cholesterol 50mg; Calcium 64mg; Fibre 0.9g; Sodium 400mg.

WARM DUCK SALAD WITH ORANGE

THE DISTINCT, SHARP FLAVOUR OF RADICCHIO, FRISÉE AND FRESH ORANGES COMPLEMENTS THE RICH TASTE OF THE DUCK TO MAKE THIS A SUPERB DISH. IT IS ESPECIALLY GOOD SERVED WITH STEAMED NEW POTATOES FOR AN ELEGANT MAIN COURSE AT A DINNER PARTY.

3 Transfer the duck to a plate to cool slightly and pour off the excess fat from the pan.

4 Peel the oranges. Separate the oranges into segments and use a knife to remove all the pith, catching the juice in a small bowl. Arrange the salad leaves in a shallow serving bowl.

5 Heat the duck juices in the pan and stir in 45ml/3 tbsp of the reserved orange juice. Bring to the boil, add the sherry and then just enough soy sauce to give a piquant, spicy flavour.

6 Cut the duck into thick slices and arrange over the salad. Pour over the warm dressing and serve.

SERVES FOUR

INGREDIENTS
  2 duck breast fillets
  salt
  2 oranges
  frisée lettuce, radicchio and
    lamb's lettuce
  30ml/2 tbsp medium dry sherry
  10–15ml/2–3 tsp dark soy sauce

1 Rub the skin of the duck breasts with salt and then slash the skin several times with a sharp knife.

2 Heat a heavy cast iron frying pan and fry the duck breasts, skin side down at first, for 20–25 minutes, turning once, until the skin is well browned and the flesh is cooked to your preference.

Energy 231kcal/971kJ; Protein 17.3g; Carbohydrate 13.3g, of which sugars 4.5g; Fat 11.1g, of which saturates 1.7g; Cholesterol 83mg; Calcium 68mg; Fibre 1.5g; Sodium 185mg

RADICCHIO PIZZA

THIS UNUSUAL PIZZA TOPPING CONSISTS OF CHOPPED RADICCHIO WITH LEEKS, TOMATOES AND PARMESAN AND MOZZARELLA CHEESES. THE BASE IS A SCONE DOUGH, MAKING THIS A QUICK AND EASY SUPPER DISH TO PREPARE. SERVE WITH A CRISP GREEN SALAD.

SERVES TWO

INGREDIENTS

½ x 400g/14oz can chopped tomatoes
2 garlic cloves, crushed
a pinch of dried basil
25ml/1½ tbsp olive oil, plus extra
   for dipping
2 leeks, sliced
100g/3½oz radicchio,
   roughly chopped
25g/1oz/⅓ cup grated Parmesan cheese
115g/4oz mozzarella cheese, sliced
10–12 black olives, pitted
basil leaves, to garnish
salt and freshly ground black pepper
For the dough
225g/8oz/2 cups self-raising
   (self-rising) flour
2.5ml/½ tsp salt
50g/2oz/4 tbsp butter or margarine
about 120ml/4fl oz/½ cup milk

1 Preheat the oven to 220°C/425°F/ Gas 7 and grease a baking sheet. Mix the flour and salt in a bowl, rub in the butter or margarine and gradually stir in the milk and mix to a soft dough.

2 Roll the dough out on a lightly floured surface to make a 25–28cm/10–11in round. Place on the baking sheet.

3 Purée the tomatoes and then pour into a small pan. Stir in one of the crushed garlic cloves, together with the dried basil and seasoning, and simmer over a moderate heat until the mixture is thick and reduced by about half.

4 Heat the olive oil in a large frying pan and fry the leeks and remaining garlic for 4–5 minutes until slightly softened. Add the radicchio and cook, stirring continuously for a few minutes, and then cover and simmer gently for about 5–10 minutes. Stir in the Parmesan cheese and season with salt and pepper.

5 Cover the dough base with the tomato mixture and then spoon the leek and radicchio mixture on top. Arrange the mozzarella slices on top and scatter over the black olives. Dip a few basil leaves in olive oil, arrange on top and then bake the pizza for 15–20 minutes until the scone base and top are golden brown.

Energy 933kcal/3910kJ; Protein 29g; Carbohydrate 94g, of which sugars 9g; Fat 52g, of which saturates 25g; Cholesterol 96mg; Calcium 781mg; Fibre 11g; Sodium 1732mg.

BAKED CHICORY WITH PROSCIUTTO

ALTHOUGH CHICORY IS SOMETIMES TOO HARSHLY FLAVOURED FOR SOME PEOPLE'S TASTES, SIMMERING IT BEFORE BRAISING ELIMINATES ANY BITTERNESS SO THAT THE FLAVOUR IS PLEASANTLY MILD. HERE, IT IS WRAPPED IN THIN SLICES OF PROSCIUTTO AND BAKED WITH A CREAMY SAUCE.

SERVES FOUR

INGREDIENTS
  4 heads of chicory (Belgian endive)
  25g/1oz/2 tbsp butter
  250ml/8fl oz/1 cup vegetable
    or chicken stock
  4 slices prosciutto
  75g/3oz/⅜ cup mascarpone
  50g/2oz Emmenthal or Cheddar
    cheese, sliced
  salt and freshly ground black pepper

1 Preheat the oven to 180°C/350°F/ Gas 4. Grease an ovenproof dish. Trim the chicory and remove the central core.

2 Melt the butter in a large pan and gently sauté the chicory over a moderate heat for 4–5 minutes, turning occasionally, until the outer leaves begin to turn transparent.

3 Add the stock and a little seasoning, bring to the boil and then cover and simmer gently for 5–6 minutes until the chicory is almost tender.

4 Remove the chicory using a slotted spoon. Lay out the prosciutto slices and place one piece of chicory on each of the slices. Roll up and place, side by side, in a single layer in the prepared dish.

5 Simmer the stock until it is reduced by about half, then remove from the heat. Stir in the mascarpone and pour the sauce over the chicory. Lay the slices of cheese over the top and bake in the oven for about 15 minutes until the top is golden and the sauce is bubbling.

Energy 322kcal/1333kJ; Protein 16g; Carbohydrate 5g, of which sugars 2g; Fat 28g, of which saturates 16g; Cholesterol 56mg; Calcium 169mg; Fibre 1g; Sodium 112mg.

ROCKET AND GOAT'S CHEESE SALAD

FOR THIS RECIPE, LOOK OUT FOR CYLINDER-SHAPED GOAT'S CHEESE FROM A DELICATESSEN OR FOR SMALL ROLLS THAT CAN BE CUT INTO HALVES, WEIGHING ABOUT 50G/2OZ. SERVE ONE PER PERSON AS AN APPETIZER OR DOUBLE THE RECIPE AND SERVE TWO EACH FOR A LIGHT LUNCH.

SERVES FOUR

INGREDIENTS
    about 15ml/1 tbsp olive oil
    about 15ml/1 tbsp vegetable oil
    4 slices French bread
    45ml/3 tbsp walnut oil
    15ml/1 tbsp lemon juice
    salt and freshly ground black pepper
    225g/8oz cylinder-shaped
        goat's cheese
    a generous handful of rocket (arugula)
    about 115g/4oz frisée lettuce
For the sauce
    45ml/3 tbsp apricot jam
    60ml/4 tbsp white wine
    5ml/2 tsp Dijon mustard

1 Heat the two oils in a frying pan and fry the slices of French bread on one side only, until lightly golden. Transfer to a plate lined with kitchen paper.

4 Preheat the grill (broiler) a few minutes before serving the salad. Cut the goat's cheese into 50g/2oz rounds and place each piece on a croûton, untoasted side up. Place under the grill and cook for 3–4 minutes, until the cheese melts.

5 Toss the rocket and frisée in the walnut oil dressing and arrange attractively on four individual serving plates. When the cheese croûtons are ready, arrange on each plate and pour over a little of the apricot sauce.

2 To make the sauce, heat the jam in a small pan until it is warm but not boiling. Push the jam through a sieve (strainer), into a clean pan, to remove the pieces of fruit, and then stir in the white wine and mustard. Heat gently and keep warm, but not boiling, until ready to serve with the salad.

3 Blend the walnut oil and lemon juice and season with a little salt and pepper to taste.

Energy 453kcal/1890kJ; Protein 15.9g; Carbohydrate 31.7g, of which sugars 10.4g; Fat 29.3g, of which saturates 11.7g; Cholesterol 52mg; Calcium 139mg; Fibre 1.4g; Sodium 592mg

CHINESE LEAVES AND DAIKON WITH SCALLOPS

A SPEEDY STIR-FRY MADE USING CHINESE CABBAGE, DAIKON AND SCALLOPS. BOTH THE DAIKON AND CHINESE LEAVES HAVE A PLEASANT CRUNCHY 'BITE'. YOU NEED TO WORK QUICKLY, SO HAVE EVERYTHING PREPARED BEFORE YOU START COOKING.

SERVES FOUR

INGREDIENTS
    10 prepared scallops
    60–75ml/4–5 tbsp vegetable oil
    3 garlic cloves, finely chopped
    1cm/½in piece fresh root ginger,
        finely sliced
    4–5 spring onions (scallions), cut
        lengthways into 2.5cm/1in pieces
    30ml/2 tbsp medium dry sherry
    ½ daikon (mooli), cut into
        1cm/½in slices
    1 Chinese cabbage, chopped
        lengthways into thin strips
For the marinade
    5ml/1 tsp cornflour (cornstarch)
    1 egg white, lightly beaten
    a pinch of white pepper
For the sauce
    5ml/1 tsp cornflour (cornstarch)
    45ml/3 tbsp oyster sauce

1 Rinse the scallops and separate the corals from the white meat. Cut each scallop into 2–3 pieces and slice the corals. Place them on two dishes.

2 For the marinade, blend together the cornflour, egg white and white pepper. Pour half over the scallops and the rest over the corals. Leave for 10 minutes.

3 To make the sauce, blend the cornflour with 60ml/4 tbsp water and the oyster sauce and set aside.

4 Heat about 30ml/2 tbsp of the oil in a wok, add half of the garlic and let it sizzle, and then add half the ginger and half of the spring onions. Stir-fry for about 30 seconds and then stir in the scallops (not the corals).

5 Stir-fry for ½–1 minute until the scallops start to become opaque and then reduce the heat and add 15ml/1 tbsp of the sherry. Cook briefly and then spoon the scallops and the cooking liquid into a bowl and set aside.

6 Heat another 30ml/2 tbsp of oil in the wok, add the remaining garlic, ginger and spring onions and stir-fry for 1 minute. Add the corals, stir-fry briefly and transfer to a dish.

7 Heat the remaining oil and add the daikon. Stir-fry for about 30 seconds and then stir in the cabbage. Stir-fry for about 30 seconds and then add the oyster sauce mixture and about 60ml/4 tbsp water. Allow the cabbage to simmer briefly and then stir in the scallops and corals, together with all their liquid and cook briefly to heat through.

Energy 259kcal/1079kJ; Protein 17g; Carbohydrate 10g, of which sugars 3g; Fat 16g, of which saturates 2g; Cholesterol 29mg; Calcium 86mg; Fibre 3g; Sodium 609mg.

RADISH, MANGO AND APPLE SALAD

RADISH IS A YEAR-ROUND VEGETABLE AND THIS SALAD CAN BE SERVED AT ANY TIME OF YEAR, WITH ITS CLEAN, CRISP TASTES AND MELLOW FLAVOURS. SERVE WITH SMOKED FISH, SUCH AS ROLLS OF SMOKED SALMON, OR WITH SMOKED CONTINENTAL HAM OR SALAMI.

SERVES FOUR

INGREDIENTS
    10–15 radishes
    1 dessert apple, peeled cored and
      thinly sliced
    2 celery sticks, thinly sliced
    1 small ripe mango
For the dressing
    120ml/4fl oz/½ cup sour cream
    10ml/2 tsp creamed horseradish
    15ml/1 tbsp chopped fresh dill
    salt and freshly ground
      black pepper
  sprigs of dill, to garnish

1 To prepare the dressing, blend together the sour cream, horseradish and dill in a small jug (pitcher) or bowl and season with a little salt and pepper.

2 Top and tail the radishes and then slice them thinly. Add to a bowl together with the thinly sliced apple and celery.

3 Cut through the mango lengthways either side of the stone (pit). Make even criss-cross cuts through each side section. Take each one and bend it back to separate the cubes. Remove the mango cubes with a small knife and add to the bowl. Pour the dressing over the vegetables and fruit and stir gently so that all the ingredients are coated in the dressing. When ready to serve, spoon the salad into an attractive salad bowl and garnish with sprigs of dill.

Energy 77kcal/324kJ; Protein 1.4g; Carbohydrate 7.6g, of which sugars 7g; Fat 4.9g, of which saturates 3.1g; Cholesterol 0mg; Calcium 44mg; Fibre 1.4g; Sodium 46mg

WATERCRESS SOUP

THIS DELICIOUS, VIVID GREEN SOUP MAKES AN ELEGANT APPETIZER OR LIGHT LUNCH.

SERVES FOUR

INGREDIENTS
15ml/1 tbsp sunflower oil
15g/½oz/1 tbsp butter
1 medium onion, finely chopped
1 medium potato, diced
about 175g/6oz watercress
400ml/14fl oz/1⅔ cups chicken
  or vegetable stock
400ml/14fl oz/1⅔ cups milk
lemon juice
salt and freshly ground black pepper
sour cream, to serve (optional)

1 Heat the oil and butter in a large pan and fry the onion over a gentle heat until soft but not browned. Add the potato, fry gently for 2–3 minutes and then cover and sweat for 5 minutes over a gentle heat, stirring occasionally.

2 Strip the watercress leaves from the stalks and roughly chop the stalks.

3 Add the stock and milk, stir in the stalks and season. Bring to the boil and simmer for 10–12 minutes until the potatoes are tender. Add all but a few of the watercress leaves and simmer for 2 minutes.

4 Process the soup in a food processor or blender, and then pour into a clean pan and heat gently with the reserved watercress leaves. Taste when hot and add a little lemon juice and adjust the seasoning.

5 Pour the soup into warmed soup dishes and swirl in a little sour cream, if using, just before serving.

COOK'S TIP
Provided you leave out the cream, this is a low calorie but nutritious soup, which, served with crusty bread, makes a satisfying meal.

WATERCRESS ^AND^ TWO-FISH TERRINE

THIS IS A PRETTY, DELICATE DISH, IDEAL FOR A SUMMER BUFFET PARTY OR PICNIC. SERVE WITH LEMON MAYONNAISE OR SOUR CREAM, AND A WATERCRESS AND GREEN SALAD.

SERVES SIX TO EIGHT

INGREDIENTS
350g/12oz monkfish, filleted
175g/6oz lemon sole, filleted
salt and freshly ground black pepper
1 egg and 1 egg white
45–60ml/3–4 tbsp lemon juice
50g/2oz/1 cup fresh white breadcrumbs
300ml/½ pint/1¼ cups whipping
  cream
75g/3oz smoked salmon
175g/6oz watercress, roughly chopped

1 Preheat the oven to 180°C/350°F/ Gas 4. Grease and line a 1.5 litre/2½ pint/ 6¼ cup loaf tin (pan) with non-stick baking parchment.

2 Cut the fish into rough chunks, discarding the skin and bones. Put the fish into a food processor with a little seasoning.

3 Process briefly and add the egg and egg white, lemon juice, breadcrumbs and cream. Process to a paste. Put the mixture into a bowl. Take 75ml/5 tbsp of the mixture and process with the smoked salmon. Transfer to a separate bowl. Take 75ml/5 tbsp of the white fish mixture and process with the watercress.

4 Spoon half of the white fish mixture into the base of the prepared loaf tin and smooth the surface with a palette knife or metal spatula.

5 Spread over the watercress mixture, then the smoked salmon mixture and finally spread over the remaining white fish mixture and smooth the top.

6 Lay a piece of buttered non-stick baking parchment on top of the mixture and then cover with foil. Place the loaf tin in a roasting pan half-filled with boiling water and cook in the oven for 1¼–1½ hours. Towards the end of the cooking time the terrine will begin to rise, which indicates that it is ready.

7 Allow the terrine to cool in the tin and then turn it out on to a serving plate and peel away the baking paper. Chill for 1–2 hours before serving.

Soup: Energy 68kcal/280kJ; Protein 1.5g; Carbohydrate 1.4g, of which sugars 1g; Fat 6.3g, of which saturates 2.4g; Cholesterol 8mg; Calcium 79mg; Fibre 0.9g; Sodium 45mg.
Terrine: Energy 236kcal/983kJ; Protein 16g; Carbohydrate 4g, of which sugars 1g; Fat 17g, of which saturates 10g; Cholesterol 91mg; Calcium 80mg; Fibre 1g; Sodium 276mg.

MUSHROOM RECIPES

CREAM OF MUSHROOM SOUP

A GOOD MUSHROOM SOUP MAKES THE MOST OF THE SUBTLE AND SOMETIMES RATHER ELUSIVE FLAVOUR OF MUSHROOMS. BUTTON MUSHROOMS ARE USED HERE FOR THEIR PALE COLOUR; CHESTNUT OR, BETTER STILL, FIELD (PORTOBELLO) MUSHROOMS GIVE A FULLER FLAVOUR BUT TURN THE SOUP BROWN.

SERVES FOUR

INGREDIENTS
  275g/10oz button (white) mushrooms
  15ml/1 tbsp sunflower oil
  40g/1½oz/3 tbsp butter
  1 small onion, finely chopped
  15ml/1 tbsp plain (all-purpose) flour
  450ml/¾ pint/1¾ cups vegetable stock
  450ml/¾ pint/1¾ cups milk
  a pinch of dried basil
  30–45ml/2–3 tbsp single (light)
    cream (optional)
  fresh basil leaves, to garnish
  salt and freshly ground black pepper

1 Separate the mushroom caps from the stalks. Finely slice the caps and finely chop the stalks.

2 Heat the oil and half the butter in a heavy pan and add the onion, mushroom stalks and ½–¾ of the sliced mushroom caps. Fry for about 1–2 minutes, stirring frequently, and then cover and sweat over a gentle heat for 6–7 minutes, stirring occasionally.

3 Stir in the flour and cook for about 1 minute. Gradually add the stock and milk, to make a smooth thin sauce. Add the basil, and season with salt and pepper. Bring to the boil and then simmer, partly covered, for 15 minutes.

4 Cool slightly and then pour the soup into a food processor or blender and process until smooth. Melt the rest of the butter in a frying pan and fry the remaining mushrooms gently for 3–4 minutes, until they are just tender.

5 Pour the soup into a clean pan and stir in the sliced mushrooms. Heat until very hot and adjust the seasoning. Add a little cream, if using. Serve sprinkled with fresh basil leaves.

SOUFFLÉ OMELETTE WITH MUSHROOM SAUCE

A SOUFFLÉ OMELETTE INVOLVES A LITTLE MORE PREPARATION THAN AN ORDINARY OMELETTE BUT THE RESULT IS VERY LIGHT YET SATISFYINGLY FILLING.

SERVES ONE

INGREDIENTS
  2 eggs, separated
  15g/½oz/1 tbsp butter
  a sprig of parsley or coriander (cilantro)
For the mushroom sauce
  15g/½oz/1 tbsp butter
  75g/3oz button (white) mushrooms,
    thinly sliced
  15ml/1 tbsp plain flour
  85–120ml/3–4fl oz/½ cup milk
  5ml/1 tsp chopped fresh
    parsley (optional)
  salt and freshly ground black pepper

1 To make the mushroom sauce, melt the butter in a pan or frying pan and fry the sliced mushrooms for 4–5 minutes until tender.

2 Stir in the flour, cook for 1 minute, and then gradually add the milk, stirring all the time, to make a smooth sauce. Add the parsley, if using, and season with salt and pepper. Keep warm to one side.

3 Beat the egg yolks with 15ml/1 tbsp water and season with a little salt and pepper. Whisk the egg whites until stiff and then fold very gently into the egg yolks using a metal spoon. Preheat the grill (broiler).

4 Melt the butter in a large frying pan and pour the egg mixture into the pan. Cook over a gentle heat for 2–4 minutes. Place the frying pan under the grill and cook for a further 3–4 minutes until the top is golden brown.

5 Slide the omelette on to a warmed serving plate, pour over the warm mushroom sauce and fold the omelette in half. Serve the omelette immediately, garnished with a sprig of parsley or fresh coriander leaves.

Soup: Energy 227kcal/939kJ; Protein 6g; Carbohydrate 10g, of which sugars 6g; Fat 18g, of which saturates 9g; Cholesterol 41mg; Calcium 155g; Fibre 2g; Sodium 304mg.
Omelette: Energy 529kcal/2197kJ; Protein 22g; Carbohydrate 17g, of which sugars 5g; Fat 42g, of which saturates 22g; Cholesterol 542mg; Calcium 221mg; Fibre 2g; Sodium 400mg.

STUFFED MUSHROOMS

THIS IS A CLASSIC MUSHROOM DISH, STRONGLY FLAVOURED WITH GARLIC. USE FLAT MUSHROOMS OR FIELD (PORTOBELLO) MUSHROOMS, WHICH ARE SOMETIMES AVAILABLE FROM FARM STORES.

SERVES FOUR

INGREDIENTS
450g/1lb large flat mushrooms
butter, for greasing
about 75ml/5 tbsp olive oil
2 garlic cloves, grated or very
   finely chopped
45ml/3 tbsp finely chopped
   fresh parsley
50g/oz/1 cup fresh white breadcrumbs
salt and freshly ground black pepper
sprig of flat leaf parsley,
   to garnish

1 Preheat the oven to 180°C/350°F/ Gas 4. Cut off the mushroom stalks and reserve on one side.

2 Arrange the mushroom caps in a buttered shallow dish, gill side upwards.

COOK'S TIP
The cooking time for the mushrooms depends on their size and thickness. If they are fairly thin, cook for slightly less time. They should be tender but not too soft when cooked. If a stronger garlic flavour is preferred, do not cook the garlic before adding it to the breadcrumb mixture.

3 Heat 15ml/1 tbsp of oil in a frying pan and fry the garlic briefly. Finely chop the mushroom stalks and mix with the parsley and breadcrumbs. Add the garlic, seasoning and 15ml/1tbsp of the oil. Pile a little of the mixture on each mushroom.

4 Add the remaining oil to the dish and cover the mushrooms with buttered greaseproof (waxed) paper. Bake for about 15–20 minutes, removing the paper for the last 5 minutes to brown the tops. Garnish with a sprig of parsley.

Energy 228kcal/943kJ; Protein 3g; Carbohydrate 7g, of which sugars 1g; Fat 21g, of which saturates 4g; Cholesterol 4mg; Calcium 26mg; Fibre 3g; Sodium 82mg.

BOEUF EN CROÛTE WITH MUSHROOM FILLING

A DUXELLES FILLING OF MUSHROOMS, SHALLOTS, GARLIC AND PARSLEY IS THE CLASSIC FILLING FOR BOEUF EN CROÛTE. THESE INDIVIDUAL VERSIONS ARE GOOD SERVED WITH NEW POTATOES AND A GREEN VEGETABLE.

SERVES FOUR

INGREDIENTS
   4 fillet steaks (beef tenderloin),
      about 115–150g/4–5oz each
   a little Dijon mustard
   25g/1oz/2 tbsp butter
   275g/10oz puff pastry
   25g/1oz/½ cup fresh white
      breadcrumbs
   beaten egg, for glazing
   salt and freshly ground black pepper
   sprigs of parsley or chervil, to garnish
For the duxelles filling
   25g/1oz/2 tbsp butter
   4 shallots, finely chopped
   1–2 garlic cloves, crushed
   225–275g/8–10oz flat mushrooms,
      finely chopped
   15ml/1 tbsp finely chopped parsley

4 Cut the pastry into four and roll out each piece very thinly to a 18cm/7in square. Cut the corners from each square and spread a spoonful of the mushroom mixture in the centre. Top with a steak and sprinkle with a spoonful of fresh breadcrumbs.

5 Bring the sides of the pastry up to the centre and seal with water. Place seam side down on a baking sheet. Decorate with pastry trimmings and brush each with beaten egg. Bake for about 20 minutes, until golden brown. Serve garnished with parsley or chervil.

1 Preheat the oven to 220°C/425°F/ Gas 7. Rub a little mustard over each of the steaks and season with pepper. Melt the butter in a heavy-based frying pan and fry the steaks for about 1–2 minutes each side, so that they are browned on the outside but still red in the centre. Transfer to a plate to cool.

2 To make the filling, melt the butter and fry the shallots and garlic briefly. Stir in the finely chopped mushrooms.

3 Fry over a fairly high heat for about 3–4 minutes, stirring, until the juices run. Lower the heat and cook gently for 4–5 minutes until the mixture is dry. Add the parsley and seasoning and cool.

Energy 559kcal/233kJ; Protein 34g; Carbohydrate 29g, of which sugars 3g; Fat 35g, of which saturates 11g; Cholesterol 161mg; Calcium 72mg; Fibre 4g; Sodium 419mg.

GNOCCHI WITH OYSTER MUSHROOMS

GNOCCHI MAKE AN UNUSUAL AND PLEASANT ALTERNATIVE TO PASTA. THEY ARE BLAND ON THEIR OWN BUT BRING OUT THE FLAVOUR OF THE OYSTER MUSHROOMS IN THIS DISH WHILE THEIR SOFT TEXTURE CONTRASTS WITH THE FIRMNESS OF THE MUSHROOMS.

SERVES FOUR

INGREDIENTS
225g/8oz oyster mushrooms
15ml/1 tbsp olive oil
1 medium onion, finely chopped
1 garlic clove, crushed
4 plum tomatoes, peeled and chopped
45–60ml/3–4 tbsp vegetable stock
   or water
salt and freshly ground black pepper
2 x 300g/11oz packet plain
   potato gnocchi
a good knob (pat) of butter
10ml/2 tsp chopped fresh parsley
Parmesan cheese, cut in shavings,
   to serve

1 Trim the mushrooms and tear into smaller pieces, if they are large. Heat the oil in a large frying pan and fry the onion and garlic over a low heat for about 4–5 minutes until softened but not browned.

2 Increase the heat, add the mushrooms to the pan and sauté for 3–4 minutes, stirring constantly.

3 Stir in the chopped tomatoes, stock or water and seasoning and then cover and simmer for about 8 minutes until the tomatoes are very soft and reduced to a pulp. Stir occasionally to prevent the mixture sticking to the pan.

4 Cook the gnocchi in a large pan of salted boiling water for 2–3 minutes (or according to the instructions on the packet) then drain well and toss with the butter. Place the gnocchi in a large warmed serving bowl and stir in the chopped parsley.

5 Pour the mushroom and tomato mixture over the top, stir briefly and sprinkle with the Parmesan cheese.

COOK'S TIPS
If the mushrooms are very large, the stalks are likely to be tough, therefore they should be discarded. Always tear rather than cut oyster mushrooms.

SHELLFISH AND OYSTER MUSHROOMS

THIS DISH IS REMARKABLY QUICK TO PREPARE. IT CAN BE MADE INTO A MORE SUBSTANTIAL DISH BY STIRRING 275–350G/10–12OZ COOKED PASTA SHELLS INTO THE SAUCE AT THE END.

SERVES FOUR

INGREDIENTS
15ml/1 tbsp olive oil
15g/½oz/1 tbsp butter
1 garlic clove, crushed
175g/6oz oyster mushrooms,
   halved or quartered
115–175g/4–6oz peeled cooked
   prawns (shrimp)
115g/4oz cooked mussels, optional
juice of ½ lemon
15ml/1 tbsp medium dry sherry
150ml/¼ pint/⅔ cup double
   (heavy) cream
salt and freshly ground black pepper

1 Heat the oil and butter in a frying pan and sauté the garlic for a few minutes, then add the mushrooms. Cook for 4–5 minutes until soft, stirring occasionally.

2 Reduce the heat and stir in the prawns, mussels and lemon juice. Cook for 1 minute, stirring continuously. Stir in the sherry and cook for 1 minute.

3 Add the cream and cook gently until heated through but not boiling. Taste and adjust the seasoning and then spoon into warmed serving dishes. Serve immediately with chunks of Italian bread, if you like.

Gnocchi: Energy 306kcal/1283kJ; Protein 7g; Carbohydrate 54g, of which sugars 8g; Fat 6g, of which saturates 2g; Cholesterol 5mg; Calcium67 mg; Fibre 3g; Sodium 1006mg.
Shellfish: Energy 487kcal/2083kJ; Protein 12g; Carbohydrate 57g, of which sugars 5g; Fat 26g, of which saturates 14g; Cholesterol 57mg; Calcium 87mg; Fibre 5g; Sodium 108mg.

TAGLIATELLE FUNGI

THE MUSHROOM SAUCE IS EASY TO MAKE AND THE PASTA COOKS VERY QUICKLY; BOTH NEED TO BE COOKED AS NEAR TO SERVING AS POSSIBLE SO CAREFUL COORDINATION IS REQUIRED. PUT THE PASTA IN TO COOK WHEN THE MASCARPONE IS ADDED TO THE SAUCE.

SERVES FOUR

INGREDIENTS
about 50g/2oz/4 tbsp butter
225–350g/8–12oz chanterelles
  or other wild mushrooms
15ml/1 tbsp plain (all-purpose) flour
150ml/¼ pint/⅔ cup milk
90ml/6 tbsp crème fraîche
15ml/1 tbsp chopped fresh parsley
275g/10oz fresh tagliatelle
olive oil
salt and freshly ground
  black pepper

3 Add the crème fraîche, parsley, mushrooms and seasoning and stir well. Cook very gently to heat through and then keep warm while cooking the pasta.

4 Cook the pasta in a large pan of boiling water for 4–5 minutes (or according to the instructions on the packet). Drain well, toss in a little olive oil and then turn on to a warmed serving plate. Pour the sauce over and serve immediately.

COOK'S TIP
Chanterelles are a little tricky to wash, as they are so delicate. However, since these are woodland mushrooms, it's important to clean them thoroughly. Hold each one by the stalk and let cold water run under the gills to dislodge hidden dirt. Shake gently to dry.

1 Melt 40g/1½oz/3 tbsp of the butter in a frying pan and fry the mushrooms for about 2–3 minutes over a gentle heat until the juices begin to run. Increase the heat and cook until the liquid has almost evaporated. Transfer the mushrooms to a bowl using a slotted spoon.

2 Stir in the flour, adding a little more butter if necessary, cook the paste for 1 minute, then gradually stir in the milk and beat to make a smooth sauce.

Energy 223kcal/922kJ; Protein 7g; Carbohydrate 4g, of which sugars 3g; Fat 20g, of which saturates 6g; Cholesterol 129mg; Calcium 58mg; Fibre 3g; Sodium 518mg.

SHIITAKE FRIED RICE

SHIITAKE MUSHROOMS HAVE A STRONG, MEATY MUSHROOMY AROMA AND FLAVOUR. THIS IS A VERY EASY RECIPE TO MAKE, AND IT CAN EITHER BE SERVED AS A SIDE DISH FOR FOUR PEOPLE OR AS A MEAL IN ITSELF FOR ONE OR TWO PEOPLE, DEPENDING ON APPETITES.

SERVES FOUR

INGREDIENTS
  2 eggs
  45ml/3 tbsp vegetable oil
  350g/12oz shiitake mushrooms
  8 spring onions (scallions),
    sliced diagonally
  1 garlic clove, crushed
  ½ green (bell) pepper, chopped
  25g/1oz/2 tbsp butter
  200g/7oz/1 cup long grain rice, cooked
  15ml/1 tbsp medium dry sherry
  30ml/2 tbsp dark soy sauce
  15ml/1 tbsp chopped fresh
    coriander (cilantro)
  salt

1 Beat the eggs with 15ml/1 tbsp cold water and season with a little salt.

2 Heat 15ml/1 tbsp of the oil in a wok or large frying pan, pour in the eggs and cook to make an omelette. Lift the sides and tilt the wok so that the uncooked egg can run underneath and be cooked. Roll up the omelette and slice thinly.

3 Remove and discard the mushroom stalks if tough and slice the caps thinly, halving them if they are large.

4 Heat 15ml/1 tbsp of the remaining oil in the wok and stir-fry the spring onions and garlic for 3–4 minutes until softened but not brown. Transfer them to a plate using a slotted spoon.

5 Add the pepper, stir-fry for about 2–3 minutes, then add the butter and the remaining 15ml/1 tbsp of oil. As the butter begins to sizzle, add the sliced mushrooms and stir-fry over a moderate heat for 3–4 minutes until soft.

6 Loosen the rice grains as much as possible. Pour the sherry over the mushrooms and then stir in the rice.

7 Heat the rice over a moderate heat, stirring all the time to prevent it sticking. If the rice seems very dry, add a little more oil.

8 Stir in the reserved onions and omelette slices, the soy sauce and coriander. Cook for a few minutes until heated through and serve.

COOK'S TIP
Unlike risotto, for which rice is cooked along with the other ingredients, Chinese fried rice is always made using cooked long grain rice. If you cook 200g/7oz/ 1 cup uncooked long grain, you will get about 450g/1lb/2⅓ cups cooked rice, which makes enough for a side dish for four people.

Energy 278kcal/1159kJ; Protein 5g; Carbohydrate 23g, of which sugars 6g; Fat 19g, of which saturates 9g; Cholesterol 50mg; Calcium 44mg; Fibre 2g; Sodium 195mg.

WILD MUSHROOMS ᴵᴺ BRIOCHES

SLIGHTLY SWEET BRIOCHES PROVIDE THE PERFECT CONTRAST TO CREAMY MUSHROOMS.

SERVES FOUR

INGREDIENTS
4 small brioches
olive oil, for glazing
20ml/4 tsp lemon juice
sprigs of parsley, to garnish
For the mushroom filling
25g/1oz/2 tbsp butter
2 shallots
1 garlic clove, crushed
175–225g/6–8oz assorted wild
  mushrooms, halved if large
45ml/3 tbsp white wine
45ml/3 tbsp double (heavy) cream
5ml/1 tsp chopped fresh basil
5ml/1 tsp chopped fresh parsley
salt and freshly ground black pepper

1 Preheat the oven to 180°C/350°F/
Gas 4. Cut a circle out of the top of each
brioche and reserve. Scoop out the
bread inside to make a small cavity.

2 Place the brioches and the tops on a
baking sheet and brush inside and out
with olive oil. Bake for 7–10 minutes
until golden and crisp. Squeeze 5ml/
1 tsp of lemon juice inside each brioche.

3 To make the filling, melt the butter in
a frying pan and fry the shallots and
garlic for 2–3 minutes until softened.
Add the mushrooms and cook gently for
about 4–5 minutes, stirring.

4 When the juices begin to run, reduce
the heat and continue cooking for about
3–4 minutes, stirring occasionally, until
the pan is fairly dry.

5 Stir in the wine. Cook for a few more
minutes and then stir in the cream, basil,
parsley and seasoning to taste.

6 Pile the mushroom mixture into the
brioche shells and return to the oven and
reheat for about 5–6 minutes. Serve as
an appetizer or light lunch.

WILD MUSHROOMS ᵂᴵᵀᴴ PANCAKES

PANCAKES MAKE AN ELEGANT ALTERNATIVE TO BUTTERED TOAST IN THIS SIMPLE RECIPE.

SERVES SIX

INGREDIENTS
225–275g/8–10oz wild mushrooms
50g/2oz/4 tbsp butter
1–2 garlic cloves
a splash of brandy (optional)
freshly ground black pepper
sour cream, to serve
For the pancakes
115g/4oz/1 cup self-raising
  (self-rising) flour
25g/1oz/¼ cup buckwheat flour
2.5ml/½ tsp baking powder
2 eggs
about 250ml/8fl oz/1 cup milk
a pinch of salt
oil, for frying

1 To make the pancakes, mix together
the flours, baking powder and salt in a
large bowl. Add the eggs and milk and
beat to make a smooth batter.

2 Grease a large griddle or frying pan
and, when hot, pour small amounts of
batter on to the griddle, well spaced apart.

3 Fry for a few minutes until bubbles
begin to appear on the surface and the
underside is golden, and then flip over.
Cook for about 1 minute until golden.
Keep warm, wrapped in a clean dish
towel. (Makes about 18–20 pancakes.)

4 If the mushrooms are large, cut them
in half. Melt the butter in a frying pan
and add the garlic and mushrooms. Fry
over a moderate heat for a few minutes
until the juices begin to run and then
increase the heat and cook, stirring
frequently, until nearly all the juices have
evaporated.

5 Stir in the brandy, if using, and season
with a little black pepper.

6 Arrange the warm pancakes on a
serving plate and spoon over a little sour
cream. Top with the hot mushrooms and
serve immediately.

COOK'S TIP
This makes a delicious and elegant
appetizer for a dinner party. Alternatively,
make cocktail-size pancakes and serve
as part of a buffet supper or as finger
food with drinks.

Brioches: Energy 278kcal/1159kJ; Protein 5g; Carbohydrate 23g, of which sugars 6g; Fat 19g, of which saturates 9g; Cholesterol 50mg; Calcium 44mg; Fibre 2g; Sodium 195mg.
Pancakes: Energy 249kcal/1037kJ; Protein 7g; Carbohydrate 20g, of which sugars 2g; Fat 16g, of which saturates 7g; Cholesterol 701mg; Calcium 97mg; Fibre 2g; Sodium 149mg.

INDEX